DIVERGING PATHS: COMPARING A CENTURY OF SCANDINAVIAN AND LATIN AMERICAN ECONOMIC DEVELOPMENT

Editors
Magnus Blomström
Patricio Meller

Published by the Inter-American Development Bank
Distributed by The Johns Hopkins University Press

1991
Washington, D.C.

The views and opinions expressed in this publication are those of the authors and do not necessarily reflect the official positions of the Inter-American Development Bank.

Diverging Paths

Comparing a Century of Scandinavian and Latin American Economic Development

© Copyright 1991 by the Inter-American Development Bank

Inter-American Development Bank
1300 New York Avenue, N.W.
Washington, D.C. 20577

Distributed by
The Johns Hopkins University Press
701 West 40th Street
Baltimore, Maryland 21211

ISBN: 0-940602-36-9

PREFACE

The great challenge confronting Latin America in the 1990s is how to combine increased economic growth with greater social equity. The major economic policy reforms instituted in the 1980s provide the basis for growth but have not addressed the social question. It is therefore interesting to examine the development experiences of other regions that have been successful in achieving both objectives simultaneously.

The Scandinavian countries provide a good example. In less than a hundred years, this region has been transformed into one of the world's most prosperous, with ambitious distribution programs that permit the benefits of economic progress to be enjoyed by all. It should be noted that Scandinavian development has been accomplished with reduced state participation in production. Private enterprise has been stimulated to optimize its profitability on both the domestic and external levels.

This collection of articles produced by distinguished Scandinavian and Latin American economists makes it possible for the first time to compare the long-term development of four countries of each region. Countries with similar natural resources have been chosen. This research project began with a meeting at the IDB (Washington, D.C.) in January 1989. Two International Seminars were later held to discuss the preliminary versions of the articles: one at the Stockholm School of Economics (Stockholm, September 1989), and the other at CIEPLAN (Santiago, January 1990). The project required tremendous coordination among the various economists from both regions, accomplished with great efficiency by Magnus Blomström, of the Stockholm School of Economics, and Patricio Meller of CIEPLAN. The coordinators are also co-authors of the introductory chapter, which provides a summary of the project. The Inter-American Development Bank congratulates both of them on the production of this interesting and excellent publication.

Nohra Rey de Marulanda, Manager
Department of Economic and Social Development
Inter- American Development Bank

CONTRIBUTORS

Galo Abril-Ojeda, Manager at the Econometric Department, Central Bank of Ecuador and Researcher at CEPLAES (Quito)

Magnus Blomström, Professor at the Stockholm School of Economics (Sweden) and Research Associate at the NBER (USA).

Tarmo Haavisto, Research Fellow at the University of Lund, Sweden.

Lennart Hjalmarsson, Professor of Economics at the University of Gothenburg, Sweden.

Helge Hveem, Professor of Political Science at the University of Oslo, Norway.

Ari Kokko, Research Fellow at the Stockholm School of Economics, Sweden.

Patricio Meller, Executive Director at CIEPLAN, Chile.

José Antonio Ocampo, Adviser to the Colombian Government on coffee matters and Researcher at FEDESARROLLO (Bogotá).

Martin Paldam, Professor of Economics at Aarhus University, Denmark.

Martín Rama, Researcher at CINVE (Uruguay) and Assistant Professor at the Universidad de la República.

Bo Södersten, Professor of International Economics at the University of Lund, Sweden.

CONTENTS

INTRODUCTION

Magnus Blomström and Patricio Meller

International comparisons of development patterns have recently gained currency. By learning from the experiences of other countries, mistakes can be avoided and earlier success stories can perhaps show the way to new successes. Over the last one hundred years, the Scandinavian countries, i.e., Denmark, Finland, Norway, and Sweden, have experienced a remarkable transformation. From having been among the poorest countries in Europe, they are now among the richest countries in the world. Few countries can exhibit a similar record, particularly as it proves that it is possible to combine growth and economic efficiency with advanced welfare states.

Although the physical characteristics of several Latin American countries have been similar to those in Scandinavia—in both regions, countries have been small in area and population and rich in natural resources—Latin America has developed very differently. While the northern countries were able to use their natural resources to generate the momentum for sustained growth, the countries of Latin America have tried different formulas without much success.

In this book, we outline and compare one hundred years of the growth experience of Scandinavia and four Latin American countries (Chile, Colombia, Ecuador, and Uruguay). Our main purpose is to examine the circumstances that led to diverging development paths between the countries and regions, and to see what lessons Latin America can draw from the Scandinavian experiences of development. Because of the many initial similarities between the two regions, it is important to compare their long-run growth performance to understand the reasons for their divergent paths.[1]

The essays in this volume have been written from a variety of points of views by scholars from Scandinavia and Latin America. Each author outlines the path of long-run growth with emphasis on development issues that have been characteristic for the country in question. In Chapter 2, the economic history of Sweden is told by Bo Södersten,who claims that an agrarian reform laid the foundation for Sweden's rapid industrialization process. The land reform not only encouraged a more efficient and intensive cultivation of land,

---

[1] The Latin American countries should, in fact, have much more to learn from Scandinavia than from the Asian countries that are currently studied all around the developing world (see e.g., Naya, et al., 1990). For several reasons, Latin American-Asian comparisons may not be very relevant. First, there are significant differences between the two regions. For example, while Latin American countries are rich in natural resources, the Asian NICs are generally not. There are also significant cultural and historical differences between the two areas. Finally, it is not obvious what the Asian countries did to become so successful. The Asian NICs have not followed one single growth model and their diversity is perhaps greater than Latin America's.

but also increased the domestic market through the demand from the agricultural sector. Also, the early and massive support for education played an important role in the Swedish transformation to a modern society. Finally, Södersten shows that a strong international orientation has been critical to Sweden's remarkable industrial development.

In Chapter 3, Patricio Meller analyses Chile's long-run development by examining the roles of the external sector and the main economic agents. He maintains that lack of domestic entrepreneurs and local capability in general, rather than deteriorating terms of trade and instability in export prices, explain why Chile benefitted so little from its early natural resource exports. He also discusses the roles of the state and the market during different historical periods, as well as why the Chilean import-substitution policy failed. In addition, he examines the effects of the introduction of a free market economy in Chile after 1973.

Martin Paldam, in Chapter 4, discusses the political economy of growth in Denmark, 1850-1990. He claims that the Danish tradition for openness in international trade has been an important factor behind the rapid development of the economy, mainly because it has efficiently curbed rent seeking. Moreover, he argues that the Danish experience shows that it is possible to create an extensive welfare system, without loosing the dynamism of the economy. It appears that redistribution causes the least amount of damage to the efficiency of the economy if it is confined to personal incomes and consumption, while the property rights and production decisions are left to the market. He notes, however, that a welfare system cannot be created until the economy has acquired a relatively high level of development.

Unlike most Latin American countries, Uruguay has not always been a less developed country. In the middle of this century, the income level there was similar to that of the richest European countries and the Uruguayan welfare system was widely known. In 1985, however, income per capita in Uruguay was still at the same level as in 1954; in Chapter 5, Martin Rama tries to explain why. He rejects the conventional explanation for the Uruguayan stagnation, which builds on the bias against natural resources arising from highly distorting trade policies. Instead, he argues that the stagnation was related to the weakening of the Uruguayan state vis-à-vis the three social groups—civil servants, manufacturers, and wage earners.

In Chapter 6, Helge Hveem outlines the development of Norway from a poor, agro-based economy to a highly industrialized country by focusing on factors related to institutions, policies, and the organization of the external sector. He asserts that the Norwegian transformation, to a large extent, resulted from a strong domestic organization that was legitimized by relative social egalitarianism and parliamentary democracy, combined with rapid adaptation to international technological changes, and heavy reliance on exports.

Compared to the other Latin American countries discussed in this volume, Ecuador is a latecomer. Despite several export booms, it was not until the

1970s, when oil was discovered in large quantities, that Ecuador really took off. In Chapter 7, Galo Abril-Ojeda tries to explain why the export booms prior to the oil era did not generate development. He claims that the main reason was that Ecuador was too far behind to profit from the stimulus generated by the booms. The country was lacking both infrastructure and a domestic socioeconomic and political organization.

Scandinavia also had a latecomer. Until the 1960s, Finland was lagging far behind its neighbors to the west, despite the fact that the standard criteria for growth (education level, savings, investment, etc.) seemed to have been fulfilled during the first part of the century. According to Tarmo Haavisto and Ari Kokko, the explanation of this Finnish experience is to be found in political factors. In Chapter 8, they argue that policies in Finland during the interwar period favored small-scale agriculture, and allowed an inefficient economic structure to survive longer than would otherwise have been the case. When policies shifted in emphasis from agriculture to manufacturing, Finland caught up rapidly with the rest of Scandinavia.

In Chapter 9, José Antonio Ocampo examines the transition from primary exports to industrial development in Colombia. He holds that in a country in which geographical fragmentation posed a basic constraint to economic growth, external economies associated with the construction of a modern transport infrastructure played the leading role. He also argues that exogenous terms of trade shocks, aside from their purely cyclical effects, played a crucial role in the transition between different phases of development. Moreover, he asserts that economic policy played a rather subsidiary role in the process and that policy shifts were largely a lagged effect of changes in the underlying economic conditions.

Finally, in Chapter 10, Lennart Hjalmarsson highlights the main features of Scandinavian industrial policy. This policy differs from the more common, pro-competitive industrial policy of the antitrust type, in that it emphasises productive efficiency more than allocative efficiency. Because of the small size of the Scandinavian economies, the attitude towards monopolies and large companies has been very different than in other countries. Industrial policy has often stressed the importance of large firms that are able to survive in international competition. Hjalmarsson also points at the insignificant role of public enterprises in Scandinavia and discusses the positive role played by the unions for economic growth.

It should be noted that the purpose of this book is neither to provide detailed analyses of the individual countries nor to completely explain the diverging development paths between Scandinavia and Latin America. To make the comparison between the regions possible, the authors of each chapter have been asked to concentrate on selected issues, and stay away from details. Some important issues have been dealt with only superficially, while others, some of them very important, have been left out completely. Among the latter are differences in savings and investment patterns, for which we did not have enough data to make the historical comparison interesting. We hope, however, that the book will open up a new perspective on development policy and that it will stimulate more research into the questions addressed here.

REFERENCES

Naya, S., M. Urrutia, S. Mark, and A. Fuentes 1990. *Lessons in Development: A Comparative Study of Asia and Latin America.* ECEG International Center for Economic Growth.

CHAPTER ONE

ISSUES FOR DEVELOPMENT: LESSONS FROM SCANDINAVIAN – LATIN AMERICAN COMPARISONS

Magnus Blomström and Patricio Meller

Introduction

The wealth and high living standards enjoyed today by the Scandinavian countries (Denmark, Finland, Norway, and Sweden) stand in stark contrast to the long-lived economic crisis that has plagued Latin America since the early 1980s. However, the present contrast hides the fact that Scandinavia developed from conditions that were not very different from those in Latin America, and that Scandinavia exhibited many of the typical characteristics of underdevelopment only a couple of generations ago. In 1870, the small, natural resource-rich Nordic countries had among the lowest per capita incomes of the present countries of the Organization for Economic Cooperation and Development (Maddison 1982, 8). With the exception of Denmark, Scandinavia was so poor that even relatively slow population growth created serious income problems, resulting in mass emigration to North America. For example, from 1850 to 1930, 1.25 million Swedes emigrated to the United States. They came from a country where population grew from 3.5 million in 1850 to 6 million in 1930.

The economic structure of Scandinavia at the turn of the century was very similar to that of today's least developed countries. Agriculture dominated the economies in 1870, and as late as the 1920s, agriculture played an important role. As much as 40 (Denmark) to 50 (Sweden) percent of the labor force was employed in agriculture (Kuznets 1971) at that time.

Income distribution was extremely skewed before the industrial revolution. During the eighteenth century, for example, virtually all Danish land was owned by a few thousand noble families, with large estates tilled by tenants/serfs who belonged to the land. By the beginning of this century, only 23 percent of the rural households in Finland owned land. In other words, the economic situation in Scandinavia a few generations ago could not have been very much different from that in many Latin American countries at the time.

However, detailed comparisons of the Scandinavian and Latin American countries before 1950 are difficult because of the lack of comparable data, and will not be attempted here. Instead, parts of each country's early development

Table 1.1. GDP per Capita

	LATIN AMERICA				SCANDINAVIA			
	(US Dollars in 1980 International Prices)							
	Chile	Colombia	Ecuador	Uruguay	Denmark	Finland	Norway	Sweden
1950	2,536	1,188	916	2,864	4,241	2,758	3,802	3,980
1960	2,932	1,344	1,143	3,271	5,490	4,073	5,001	5,149
1970	3,687	1,711	1,403	3,453	7,776	6,186	7,104	7,401
1980	4,271	2,552	2,607	4,502	9,598	8,393	11,094	8,863
1985	3,486	2,599	2,387	3,462	10,884	9,232	12,623	9,904
	(US Dollars in current prices)							
	Chile	Colombia	Ecuador	Uruguay	Denmark	Finland	Norway	Sweden
1985	1,235	1,208	1,437	1,454	11,310	11,009	13,944	12,006

Source: Summers and Heston (1988) and World Development Report 1987.

Table 1.2. Annual Growth Rates of Real GDP per Capita
(Percent)

	LATIN AMERICA				SCANDINAVIA			
	Chile	Colombia	Ecuador	Uruguay	Denmark	Finland	Norway	Sweden
1950–60	1.5	1.2	2.2	1.3	2.6	4.0	2.8	2.6
1960–70	2.3	2.4	2.1	0.5	3.5	4.3	3.6	3.7
1970–80	1.5	4.1	6.4	2.7	2.1	3.1	4.6	1.8
1980–85	−4.0	0.4	−1.7	−5.1	2.5	1.9	2.6	2.2
1950–80	1.8	2.6	3.5	1.5	2.8	3.8	3.6	2.7
1950–85	0.9	2.3	2.8	0.5	2.7	3.5	3.5	2.6

Source: Summers and Heston (1988).

Table 1.3. Annual Growth Rates of Real GDP and Population
(Percent)

	LATIN AMERICA				SCANDINAVIA			
	Chile	Colombia	Ecuador	Uruguay	Denmark	Finland	Norway	Sweden
GDP								
1950–80	3.9	5.3	6.4	2.5	3.4	4.4	4.4	3.3
1950–85	3.0	4.9	5.6	1.5	3.2	4.1	4.2	3.1
Population								
1950–80	2.1	2.7	2.8	0.9	0.6	0.6	0.8	0.6
1950–85	2.0	2.6	2.8	0.9	0.5	0.6	0.7	0.5

Source: Summers and Heston (1988).

story will be told in the following chapters. The purpose of this chapter is to present some comparative data on production, incomes, population, and trade after 1950 for the eight countries, as a background or benchmark for the country studies. The main findings from the country essays will also be summarized around six central development-related topics so as to provide a comparative perspective and hopefully some lessons for development.

Development Paths after 1950

In 1950, real GDP per capita in the Scandinavian countries, with the exception of Finland, was close to $4,000 in 1980 international prices[1] (see Table 1.1). Although two of the Latin American countries (Chile and Uruguay) had surpassed that level by 1980, none of the Latin American countries had a real GDP per capita above $3,500 in 1985, after the structural adjustment processes. Thus, these figures seem to suggest that there is currently a gap of more than thirty years between the Latin American and the Scandinavian countries in terms of income levels.

It is worth noting that in 1950 Uruguay and Chile had real GDP per capita levels similar to Finland, i.e., around $2,700 (in 1980 international prices). However, thirty-five years later, Finland's real GDP per capita was 2.7 times higher than that in the two Latin American countries.

The annual increase in real GDP per capita has been relatively homogeneous and stable among the Scandinavian countries since 1950. According to Table 1.2, their annual growth rates were mostly in the 2 to 4 percent range. Growth rates in Latin America, on the other hand, have fluctuated from year to year and have differed among the countries. Uruguay and Chile, the two slowest growing economies, grew by less than 1 percent per year between 1950 and 1985. By contrast, Ecuador and Colombia had annual growth rates larger than 2.3 percent during the same period.

A more interesting difference between the two regions, however, is found if we compare the evolution of the two components of their real GDP per capita: growth of real GDP and population. GDP grew at similar, or even faster, rates in the Latin American countries than in Scandinavia, Uruguay being an exception (see Table 1.3). Between 1950 and 1985, Scandinavian annual GDP growth rates were in the 3.1 to 4.2 percent range, as were Chile's, but Ecuador and Colombia had economic growth rates of 5.6 and 4.9 percent, respectively. However, while GDP growth showed little difference between the two regions, there were huge differences in the growth of population. While the annual

---

[1] International prices are based on purchasing power parities as calculated by Summers and Heston (1988). These are corrected for cross-country differences in prices, so that domestic currency to a value of x international dollars can buy the same basket of goods and services in all countries.

Table 1.4. Population
(Thousands)

	LATIN AMERICA				SCANDINAVIA			
	Chile	Colombia	Ecuador	Uruguay	Denmark	Finland	Norway	Sweden
1950	5,950	11,597	3,307	2,194	4,271	4,009	3,265	7,014
1960	7,585	15,754	4,422	2,538	4,581	4,430	3,581	7,480
1970	9,368	21,266	5,864	2,908	4,929	4,606	3,877	8,043
1980	11,104	25,892	7,593	2,908	5,123	4,780	4,091	8,310
1985	12,074	28,468	8,735	3,013	5,114	4,908	4,153	8,350

Source: Summers and Heston (1988).

Table 1.5. Exports per Capita
(US Dollars/Person in constant 1980 prices)

	LATIN AMERICA				SCANDINAVIA			
	Chile	Colombia	Ecuador	Uruguay	Denmark	Finland	Norway	Sweden
1950	217	125	72	213	876	648	1,282	1,029
1960	215	148	142	209	1,636	1,146	2,230	1,641
1970	273	149	136	266	2,808	2,197	4,149	3,174
1980	575	225	389	524	4,242	3,558	6,674	4,456
1985	566	219	440	587	5,268	4,001	8,442	5,660

Source: United Nations.

Table 1.6. Export Share of GDP
(Percent)

	LATIN AMERICA				SCANDINAVIA			
	Chile	Colombia	Ecuador	Uruguay	Denmark	Finland	Norway	Sweden
1950	12.6	10.7	18.6	13.7	26.9	19.0	39.2	21.9
1960	13.8	15.4	27.4	14.3	32.3	22.5	42.1	22.8
1970	15.0	14.0	14.8	12.1	27.9	26.0	41.8	24.1
1980	22.8	17.4	25.2	15.0	32.7	33.0	47.3	29.8
1985	29.1	14.2	27.7	24.6	37.5	29.5	48.3	35.3

population growth rates in Latin America were in the 2.0 to 2.8 percent range, Uruguay excluded, the Scandinavian population grew by only 0.5 to 0.7 percent per year.

The outcome of these differences in population growth can be seen in Table 1.4. In the span of only thirty-five years, the population in Colombia and Ecuador increased by 150 percent. During the same time, the Scandinavian population increased by less than 25 percent. Ecuador's population, for instance, was 23 percent smaller than Denmark's in 1950, but 70 percent larger in 1985.

Rapid growth in population is normally thought of as a poor country phenomenon, but it is worth noting that the population growth in Scandinavia never has been close to the Latin American levels, not even when these northern countries were poor. Between 1820 and 1913, the Scandinavian population increased somewhat less than one percent a year, and for the 1820 to 1979 period, the average yearly growth varied between 0.7 percent (Sweden) and 1.0 percent (Denmark) (Maddison 1982, 49).

Most likely, the rapid demographic growth in Latin America has diverted savings into widening rather than deepening capital, with possible negative effects on economic growth. As an experiment we have asked the following hypothetical question: What would GDP per capita have been in our four Latin American countries in 1980, before the structural adjustment processes, if these countries had kept their own GDP growth, but had had the Scandinavian demographic growth between 1950 and 1980? GDP per capita in Chile would then have been close to the level of Italy and above the level of Spain, while the other three Latin American countries would have had higher income per capita than Portugal.[2] This means that all four Latin American countries would have been "developed" today.

While the Latin American countries, in general, have larger populations than the countries in Scandinavia, their level of exports is considerably lower. In 1985, exports per capita in the Latin American countries varied between $200 (Colombia) and $600 (Chile and Uruguay) (see Table 1.5). In Scandinavia it was in the $4,000 (Finland) to $8,500 (Norway) range. In fact, the Scandinavian countries exported more in per capita terms in 1950 than the Latin American countries did in 1985.

---

[2] Income per capita in 1980 international prices would have been as follows:

Italy	$7,164	Uruguay	$4,972
Chile	$6,642	Colombia	$4,748
Spain	$6,131	Portugal	$3,733
Ecuador	$4,988		

Of course, these figures are only hypothetical, since the labor force has also contributed to the national product.

The export share of GDP has also been much higher in Scandinavia than in Latin America (see Table 1.6). Although the export share of GDP in the Latin American countries has increased rapidly since the 1970s, it was still only in the 14 to 30 percent range in the mid-1980s. This should be compared to Scandinavia, where the export share of GDP in 1985 was in the 30 to 37 percent range (with the exception of Norway, where it was almost 50 percent). This indicates that international trade has played an important role in Scandinavian development. Economic growth has been export led. Exports have served both as an outlet for the output of the countries and to facilitate imports of goods and services, including technology, that could not be produced domestically.

Lessons for Development

Why then did the Scandinavian countries develop so differently from those in Latin America? And what are the main lessons that Latin America can draw from these growth experiences? We have already hinted that an increase in exports and a lowering of the Latin American population growth rate are important issues for the future. As we mentioned above, demographic growth in Scandinavia has never even been close to the growth rates of the Latin American countries. But there are other important factors that to a large extent seem to explain the diverging development paths between the two regions. From the country studies in this book we have extracted the most important ones, and grouped them into six areas.

Agriculture and Agrarian Reforms

What laid the foundation for the Scandinavian transformation to modern and wealthy societies were the agrarian reforms. The Danish reform, which was the first in Europe, was already underway by 1788 and extended over a period of about 100 years. In Norway and Sweden, important changes in agriculture started to occur by the 1850s. In Finland land reforms were not introduced until the 1920s. This probably slowed down overall economic growth for a period, but it was also an absolute prerequisite for the development of the welfare state.

The land reforms in Scandinavia created small and medium-sized, privately-owned farms, which encouraged a more efficient and intensive cultivation of land. The additional income derived from agricultural modernization increased the propensity to invest and innovate, thereby creating the basis for sectors that support agriculture. To begin with, the modernization of Scandinavian agriculture drew upon growing linkages with local craft-based production. Gradually, however, these craftsmen were overtaken by growing industrialization.

With the land reforms, income also became more equally distributed. This gave rise to a domestic market for consumption goods, and provided one of the foundations for the Scandinavian industrialization process, as will be discussed below. For example, in the case of Denmark, at least half and maybe as much as three-quarters of the early industrialization boom during the end of the last century was somehow connected with the agricultural boom.

In Latin America, land reforms did not come until the 1960s or 1970s, if they came at all. The hacienda system prevailed, with negative effects both on productivity growth in the agricultural sector and on domestic demand. Thus, an internally consolidated national economy emerged very slowly in Latin America and when the import-substituting era began, lack of domestic demand soon turned out to be an important obstacle for the industries.[3]

Education

A second important prerequisite for Scandinavia's success is undoubtedly the high level of education of its population. At a very early stage, the Scandinavian countries began to support education. For example, Denmark introduced general schooling in 1814. By the mid-nineteenth century, illiteracy in the Scandinavian countries, with the exception of Finland, was confined to some 10 percent, and by the turn of the century, high quality elementary education was in force in all the countries and illiteracy was practically non-existent. This situation should be compared to the one in Latin America, where the illiteracy rates around 1950 were as follows: Chile, 19.8 percent; Colombia, 37.7 percent; and Ecuador, 44.3 percent. The illiteracy rate in Uruguay was 9.5 percent in 1963, the closest year for which comparable figures are available.

Another factor that characterizes the Scandinavian model of education, particularly higher education, is the strong emphasis on applied science. The University of Oslo, founded in 1811, began as a learning place mainly for law and humanities: towards the end of the century, however, greater emphasis was placed on the natural sciences. An agriculture college was created in 1897, and the Institute of Technology, modeled after the German polytechnical universities, was established in 1910. In Sweden, a redirection towards more "useful" and applied education began in the 1870s. By the turn of the century, the two Swedish Institutes of Technology (Chalmer's and the Royal Institute of Technology) had educated so many civil engineers that many had to leave for the United States, because they could not find a job in Sweden.[4]

---

[3] To some degree, Colombia is an exception to this rule. The coffee production took place in small and medium-sized farms in the western part of the country, and laid the foundation for a relatively faster structural transformation of the Colombian economy.

[4] This migration resulted in an important technology transfer from Sweden to the United States. A third of the Swedish engineers that came to the United States were skilled in mechanics and machinery. They came to construct machines, turbines, and instruments for their American employers, and they left many important landmarks. For example, Swedish engineers constructed the first hopperbottom freight car and the first steel skyscraper in New York. Chester Carlsson invented the Xerographic dry copy process. John Ericsson constructed locomotives, the ship propeller, and the Monitor, one of the first ironclad warships and the one that ended the Confederate hopes of breaking the Union blockade in the U.S. Civil War (see Blomström et al. 1988).

Adult education is another unique Scandinavian feature. The first boarding school for adults was established in Denmark as early as 1844, and this
tradition soon spread to the other Nordic countries. Today, adult education is
an important part of the Scandinavian labor market policy. With training and
education programs provided by the governments, labor mobility has increased tremendously. This has not only helped to keep unemployment low
(Scandinavia has some of the lowest unemployment rates in the world), but it
has also facilitated and spurred structural changes. It has been easier to move
resources from low to high productivity sectors and firms.

Of the Latin American countries in our sample, Uruguay has had the most
advanced educational system. In terms of illiteracy, Uruguay was at a European level at the turn of the century. However, the emphasis of Uruguayan
education has differed substantially from the Scandinavian model. While the
students in the northern countries were preparing for examinations in math and
science, the Uruguayan students were studying law and discussing literature.

Technical education seems to have been neglected throughout Latin
America. In Chile, for instance, during the mid-1950s one could have learned
more about Chilean copper in foreign libraries than in Chilean ones, despite the
importance of copper in the Chilean economy. Neither was there training of
Chilean engineers and technicians specializing in copper. The technical
education that has existed in Latin America appears to differ significantly from
that in Scandinavia. In the Scandinavian countries, engineering students are
generally required to participate directly in production activities after their
formal training is completed in order to develop a deeper understanding of the
production processes. In contrast, the Latin American system of technical
education places more emphasis on formal learning in the classroom and
laboratory rather than practical, hands-on experience.

Furthermore, it seems that Latin American education, in particular higher
education, has not been able to meet the needs of the countries, and the benefits
of education have generally gone to only a small segment of the population.

Natural Resources and Industrialization

The wealth of natural resources is one of the common features of all the
countries studied in this book. But these resource endowments have played a
very different role in the various economies. While the Scandinavian countries
based their future industries and comparative advantages on these endowments, the Latin American countries did not.

Denmark and Sweden were the first to show how industries can develop
out of natural resources. Denmark began as a large grain exporter. By the mid-
1870s, however, Danish grain exports were drastically reduced by the emergence on the world market of new and more efficient grain exporters (particularly the United States). Faced with this situation, Denmark began to seek new
comparative advantages, and found them in animal husbandry and local

processing of meat and dairy products. In other words, out of agriculture grew an agricultural processing sector, which today still plays an important role in the Danish economy.

The Swedish success story is based on iron and timber, which the country began to export in large quantities during the early 1870s. Since that time, these two raw materials have been the mainstay of Swedish exports. The raw materials have been refined and improved and continue to be major export items for Sweden. But they played their most important role in the backward and forward linkages that they created. Tools and machines were needed in the forests and mills. Out of timber grew the paper and pulp industry, and iron provided the basis for the Swedish steel and machine-tool industries.

It is important to remember that the Scandinavian transformation toward processing economies did not take place overnight. The industries grew very slowly out of the natural resources and were, at first, typically more local handicraft production than modern factories. The continuous improvements, elaborations, and refinements of production, however, gradually gave rise to modern, internationally competitive industries.

The Latin American industrialization route is strikingly different. Few competitive industries there have grown out of natural resources. In fact, ever since the days of Prebisch's first writing, natural resources have been treated with suspicion. The fact that foreign firms controlled most of the exports of natural resources in several Latin American countries helps to explain this attitude. These firms remitted substantial profits abroad. When Latin America decided to force industrialization by import substitution, it was not an industrialization based on the countries' endowments that was supported. While the Scandinavian countries slowly and gradually filled in the empty slots in their input-output tables, the Latin American countries filled in all the numbers at the same time; and even worse, they tried to fill in the U.S. numbers! Suddenly there were several small Latin American economies with production structures similar to that of the United States. For example, Ecuador, with only a fraction of the United States' GDP, had almost as many car producers during the 1960s as the big country to the north.

Trade and Industrial Policy

Prior to the Great Depression in the 1930s, both the Scandinavian and Latin American economies were fairly open. Thereafter, they went different ways. While the Scandinavian economies remained open and, as discussed above, used the export sector as an engine of growth, the Latin American countries began to substitute their imports and close their economies.

Since the Scandinavian trade policy is not unique, except that it has always been very open, and since the negative effects of import substitution are well known, these issues will not be further discussed. Instead, the discussion will center on some other features of the Scandinavian industrial policy that differ notably from the Latin American variants. These features include the incentive structure, antitrust policies, and policies promoting structural change.

In Latin America, governments have usually used proscriptions to force firms to act. Such policy measures have been much less common in Scandinavia. There, governments have relied more on incentives and infrastructure support. For example, in Sweden, the government has provided many "basics" for the private sector. Government institutions have been created for improving seeds and spreading knowledge of new plants and new methods of cultivation among the private farmers, and free education has, of course, accelerated the diffusion of technology and economic growth.

Another example of government incentives for the private sector is the corporate tax system. As long as firms in Scandinavia invest their profits, they pay very low taxes. If, however, they decide to distribute the profits to their stock owners, the tax share increases dramatically since the owners have to pay income taxes. Such a tax system favors and stimulates investment, and it has played a very important role in the Scandinavian industrialization process.

Latin American governments, on the other hand, lack the infrastructure to implement and collect personal income taxes. The tax burden is, therefore, on firms rather than individuals: a large share of taxes are collected from external sector activities, particularly from large and medium-sized firms.

When it comes to an antitrust policy, we again find some notable differences between Latin America and Scandinavia. Latin American countries have for the most part followed U.S. antitrust policy, without considering that the policy was developed for a "large" economy, where both productive and allocative efficiency can be achieved by competition in the domestic product and factor markets.

The Scandinavian countries chose a completely different strategy, mainly because of the small size of their domestic economies. Just like the Latin American countries, the Scandinavian ones are too small to support several firms of efficient size, since economies of scale are normally very important. Therefore, their industrial policy has always supported the creation of large firms, and the potential negative effects of monopolies have been taken care of by promoting free trade. In other words, industrial policy in Scandinavia has stressed the importance of large firms that are able to survive in international competition.

Another feature of the Scandinavian model of industrial policy is its focus on so-called structural rationalization. Clearly, rapid growth is not only a result of creating new capacities, but also of destroying old ones. This type of "creative destruction" in Scandinavia has been facilitated by the training and education programs for adults, which have already been discussed. Textiles and shipbuilding are examples of Scandinavian industries which have contracted in this way.

The normal policy response toward declining industries in Latin America has, on the other hand, involved increased protection and subsidies. There, medium and large-sized firms seldom die, even if they are inefficient or located in sectors without comparative advantages, because closing down results in unemployment. To some extent, this policy is a result of the lack of a welfare system in Latin America. Unemployment benefits are rare and there are no retraining programs for workers comparable to those in Scandinavia.

Foreign Technology and Capital

Small countries have to rely on the international community much more than large countries. This is particularly true for technology. Technology, or knowledge in general, can be acquired from abroad through a variety of channels. People move from one country to another, and goods and services cross international borders through trade. Multinational firms establish subsidiaries abroad, but they may also transfer technology through a number of other arrangements, including licensing and franchising.

In Scandinavia, foreign technology has always played an important role, but the channels through which this technology has been imported have varied between the countries and over time. In the early days of the industrialization process, the importing of skills through immigration was important. For instance, Sweden imported blacksmiths from Belgium during the creation of the iron industry, and later on, immigrants from Scotland and Germany played a crucial role in developing the mining and forest industries. The same was true for Norway. For example, when creating the country's textile industry, Norwegian entrepreneurs sought out English textile firms, purchasing not only the production equipment, but also specific production skills, sometimes even hiring English foremen, engineers, or other specialists.

The only Scandinavian country which did not import technology via immigration to any large extent during this period was Denmark. Given the importance of agriculture and agricultural processing in the Danish economy, this is not surprising. There was no need for foreign knowledge to build up new industries.

During the twentieth century, the main technology import channel in Scandinavia has been international trade. By allowing free imports of most goods and services, Scandinavian firms have had access to the latest technology, which in turn has been decisive in their ability to stay competitive in world markets.

Foreign firms have always played a limited role in Scandinavia. In the early days, this was simply because not very many multinational firms existed. At that time, channels of technology transmission other than foreign investment were much more important. When the multinationals eventually entered the world arena on a larger scale, the Scandinavian countries had already developed their own firms of that kind.

The Latin American countries have also had access to foreign technology and have received it in a variety of ways. There has been substantial immigration. Foreign firms have invested much more in Latin America than in Scandinavia, and at least until the 1950s, foreign technology could enter these countries to a large extent through imported goods and services. Still, this technology has never had the same impact on Latin American development as it had on Scandinavian development, and the question is, why?

The so-called convergence school, based on Gerschenkron's (1952) advantages of backwardness thesis, suggests that the more backward the country, the higher the rate of productivity growth achievable by acquiring the technology of the advanced nations. Our comparison of Scandinavia and Latin America, however, suggests that the realization of the potential for productivity catch-up simply because of backwardness depends heavily on another set of causes. In other words, backwardness only carries a *potential* for rapid growth, and certain conditions have to be fulfilled in order to realize that potential.

Obviously, a country cannot be too far behind the leaders to profit from the leaders' knowledge. This has clearly been the case of Colombia and Ecuador. Until fairly recently, these countries were not able to take advantage of the possibilities created by their different economic booms. For the more advanced developing countries, our study points to the importance of education in creating the capacity to successfully exploit technologies already employed by the developed countries. The heavy investment in learning and human capital in Scandinavia not only facilitated the emergence of domestic entrepreneurs, capable of absorbing new ideas from abroad, but it also provided the entrepreneurs with an educated and skilled work force. This never happened in Latin America. The chapter on Chile suggests, for instance, that if Chilean governments had more actively promoted the development of domestic human capital and entrepreneurial capacity, the Chilean economy could have gained much more than it did from the nitrate and copper exploitation of the foreign investors.

A country's potential for productivity growth is also strongly influenced by political institutions, as discussed in the following section.

Socio-Political Aspects and the Role of the State

One salient feature of the Scandinavian model of development is the special relationship between the role of the state and that of the market. At an early stage of development, the governments in Scandinavia assumed the role of producing infrastructure, high-quality administration, and social services, but left the goods-producing sectors to private enterprises and the market. Thus, a heavy taxation of income and consumption has provided free or inexpensive public services (health, education, culture, etc.) and large-scale redistribution of income (between 25 and 35 percent of GDP is redistributed). Industry, agriculture, trade, and banking have, however, remained almost entirely in private hands.

This is in sharp contrast to the situation in Latin America where the governments have participated much more actively in the productive sphere. The most extreme case in our Latin American group of countries is Chile. After 1940, the Chilean government began to acquire new tasks in the economy. At the beginning, the government provided credits to the private sector. Then came the state entrepreneur, followed by the state programmer, who defined the long-run horizon for Chilean economic growth and specified future investment. Finally, in the beginning of the 1970s, the programmer was substituted by a central planner, whose task was to prepare for the socialist society.

Another Scandinavian feature is the consensus among organized labor, capital, and government. This has resulted in political stability which has been very important for economic development. Dramatic political shifts, as those we have seen in so many Latin American countries, have not taken place in Scandinavia since the 1920s.

Meanwhile, relations between labor and capital in Latin America have been characterized as a zero-sum game, which has perhaps been mandated by the very unequal income distribution. Changes of government—either through elections or otherwise—have meant that policies have fluctuated between radical programs for redistribution of income and forceful efforts to restore earlier conservative policies to maintain the status quo. These fluctuations have, in turn, created both internal and external disequilibria that have retarded growth.

The Scandinavian welfare states are well known, but it is worth pointing out that they were founded recently, after the countries had become relatively rich. As late as 1950, the public sectors were below 25 percent of GDP in all Scandinavian countries. In other words, the governments remained satisfied with the golden eggs and were careful to keep the hens alive (at least until the 1970s). This was not the case in our Latin American welfare state, Uruguay. There, the government went for the hen as well.

Conclusions

Latin America is currently experiencing one of its deepest crises in history. The 1980s has been a lost decade, with most countries struggling with short-run macroeconomic problems. However, it is now time to begin to look forward again and take more interest in long-term issues. The current crisis is not only a debt crisis, but a crisis for the traditional Latin American model of development. Countries that have followed other development models have generally never experienced crises such as those in Latin America.

The analysis of Scandinavian economic development is very relevant for Latin America. In addition to having similar natural resource endowments, Scandinavian countries have achieved a high standard of living coupled with an equitable distribution of wealth, which have always been important objectives of Latin American countries. The Scandinavian experience challenges deeply rooted myths in Latin American countries and illustrates possible alternatives for their development.

REFERENCES

Blomström, M., R.E. Lipsey, and L. Ohlsson. 1989. *Economic Relations Between the United States and Sweden,* Stockholm: Industriförbundet.

Gershenkron, A. 1952. "Economic Backwardness in Historical Perspective." In *The Progress of Underdeveloped Areas*, edited by Bert F. Hoselitz. Chicago: University of Chicago Press.

Kuznets, S. 1971. *Economic Growth of Nations.* Cambridge, Mass: Harvard University Press.

Maddison, A. 1982. *Phases of Capitalist Development.* Oxford and New York: Oxford University Press.

Summers, L. and A. Heston. 1988. "A New Set of International Comparisons of Real Products and Prices: Estimates of 130 Countries, 1950-85." *Review of Income and Wealth*, March.

CHAPTER TWO

ONE HUNDRED YEARS OF SWEDISH ECONOMIC DEVELOPMENT

Bo Södersten

This chapter surveys Swedish economic development during a period of 100 years. The history of every country is, of course, unique. The most striking feature of modern Swedish history is its economic success, specifically between 1870 and 1970. Only one country, Japan, has had a more rapid sustained growth. Since a basically historical approach is being taken, emphasis will be placed on the above-mentioned period. Therefore, the specific combination of external events and internal behavior that were unique to Swedish development during the period will be examined.

The Starting Point: Improving Agriculture

Although emphasis will be placed on economic development after 1870, a few remarks should be made about the earlier historical background. In the middle of the nineteenth century, Sweden was a poor, predominantly agricultural country. In 1840, 81 percent of the population was engaged in agriculture. There was a dual economy with a small export sector consisting of iron ore and other minerals. Economic development was minimal, although a certain amount of population pressure began to build up in the early nineteenth century.

By the 1850s, changes were underway, especially within the agricultural sector. One crucial prerequisite for these changes was the enactment of enclosure laws that shifted lands into more homogeneous plots that encouraged more efficient and intensive cultivation. The farmers, in turn, received incentives to improve their methods of cultivation and to clear new land.

The new enclosure laws also had implications for the supply of labor. In earlier times, landless people were allowed a certain amount of "squatting," and their animals were allowed to graze on common land. This came to an end with the new enclosure laws and the new and stricter rights of property that they entailed. In order to feed themselves, the "squatters" had to find employment as farm hands, working for an increasingly established farming class.

Technical improvements began to be made within agriculture. Better

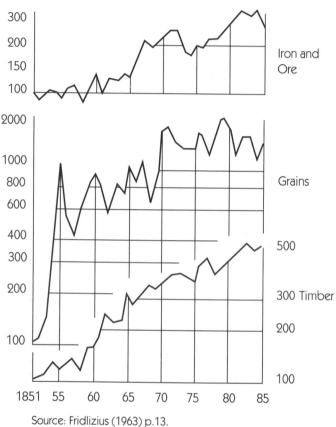

Figure 2.1
Growth of the Volume of Exports of Iron and
Ore, Grains, and Timber, 1851-1885.
(Logarithmic Scale. Index 1851=100)

Source: Fridlizius (1963) p.13.

methods of farming were introduced. Fallow and idle land was gradually eliminated. Improvements in drainage created new agricultural land. The use of fertilizers became more widespread. Simple forms of mechanization were applied. The first reaping machine, for instance, was introduced in Sweden in 1852.

These technical improvements led to a substantial increase and change in agricultural production. During the 1850s, Sweden became an exporter of grain—a fact due also to changes in international markets, especially in the English market, which was by far the most important for Sweden. About 90 percent of Sweden's agricultural exports were oats used to feed horses in the streets of London at a time when horses were the most important means of transportation.

The era of grain exports was comparatively short, lasting basically from the 1850s to the 1880s. It was important, however, since it introduced technical progress and changing methods of production in agriculture. Even the domestic market expanded through increased demand from the agricultural sector. Although production increased substantially, it was still possible to release labor from the agricultural sector. The proportion of the population engaged in agriculture decreased from 80 to 70 percent between the 1850s and the 1870s. A pattern was thereby established that would become increasingly important during the coming periods of rapid Swedish growth.

Another sector important during this "pre-growth" phase of Swedish development was forestry and the production of timber. The latter began to expand in the 1850s. Exports of timber started to increase and became, together with grains and iron ore, the most important export product. This development is illustrated in Figure 2.1. During the 1870s, these three major lines of exports each comprised between 25 and 30 percent of total exports.

The explanation for the growth of timber exports was twofold. First, there was an increase in demand in overseas markets, especially the English market. English tariffs were lowered and other barriers to trade removed. At the same time, England experienced a building boom during the 1850s. A demand-driven export expansion ensued, and the general growth in the world economy created incentives for exports of grains and timber. In both cases, exports grew rapidly.

The second reason for the growth of timber exports was the fall in transport costs, especially in relative terms. In earlier times, most timber had come from the southern and western parts of Sweden. Lower transport costs now made it profitable to exploit the forests of northern Sweden. The introduction of steamships made profitable the transport of even bulky goods, such as timber. Virgin lands of endless forests in the northern parts of Sweden were exploited. A new entrepreneurial and business class ("the tree barons") was formed. These developments began to prepare Sweden for the phase of sustained growth based on industry that took off in the 1870s.

Exploiting Raw Materials, 1870-1890

The beginnings of Swedish industrial development and sustained economic growth are usually dated from the early 1870s. At the time, Sweden was basically an exporter of raw materials. The two major export items were, on the one hand, pig and bar iron, and on the other hand, timber and

Table 2.1. Sectoral Growth of Production in Sweden

Sector	1870–1890	1890–1910	1910–1930	1930–1950	1950–1960	1960–1965	1965–1970	1970–1975	1975–1978
Total	2.1	3.1	3.1	2.6	3.4	5.3	4.0	2.6	0.5
Industry	2.2	3.3	3.1	2.6	3.4	5.3	3.7	2.3	−0.1
Agriculture, etc.	1.5	1.4	0.7	1.1	−0.4	0.4	0.8	1.3	−1.6
Manufacturing	3.6	5.6	4.0	3.8	3.9	7.1	5.4	2.4	−2.7
Construction	2.1	1.4	3.5	2.5	2.3	6.8	3.0	0.5	0.5
Trade, etc.	2.4	3.3	3.4	1.5	3.7	4.7	3.0	2.3	0.2
Transport	5.9	5.5	4.3	3.8	3.9	4.7	3.1	2.4	2.5
Housing services	1.1	1.3	1.3	2.1	5.7	2.6	2.6	1.5	1.2
Public adm.	1.6	0.5	2.4	3.0	3.5	5.5	5.9	3.7	3.4

Sources: For the period 1870–1950: Krantz and Nilsson, Swedish National Product 1861–1970.
For the period 1950–1960: Long Term Plan, 1970.
For the period 1960–1970: Long Term Plan, 1975.
For the period 1970–1979: Long Term Plan, 1978 and *Konjunkturinstitutets rapporter*.

wood products from the sawmills that had sprung up, especially along the eastern Baltic coast.

As previously discussed, this development was already underway. However, by the early 1870s, growth became more systematic, and important linkages were created with the rest of the economy.

Growth was basically export led and trade functioned as an engine of growth. The income elasticity of imports was very high, around 2.0 (Södersten 1959). The most important import branches were food items, agricultural products, and textiles. They each comprised between 25 and 30 percent of total imports and their shares were markedly constant during the whole period. The growth of imports indicated that Sweden, during this period, began to progress from basically a subsistence farming economy, with small export enclaves, to a market economy, in which products such as food and textiles were no longer provided within the scope of traditional farming, but rather were bought in the marketplace and often imported.

The growth of imports is an important but basically derived phenomenon. Exports were the driving force. However, exports consisted largely of basic raw materials. Exports of wood products were most important and comprised roughly 35 percent of total exports during the entire period. Exports of basic iron products fell somewhat, from 25 to 15 percent. Agricultural products were still important, comprising approximately 30 percent of exports.

A significant change, however, occurred in agriculture. The earlier predominance of grain exports vanished. Swedish agriculture could not compete in the long run with such grain exporters as Russia and France, and later the United States and Canada, because of declining transport costs resulting from the use of steamships and railways. Placed in this somewhat awkward position, Swedish agriculture responded with a remarkable feat of adjustment. Instead of producing grains, a switch into animal production was made. Production of milk and, especially, butter, became important. The single most rapidly expanding export item during the period was butter. Here, the relative proximity to the important English market was decisive. The share of butter in total exports increased from 5 to 15 percent. These changes in agriculture were an essential concomitant to the embryonic industrialization and the developing pattern of sustained growth.

As seen in Table 2.1, the overall economic growth rate was 2 percent at this time. This was not particularly high, but the important fact is that it was even and sustained. Thus, Sweden was able to break out of its traditional pattern of being a basically stagnant or very slow-growing economy, with a few export enclaves, to become a more industrial, market-oriented economy.

In the background, certain small but potentially very important changes took place. In connection with trade, international financial links were established and Sweden became an importer of international capital. This capital was largely devoted to investment in infrastructure. Railways were built on quite a large scale. This led to substantial improvements in communications in a country that is geographically large and sparsely populated.

Traditionally, the "bruk," an integrated type of production unit where iron, wood, and agricultural products are jointly produced, has played an important role in the Swedish economy. The "bruks" were often established in the countryside near to raw materials and access to rivers and lakes for transportation. During the latter part of the nineteenth century, a considerable number of these "bruks" were overtaken by competition and closed. However, many others were able to adapt to more modern forms of technology. They survived and prospered, partly due to the existence of raw materials, and partly due to the existence of a work force of people with elementary industrial skills who could be taught modern forms of production. The introduction of railways provided the "bruks" with new means of production. As a result, Sweden continued to have a markedly dispersed production pattern in geographical terms. Quite a few social problems were thereby avoided, as the traditional forms of social control in these often remote areas continued to be preserved even though the means of production underwent rapid changes.

The central cities of Sweden were still small and rather primitive at this time, but a certain urbanization did take place. Cities like Stockholm and Göteborg grew. Capital imports were important in providing financing for the era's building boom.

A certain number of significant "hidden" developments also occurred. The boom of the 1870s gave impetus to the engineering industries. Traditional firms blossomed and expanded. One firm (Nydquist and Holm) that had earlier built four locomotives now built 150, while another (Motala verkstad) built 400 (Gårdlund 1947). A more modern type of engineering industry was established. However, during this time, most firms were not specialized, but instead made a range of iron and metal products within an almost handicraft tradition associated with the "bruk."

An important change in Sweden's educational structure also took place at this time. This was the era when modern methods of instruction spread very rapidly. The structure of the universities changed drastically. Polytechnical universities (*technische hochschulen*) were established in Stockholm and Göteborg. Quasi-state organizations were created and upgraded to foster agricultural and industrial improvements. This is an overlooked and poorly understood aspect of Swedish development that economic historians have tended to neglect. This theme will be discussed in more detail below after further discussion of the historical overview.

Innovations and the Establishment of New Industries, 1890-1913

As previously mentioned, Swedish development until the 1890s had been export led. During the early phases of industrialization, growth was geared to the foreign demand for wood and iron products of various qualities. The increase in demand led, through an accelerator effect, to increased investment. This process had a positive effect on the domestic market, even though development was slow at the outset. Sweden at the time was a poor country with a low national income and a poor system of communications. However, the latter underwent a rapid improvement, as about 3 percent of the GDP was invested in railways during the 1870s. Moreover, 16,000 persons were employed in building railways out of an industrial work force of roughly 100,000 (Jörberg 1984, 30). During this early phase, it was easier for exports to expand than for domestic industries.

The 1890s saw a change in this pattern. From 1890 to 1913, the growth of imports slowed and the income elasticity of imports decreased to 0.8 as compared to 2.0 during the earlier period (Södersten 1959, 12). The change in the import pattern seems to have occurred around 1890. At this time, tariffs were raised because of a change in Swedish trade policy. However, it is doubtful that this change had any real impact (Montgomery 1947). A more plausible explanation is that Sweden had now reached a more mature state of development as a result of the more general establishment of domestic industries.

To a certain extent growth was characterized by import substitution. It is important to realize, however, that this was due not to a change in economic policy but to forces inherent in the development process.

The increase in income from the expansion of export industries, the building of railways, agricultural exports, and the building boom, paved the way for domestic industries. As can be seen from Table 2.1, industrial production grew by over 5 percent per annum during this time. The growth rate also increased to 3 percent per annum. Among domestic industries that underwent rapid expansion were textiles, breweries, and flour mills.

The 1890s was the first period in Swedish economic history when the rate of industrial expansion was faster than that of agriculture. Even though growth became more balanced, expansion and changes in the export sector were absolutely critical. This was the time when the foundations of modern Swedish industry were laid. Exports of timber and wood products maintained their relative position to total exports until the turn of the century. However, their share of exports subsequently fell from about 35 to 25 percent, to be replaced by the growing export of paper and pulp. This change is highly significant as an example of a typical change that took place. Timber and sawmill products were essentially raw materials that required technically simple methods of production. The production of paper and pulp demanded a more advanced technology. This was also a time when production methods changed significantly from mechanical to chemical-based. Sweden was at the forefront of this development. It is significant that productivity hardly increased in the wood industries. Nevertheless, profitability was maintained—prices increased by about 50 percent from the turn of the century to the First World War.

The paper and pulp industry showed a different pattern. Here productivity increases were very rapid. The industry's terms of trade were, however, stagnant. A "profitability index" that weighs these factors showed a fairly comparable development in the two sectors (Södersten 1959, 98). The underlying factors were very different. This is also reflected in the growth of volumes. Exports of wood products were determined by demand factors, while exports of paper and pulp products were supply determined. For an expanding industry that wants to control its expansion, the supply side should be the parameter side. This was the case with the paper and pulp industry, where there was rapid technological improvement and the opportunity to make more sophisticated products suited to a steadily increasing demand. While the export volume of timber and sawmill products reduced imports of such products from 35 to 25 percent during the fifteen years leading up to the outbreak of war, exports of paper and pulp increased their share of exports from 5 to over 15 percent during the same period.

Interesting developments also occurred in mining and engineering. New methods for using and refining iron ore were invented. As a result, ore with a fairly high content of phosphorus could be used. This led to the opening of mines in Lappland and Grängesberg in central Sweden. In engineering, this was the era when domestic innovations began to yield results. The earlier period was characterized by trial and error. Domestic innovations now became the foundation for Swedish firms that would become the cornerstones of Swedish development until present times. It was during this period that multinational corporations such as ASEA (now

ABB), SKF, Eriksson, Separator, Alfa-Laval, and several others were founded.

The increase in exports of iron ore and engineering products from 2 to 8 percent of total exports was important but not predominant during this time. However, the importance of the creation of an internationally competitive Swedish engineering industry based on domestic innovations cannot be overestimated. This period marked the era when the foundations of modern Sweden were laid.

Finance, Entrepreneurs, and Changing Institutions

In the early stages of Swedish development, traders and trading houses played an important role in the financing of agriculture and industry. The family trading houses, based in Goteborg, were active in the expansion of textile and glass industries in western Sweden, in the expansion of forestry and iron works in the province of Värmland, and in the development of sawmills on the northeastern Baltic coast. A parallel role was played by the trading houses in Skåne (usually owned by well-known families) in the southern parts of the country and by the Stockholm traders in the eastern parts and the valley of Lake Mälaren. The traders not only founded industries, but also usually provided the necessary financing before the banks entered onto the scene.

In the middle of the nineteenth century, traders provided financing for the iron ore industry, forestry and sawmills, and textile and other domestic industries. In 1857, the most important industrial bank, the Stockholm Enskilda Bank, was created. The banks started to play a larger role in financing industrial expansion. The capital of the banks initially consisted of their own share capital plus the issuance of bank notes. After a time, borrowing (*inlåningen*) became more important. This was especially the case after the boom of the 1870s.

The growth of provincial commercial banks was particularly notable. Each of the industrially expanding regions had its own privately-owned bank (usually called "enskilda"). The Skåne bank supplied credits to the industrial firms of that region, while the major clients of the bank in Norrköping were the city's textile firms. The bank of Göteborg supplied funds to local industry. In western Sweden, the "enskilda" bank of Värmland financed the iron and wood industries typical of that region and shared in their fluctuating trading conditions. Thus, the banks started to play an important role in the financial and industrial development of the country by channeling the savings of the local bourgeoisie to each region's industrial and commercial undertakings.

A primitive stock exchange for the trading of shares and bonds was established in Stockholm in the 1860s. It initially met once a month; however, by 1895, the number of meetings had been increased to four a month. It had no practical role during the periods under discussion.

The import of capital was very important during the mid-nineteenth century. The primary impact of imported capital was in the financing of infrastructure such as railways and housing. The joint stock companies expanded rapidly as this became the major vehicle both for spreading risks and for financing. In 1881, there were 658 share companies in the country, with a total share capital of 283 million Swedish Kronor (SEK). By 1908, the number of share companies had increased to 2,528 and the total capital to 1,215 million SEK; in other words, the numbers increased by 284 percent and the capital by 329 percent (Gårdlund 1947, 198).

Foreign ownership played a limited role. About 12 percent of industrial companies were foreign owned; in only 2 percent of these companies did foreign owners exert a controlling interest. Nevertheless, in 1895, one of the leading bankers, A.O. Wallenberg, presented a motion to Parliament suggesting that shares only be issued to specific persons, and not anonymously, in order to limit foreign ownership. The motion was denied by Parliament.

Swedish economic development certainly had its genuinely nationalistic streaks. At the same time, trade played an important role as an engine of growth, and many of the technical impulses came from abroad. When it came to establishing the "new" industries such as textiles, food processing, engineering, and, to a certain extent, the pulp industry, imported skills played a key role in the technological development and training of the work force. This was also partly true of the iron and mining industries, even though here the indigenous tradition was much stronger.

In 1957, the trader C.F. Göransson bought the patent for the newly developed Bessemer process while visiting England. Attempts to establish and adapt the new process to Swedish conditions followed immediately. After some failures, successes followed and laid a firm foundation (together with some local improvements) for the renewal of the Swedish iron industry. Swedes were also pioneers in the related area of mineral prospecting. This activity was strongly supported by the state and, as in many of the earlier cases, the impulse came mainly from England and, to some extent, from the United States.

Similar conditions existed in the engineering and textile industries. Early engineering plants, such as the important plant in Motala, were practically built by the English. Aspiring young engineers and workers often went to England for years of study. The Swedes also learned organization and management techniques from the English. These skills were of considerable value, since Swedish plant organization during these early years was rudimentary.

From the 1870s on, the United States became more important as a provider of skills. A domestic weapons industry was established in Eskilstuna and Husqvarna. Typically, when the weapons factory received a state order (a well-established tradition in Sweden), the manager and the leading engineer were sent to the United States to learn the appropriate skills. When the factories in the two cities received substantial state orders, two other engineering firms began to manufacture the machines (from American copies) necessary to produce the weapons.

Later, an increased emphasis was placed on trade and interchange with the new emerging industrial power of Germany. In the last two decades of the nineteenth century, the German influence could be seen in the development of food and related industries: two cases in point were breweries and the sugar industry.

With the passage of time, a fairly strong domestic industrial tradition emerged. As previously mentioned, technical impulses and imports of know-how from abroad were important. However, a domestic tradition of innovation was also increasingly important. The most significant feature of Swedish economic development is probably the blend of foreign impulses with the domestic tradition of innovation and technical skills.

A list of the more illustrious names of Swedish innovators includes de Laval, Nobel, C.E. Johansson, Wenström and Dalén. Some of the inventors and innovators were "village geniuses," while others had solid academic training. De Laval belonged to the latter group. He was a doctor of technology and ran his own laboratory with twenty-five qualified employees. His innovations involving separator technology and food processing were undoubtedly significant. He laid the foundations for the still important Swedish multinational company Alfa-Laval (Eriksson 1978, 90).

Nobel hardly needs an introduction. His most important innovation was dynamite. In 1889, he created AB Bofors, which today remains the most important, albeit slightly infamous, Swedish weapons producer. Nobel had a very high opinion of science and research, as evidenced by his will. Johansson, on the other hand, had no formal education. His great invention was a universal combination of measures (made of incredibly minute polished pieces of steel) that were of great importance in the development of precision tools, particularly those essential to the weapons industry.

Wenström and Dalén were also well-educated. Dalén invented a new type of lighthouse that became standard throughout the world, while Wenström made groundbreaking inventions in the field of electrical engineering. He was an ingenious constructor of electrical generators. His approach was completely theoretical and he had no use for laboratory tests. His inventions formed the basis for ASEA (presently ABB).

An extremely important aspect of Swedish economic development that has been somewhat neglected by historians was the creation of an institutional research structure to support development of natural resources. This aspect has been described, and to some degree analyzed, in a book by Gunnar Eriksson, *Kartläggarna* (The Mappers), published in 1978. The state became very active in developing these institutions between 1870 and 1914. In fact, the government and the Riksdag (the Parliament) created several institutions to map and survey the country to find all its riches and natural resources. A state organization, SGU, was created to conduct geological surveys. Prospecting for minerals became a Swedish speciality and was important to both domestic and foreign mining industries. An organization for sea research, hydrography, and water technology was created, as was an organization for meteorology. Even botany and zoology were supported in a mixed search for applied scientific and economic purposes. Medicine had its own surveys and even arctic expeditions were commissioned (Eriksson 1978, 103).

Cooperation between the state and industry was substantial, intense, and viewed as a very natural and uncomplicated issue. Agriculture was also supported since the state created institutions for improving seeds and spreading knowledge of new plants and methods of cultivation.

This was also an era of a great transformation within the universities and other institutions of higher learning. In earlier times, the universities had been dominated by law and theology. The two state universities at Uppsala and Lund were backward and sleepy. Their purpose was to educate teachers, bureaucrats, and Lutheran priests. During the 1870s, a great change occurred. The emphasis shifted rapidly and drastically to the sciences. A small amount of resources even trickled down to economics and the social sciences. Two private universities were created in Stockholm and Göteborg. Both aimed at being modern places of education and refused to teach theology and law. Technological universities were also established in these two cities. They soon became very important in educating engineers and managers. In Stockholm, an advanced private business school was created.

This was the heyday of the Swedish bourgeois class, although Sweden was a pluralistic and quite egalitarian society. Its industry was geographically dispersed. Although the system of education may have been considered elitist since relatively few received a higher education, all those fortunate enough to attend received a uniform education. There were few private schools and they were of little importance.

The Swedish bourgeoisie had made a very important contribution to the rapid development of the country. However, its reign was brief. Bourgeois values were not firmly established and the middle and upper-middle classes lost their hegemony within a few decades.

Expansion of Trade with Stable Exchange Rates

It has already been established that international trade played an important role in Swedish development during the periods examined. It is appropriate to now return to the theme of international dependence and discuss some specific aspects that might be of special interest to a Latin American audience. Sweden experienced a rapid growth of exports during both periods discussed. From 1870-1890, the export volume increased by 60 percent and from 1890-1930, the export volume again doubled. At the same time, the terms of trade improved. This also led to a very rapid increase in imports.

It may be useful to construct an index over what is sometimes called a country's import capacity or income terms of trade. This consists of the export volume multiplied by the net barter terms of trade (Södersten 1959, 81). Thus, the index takes into account both export performance and changes in the terms of trade. If two countries have the same export performance, their outcome in terms of import capacity may still differ greatly due to changes in the terms of trade.

A significant feature in the Swedish case is that its income terms of trade increased rapidly during this entire period. This is the natural result of the combination of fast-growing exports and improving terms of trade. The income terms of trade increased by 100 percent from 1870 to 1890, and by 200 percent from 1890 to 1913. The increase in the latter period is also partly explained by the increase in overall growth. There is little doubt that trade served as an engine of growth during these periods. One study has attributed as much as 60 percent of the growth of income during these periods to the direct and indirect growth effects of exports (Ohlsson 1969, 53).

Even though Swedish import capacity increased rapidly, the current account balance showed a substantial deficit during most of the years between 1870 and 1913. In 1871, the balance of payments showed a modest surplus of 2 million SEK. This was followed by a twenty-year stretch of continuous current account deficits that amounted to 50-60 million SEK each year, or roughly 2-3 percent of GDP.

The following twenty years showed much the same picture. After a break between 1882 and 1887, when the current account showed a modest surplus, a series of new deficits lasted until 1910. This was followed by two years of equilibrium.

On closer scrutiny, it is evident that there was a certain connection between the growth of import capacity (or increase in income terms of trade) and the current account balance, especially during the latter period. From 1891 to 1897, economic growth was very rapid. The import capacity also increased by over 50 percent. With the exception of the first two years, when a small capital import occurred, the current account was otherwise in balance. From 1897 to 1901, the import capacity was stagnant, and from 1897 to 1909 it increased by a modest 30 percent. These were also years of heavy capital imports. During the final years of the period, from 1901 to 1913, the capacity to import increased at the incredible rate of 50 percent. During these years, the current account also showed a small surplus.

What can be inferred from this scenario? One important figure in the play has so far been missing, namely the exchange rate. Until 1873, Sweden adhered to a silver standard. In that year, the Riksbank (the central bank) announced that Sweden would enter the gold standard. The Riksbank made the transition to the gold standard very smoothly by exchanging silver against gold (which it kept in its reserves). From then on, the krona was kept at a fixed rate against the other major international currencies until the First World War. In practice, this meant that during this entire period neither the authorities nor the economic agents had to worry about exchange rates. Indeed, the era was characterized by an unbelievable innocence about exchange rate matters.

A small caveat should, however, be admitted. As already mentioned, this entire period was characterized by a sustained and rapid growth led by exports. The import capacity also grew at a phenomenal pace. But naturally problems occurred and a moment of crisis existed. It was in this context that capital movements played a major role. One of the more important disturbances occurred in the latter half of the 1870s when exports stagnated. Here the state and the Riksbank intervened by taking a large loan to finance the building of railways. Another crisis occurred in 1907, when the Riksbank was under heavy pressure and losing exchange reserves. Again, a large international loan was floated by Riksgäldskontoret (the national debt office) and the problems were temporarily solved until there was another export boom a few years later.

How much of these capital imports were planned and how much were unplanned? This is a poorly researched area and no firm answers can be given. It seems, however, that during the early period, 1870-1890, a substantial proportion of these capital imports were planned in connection with the financing of railways and other forms of infrastructure. During the latter period, the Swedish economy had become somewhat more diversified and international. The expanding parts of industry financed more of their investment abroad and capital imports became more accommodating, to use James Meade's phrase. The capital imports between 1897 and 1910 were hardly planned or foreseen, thereby producing the currency crisis of 1907 that the authorities had to solve *ex post*.

The Interwar Years: Keeping the Record Intact

Sweden managed to stay out of the First World War. During the first two years of war, Swedish production increased sharply and reached a peak in 1916. The export surplus was very large, about 1 billion SEK. Then the war changed character and Sweden became affected as well. Both exports and imports fell. Industry was unable to acquire the necessary raw materials and input factors. By 1918, industrial production was 25 percent below the 1913 level.

Nevertheless, Sweden was very fortunate. At the outbreak of war, the Riksbank stated that bank notes could no longer be converted to gold. But instead of an outflow of gold, a large inflow ensued. This was created by the large surplus in the current account. The large stock of foreign debt that had been acquired during the forty years of capital imports could now be rapidly repaid at inflationary prices in depreciated currencies. Before the war, interest payments amounted to 10 percent of total exports. After the war, as the international debt was repaid, interest payments were negligible. Thus, neutrality and international inflation gave Sweden an unexpected windfall gain that increased welfare in the interwar years.

In 1919, a certain recovery was underway. This was broken by the deflationary crisis which erupted in 1921. From 1921 to 1922, prices were halved. This resulted in the disorganization of production and a sharp increase in unemployment. By 1923, the 1913 level of production had still not been reached. From then on, the growth process started again.

Production began to increase and grew at a fairly even pace during most of the interwar period. The annual growth of GDP was about 2.5 percent, somewhat lower than in the preceding period and in the years to come after the Second World War. The eight-hour work day was introduced, which meant that the labor supply fell by 15 percent (Jörberg 1984, 33). The 1920s were characterized by the "rationalization" of work and an increase in labor productivity. Overall productivity increased somewhat less, by 2 percent per annum, as compared to 2.5 percent during the earlier period.

Industrial production soon began to increase. From 1923 to 1929, it increased by 64 percent and from 1929 to 1939 by another 66 percent. Overall incomes increased annually by roughly 2.5 percent during the interwar years. During the 1920s, economic growth continued to be export oriented while during the 1930s, it was domestic markets that expanded. The international depression came to Sweden between 1931 and 1932. Its effects were comparatively mild.

The even pattern of growth persisted, partly due to a policy of active demand management by the Social-Democratic government elected in 1932. It remained in power for the next forty-four years. Persistent unemployment continued, however, during the entire interwar era. It was never a question of mass unemployment (except perhaps for a brief period in the winter of 1933), although unemployment never fell below 10 percent.

The 1920s were characterized by surpluses in the current account balance. Sweden became a capital exporter. In the early 1930s, the currency situation was somewhat tenuous as international reserves only covered two months of imports. When England devalued its currency in 1931, the Riksbank decided to follow suit and let the krona float. In 1933, the krona was again pegged against the new rate of pound sterling. That meant an effective devaluation of the krona against the dollar and gold by 44 percent. During the remainder of the 1930s the krona was somewhat undervalued. A small surplus in the current account balance remained. The tradition of currency innocence continued together with a reasonably rapid and even pattern of growth.

Table 2.2. **Increase in Total Population and the Labor Force**
(Thousands of persons)

	A Increase in Population	B Increase in Labor Force	C Due to Factor A	D Due to Change in Work Activity
1870–1890	616	254	209	45
1890–1920	1,120	848	509	339
1920–1940	467	532	489	43
1945–1965	904	425	323	102

Sources: Jörberg 1984, 19; Silenstam 1970, 31 ff.

Population, Labor Force, and the Labor Market

Sweden underwent a fairly rapid increase in population and in the labor force during the first two periods studied. This is illustrated in Table 2.2.

However, there were differences between the decades. The 1870s, for example, showed almost twice as rapid a rate of growth in population as the 1880s. The next three decades, leading up to the 1920s, showed a remarkably steady increase in population. On average, during these fifty years, the growth rate of the population amounted to 0.7-0.8 percent per year.

The interrelationships between population increase and economic growth are complex. Economic development determines population factors such as fertility, mortality, and the marriage rate. But population growth also affects economic growth. Population waves span a long period of time and an increase in fertility, for example, may have its major economic impact twenty or thirty years later.

Sweden was under a certain amount of population pressure during the latter half of the nineteenth century. This is also demonstrated by the figures in table 2.2. The increase in the labor force between 1870 and 1890 was much less than the increase in population. As the preceding decades, especially the 1850s, had also witnessed a rapid increase in population, the increase in the labor force could not absorb the increase in population. The 1870s were characterized by large-scale emigration, especially to the United States. Emigration also continued during the next two decades.

Between 1850 and 1910, 1.2 million people—one-fourth of the population—emigrated to the United States. This enormous exodus enabled the country to avoid instances of extreme poverty and famine. While this inevitably lowered GDP, it also increased capital and land per head and, thereby, income per head. The emigration of so many people led to increased savings that were invested in fixed capital as a prerequisite for industrialization.

As already mentioned, Swedish economic growth was well established during the 1870s and 1880s, but it was not rapid enough to absorb the

Figure 2.2
Unemployment in Sweden, 1911-1967
(Percent of Labor Force)

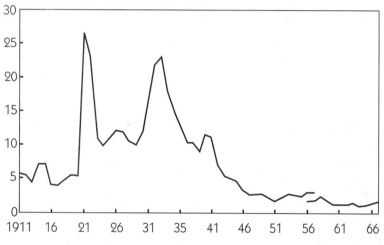

Source: Silenstam (1970), p. 85.

increase in the labor force. This was an important reason behind the emigration during this period. A certain expansion of the labor force occurred, but it is also significant that neither employment nor participation rates increased to any great extent. The unemployment or underemployment hardly decreased at all; in fact for women, it even showed a slight increase (Silenstam 1970, 33).

From the 1890s on, however, the employment creation capacity of the growth process expanded. The increase in the labor force was close to one million and the degree of labor force participation also increased substantially. Thus, the number of dependent members of a family household decreased, as both men and women were increasingly drawn into the market economy and wage employment.

The interwar period, from 1920 to 1940, was again one of relatively slow employment growth. During this era, the birth rate fell drastically and population growth was halved. Due to lag effects, the increase in the labor force was, in fact, larger than the increase in population. Even though economic growth was reasonably high during this era, the labor market was fairly slack. This is shown by Figure 2.2

Unemployment showed two peaks, one in the early 1920s and one in the early 1930s, although it remained fairly high throughout this period and never really fell below 10 percent. This explains why there was little increase in participation rates; in fact they fell for men. The rather stagnant participation rates were due to an increase in the age for schooling and increased education. They were also related to the slack labor market. For women, however, work activity increased, due basically to an increase in the marriage age (Silenstam 1970, 41).

The postwar era is different again. Once more the rate of population increased. This was particularly true during the 1940s, despite the adverse international conditions. Economic growth was rapid, the labor force increased, and Sweden approached full employment.

An important transformation of the labor market also occurred. During the 1920s, trade unions expanded and became increasingly important. Also during this decade, the Swedish labor market was beset by industrial conflicts (Korpi 1974). During the 1930s important changes took place. Collective bargaining on an industry-wide scale became widespread. In 1936, the so-called Saltsjöbad Agreement was signed. This was an agreement between the employers' organization (SAF) and the blue-collar workers' organization (LO) to seek to abstain from strikes on a nationwide basis and to opt for agreements via peaceful negotiations. The signing of this agreement benefitted from the fact that the Social Democrats had come to power in 1932. Close cooperation existed between the government and the trade unions. (In fact, the Social Democratic Party may still be characterized as the political arm of the labor movement.) Thus, a pattern of peaceful negotiations was introduced (for further discussion, see Chapter 10).

This striving for negotiated agreements and a lowering of unemployment laid the foundations for the rapid economic expansion that was to characterize the postwar era and to which the discussion will now turn. In fact, the social and economic developments can be viewed as part of a cumulative process in which one depends on and reinforces the other in a complex interplay of a general equilibrium.

The transformation of the labor market and the search for peaceful negotiations of labor conflicts was an important prerequisite for the rapid economic development that took place in the postwar period. This is also partly explained by the rising hegemony of the labor movement and the Social Democratic Party in Swedish society.

The Golden Era of the Swedish Model, 1945-1970

At the end of the Second World War, the Swedish economy was in good condition, especially in relative terms. Sweden had been able to keep its neutrality during the war and the industrial production system was intact. The first postwar years were somewhat turbulent. Imports were regulated, but tended to grow rapidly. There was a certain fear of inflation. The

Minister of Trade, Gunnar Myrdal, warned against both depression and inflation. In 1946, at the request of Myrdal, the government took the unusual step of revaluing the krona. The logic behind this policy was simple. An appreciation of the currency would combat inflation.

It is hard to dispute this contention per se. However, it is founded on a partial argument. The combination of a natural shortage of imported goods in the aftermath of war and an overvalued currency led to a large increase in imports. Sweden developed a sizable current account deficit. At the same time, it was difficult to find new realistic parities among currencies shortly after the war when most countries relied on various forms of rationing and restrictions. These postwar years were also characterized as years of "dollar crisis" in the form of large surpluses in the U.S. current account and corresponding deficits in the European trade balances. In 1949, England took the lead and devalued the pound by 30 percent. Sweden followed suit without any hesitation. Thus, in the immediate postwar years, exchange rate policies briefly played an important role.

Soon after the devaluation came the Korean boom. The devaluation and the boom jointly led to a sharp rise in inflation in 1950 and 1951. In these two years, prices rose by 14 and 16 percent, respectively. Those were the years of "one time inflation." In 1952, the rate of inflation was down to 8 percent and by 1953, it was 2 percent. Sweden became part of the IMF and adhered to the Bretton Woods system. Exchange rate innocence once again set in, and for the next twenty years exchange rates were stable and, for some reason, the balance of payments was always in equilibrium.

Exports had begun to increase sharply in 1949. During the next two years, the value of exports doubled. The combination of the large devaluation and the Korean boom had a marked impact on exports. Imports also grew, but not as rapidly, and Sweden achieved a surplus on its current account. For the next twenty years, Sweden had no problems with its balance of payments. It was not until the late 1960s that problems with the external balance again occurred.

Exports grew rapidly during both the 1950s and 1960s. During the first few years, the export impetus was due to a change to a more normal economy. As regulations and controls were dismantled, the export share of the economy increased. During the 1960s, the liberalization of trade continued, partly due to the creation of two customs unions, the European Free Trade Association (EFTA) and the European Community (EC), and partly to a general reduction of tariffs and the removal of trade controls and impediments among the western industrialized nations. From 1946 to 1970, Swedish exports increased by over 10 percent per year.

In the late 1940s, exports of paper and pulp expanded. They then settled down to a more stable level of about 25 percent of total exports. In value terms, exports from this sector increased by four times during this period.

The most important export group was that of engineering products.

Their share increased from 25 to 40 percent of total exports from the late 1940s to the late 1960s. The most rapidly expanding single group within the engineering sector, especially during the latter part of the period, was automobile exports (Volvo and Saab). In 1966, exports of cars surpassed imports. Another expansive export group was that of iron and steel products. The growth of exports from this sector mainly included technically advanced, high quality products.

In summary, Swedish exports continued to rely on the country's traditional raw material base. As in the 1870s, exports 100 years later were based on the most important raw materials of iron and timber. Naturally, there were significant differences between the exports of each period. The degree of improvement, elaboration, and refinement was infinitely higher in the late 1960s than in the early 1870s. However, the structure of Swedish industry was quite traditional. The hallmark of the Swedish success story was marked more by a continuous improvement of existing structures and lines of production than by major new innovations. The revolutionary period of Swedish change and development was the period leading up to the First World War. The period after the Second World War was one of developing, refining and adapting the existing structure of firms—especially the very important large Swedish multinational firms—to the changing conditions of the world economy.

When it came to export markets, the other Scandinavian countries played an increasingly large role. The export share attributable to them increased from 15 to 25 percent. However, the major share of Swedish exports went to other Western European countries. In fact, roughly 70 percent of total Swedish exports went to Western Europe, including the Nordic countries. The United States was also fairly important and took 10 to 15 percent of Sweden's exports. Swedish trade with developing countries was insignificant. About 10 percent of overall trade went in this direction. About 12 percent of imports came from the developing countries and half of this consisted of oil (Södersten 1989).

As Swedish comparative strength had been the evenness of its development, Sweden found itself in a very good position in the late 1940s. Swedish economic growth reached its peak between the 1950s and 1970s. As can be seen from Table 2.1, the average rate of growth reached 4 percent per annum, as compared to 3 percent during earlier periods; the early 1960s experienced an especially unprecedented rapid growth. This was internationally a time of rapid development. In comparison to earlier periods, these years were not marked by wars or deep depressions. Sweden managed to keep its relatively advantageous position during these years. Around 1970, Sweden was also at the top of most international comparisons and enjoyed one of the highest per capita incomes in the world.

Most subgroups of the economy grew rapidly during this era, as shown in Table 2.1. Industrial production increased by over 6 percent per annum

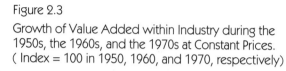

Figure 2.3

Growth of Value Added within Industry during the 1950s, the 1960s, and the 1970s at Constant Prices. (Index = 100 in 1950, 1960, and 1970, respectively)

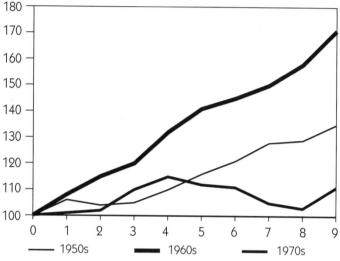

——— 1950s   ▬▬ 1960s   ▬▬ 1970s

Source: Langtidsutredningen 1980.

and most other sectors grew by 4 to 5 percent. A new, distinctive feature was the rapid growth of the government sector. It grew by almost 6 percent per annum during the 1960s. It was at this time that the welfare state became firmly established in its Swedish form.

Industrial development was at the core of the general expansion. Figure 2.3 provides a picture of expansion of industrial production in the 1950s, 1960s, and 1970s. The rate of expansion accelerated during the 1950s and took off during the 1960s. In 1965, the number of persons employed in industry also reached a peak with 743,000 persons employed in industry. Subsequently, industrial employment began to fall, and during the 1970s, declined quite markedly.

The postwar years were also a period of rapid growth in productivity. This period witnessed the most rapid increase in labor productivity ever. During the earlier periods, labor productivity increased by 1 to 2 percent yearly. In the 1950s, the increase was 3 to 3.5 percent per annum and in the 1960s, the figure increased to 4 to 6 percent. In 1970, production per employed in the Swedish economy was seven times as high as in 1870 (Bentzel 1980, 171).

The postwar era was unusually harmonious and prosperous. The rate of inflation was under control: it amounted to 4 percent per annum between 1950 and 1970. The rate of capital accumulation also increased. Total investments rose by 4.5 percent during the 1950s. During a few years of the investment boom that started in 1958, the capital stock in industry increased by 50 percent. The combination of a high rate of expansion in labor productivity and an increase in overall capital intensity led to a rapid growth of real wages, which increased by roughly 3 percent per annum in the 1950s, and 4 to 5 percent per annum in the 1960s. The Swedes began to look upon themselves as a kind of chosen people, and upon their country as a *Schlaraffenland* (paradise). A political and social hegemony under the social-democratic banner became firmly established. The reputation of the perfectly working Swedish model was spread around the world. Social harmony prevailed, built on a rapidly expanding economy. Conflicts were solved by negotiations. Very little opposition to prevailing values were voiced and labor disputes were few and far between. Sweden became known as the home of egalitarian democracy.

The incisive observer could, however, notice some slightly disturbing features during the late 1960s. One was related to the workings of the labor market and the so-called Scandinavian model for wage negotiations (or, as it is called in its Swedish context, the EFO model). According to this model, the competitive sector should have guided wage policy. If, for example, labor productivity increased by 5 percent in the competitive sector and prices by 2 percent, wages could increase by 7 percent.

Due to the solidaristic wage policy, wages were able to increase by the same percentage in the internationally protected sector (comprising building activities, non-traded services, government services, etc.). This, however, produced a slight built-in inflationary bias to the economy. The model worked well for a long time, but towards the end of the 1960s, strains could be observed. The rate of inflation tended to increase, and the competitive sector became too small because of rationalization by firms to maintain labor productivity. Hence, two strains emerged: on the one hand, a tendency towards an inflationary bias and, on the other hand, a tendency towards deficits in the balance of payments. In 1971-1972, a deficit of around 2 percent of GDP emerged.

The Social-Democratic government changed its priorities. A certain amount of unemployment was allowed in order to pursue deflationary policies aimed at closing the current account deficit. The rate of unemployment, which had been about 1.5 percent and was deemed to be the natural rate of unemployment (or perhaps, even a figure below that rate), was increased to 2.7 percent. The balance of payments was again brought into equilibrium, but the higher rate of unemployment tended to persist. The strains witnessed by the slightly inappropriate workings of the EFO model did not disappear. In fact, the days of the Swedish success story were over.

The unique Swedish success story ends with the early 1970s. The last twenty years have been filled with numerous problems and the growth rate has tended to decline. But to concentrate on Swedish development during the golden 100 years, as this chapter has done, shows how luck, ingenuity, and social harmony can contribute to long-term successful development.

REFERENCES

Bentzel, R. 1980. "Svensk ekonomisk tillväxt 1870 till 1975." In *Industriell utveckling i Sverige*, edited by D. Damén and G. Eliasson. Stockholm: Almqvist & Wiksell.

Gårdlund, T. 1947. *Industrialismens samhälle*. Stockholm: Tiden.

Eriksson, G. 1978. *Kartläggarna*, Umeå.

Fridlizius, G. 1963. *Sweden's Exports 1850-1960: A Study in Perspective*. Lund, Ekonomisk-historiska institutionen.

Jörberg, L. 1984. *Den svenska ekonomiska utvecklingen 1861-1983*, Lund : Ekonomisk-historiska institutionen.

Krans, O. and C.A. Nilsson. 1975. *Swedish National Product 1861-1970*. Lund, Sweden.

Korpi, W. 1978. *Arbetarklassen i välfärdskapitalismen*, Stockholm: Prisma.

Lundberg, E. 1953. *Kapitalbildningen i Sverige 1861-1965*. Stockholm: Almqvist & Wiksell.

Långtidsutredningen. 1970, 1975, 1978, and 1980.

Montgomery, A. 1947. *Industrialismens genombrott i Sverige*, Stockholm

Ohlsson, L. 1969 *Utrikeshandeln och den ekonomiska tillväxten i Sverige 1871-1966*. Stockholm: Almqvist & Wiksell.

Silenstam, P. 1970. *Arbetskraftsutbudets utveckling i Sverige 1870-1965*. Uppsala: Almqvist & Wiksell.

Södersten, B. 1959. *Studier i den långsiktiga utvecklingen av svensk utrikeshandel*. Uppsala: Nationalekonomiska institutionen.

_____. 1989 "Sweden: Towards a Realistic Internationalism." In *Internationalism under Strain; the North-South Policies of Canada, the Netherlands, Norway, and Sweden*, edited by C. Pratt. Toronto: Toronto University Press.

CHAPTER THREE

CHILEAN ECONOMIC DEVELOPMENT, 1880-1990

Patricio Meller*

Introduction

Few developing economies have been more studied and debated, with larger disagreement, than the Chilean economy. Chile was one of the most backward Spanish colonies until the War of Independence (1810), but it became one of the most developed Latin American countries by the beginning of the twentieth century. Political stability with an orderly sequence of elected governments prevailed (with only minor interruptions) from 1831 until 1973; being one of the oldest and most stable democracies of Latin America used to be a hallmark for Chile.

Natural resources, especially minerals, have always played an important role in the Chilean economy. During the discovery period (the sixteenth century) silver and gold were important. Later, and until the first half of the nineteenth century, it was copper. During the eighteenth and nineteenth centuries, Chile was an important exporter of wheat. But what really led to a major change in Chile's relationship with the world economy was its export of nitrate, which became substantial during the 1880s. This chapter will cover Chilean economic development from 1880 until the present.

Concentrating on long-term development, two issues have played a decisive role in shaping the Chilean economy. These are the degree of openness of the economy (i.e., outward or inward orientation) and the nature of the main economic agent. Limiting the discussion to these topics means excluding other important economic, historic, political, and socio-logical variables. Yet, in the long-run perspective, the chosen topics have been of central importance for how Chilean development has been shaped.

This chapter is divided into three sections. The first section discusses exports of natural resources and the role of foreign investment between

* Comments by Ari Kokko, Sol Serrano, Aníbal Pinto, Gabriel Palma, Oscar Muñoz, Bo Södersten, Mats Lundahl, Alberto Izquierdo, and the other participants of the project are gratefully acknowledged. The author would like to thank the highly efficient assistance provided by Fernando Lefort.

1880 and 1970, including separate discussions for nitrate (1880-1930) and copper (1920-1970) exports. The second section reviews Chile's import-substitution industrialization strategy and the increasing role of the state (1930-1973). The third section describes the recent structural liberalization reforms and the role of the private sector (1973-1990).

Exports of Natural Resources and Foreign Investment, 1880-1970

Chilean economic history may appear to be a traditional caricature of a developing country in which the main engine of growth and the key link to the international economy is the export of some foreign-controlled basic commodity. During the period 1880-1930, nitrate exports dominated the Chilean economy, and a large share of the nitrate industry was controlled by British capital. From 1940 to 1970, copper was the main export product, and U.S. companies owned the largest Chilean copper mines. During the entire period, nitrate or copper has stood for more than half of total exports.

In this section, the roles of nitrate and copper exports in Chile's development will be examined. The problems and difficulties of a developing country where foreign firms control the main economic activity are analyzed. Some of the development problems posed by a dominant natural resource (NR) sector with a higher productivity level than the rest of the economy are also discussed.

Nitrate (1880-1930)

The large nitrate deposits in the provinces of Tarapaca and Antofagasta, which belonged to Bolivia and Peru, were discovered by Chilean entrepreneurs in the 1860s. The first nitrate mines were also established by Chileans, but the early stages of the nitrate era were dramatic and the large-scale exploitation of the deposits could not begin until some years later. The reason for the delay was that the governments of Peru and Bolivia tried to replace the Chilean entrepreneurs and take over the mines, which were the world's most important sources of nitrates at the end of the nineteenth century. This led to the so-called South Pacific War (1879-1884) in which Chile acquired the northern territory and the nitrate deposits.

However, the war did not win the nitrate mines for Chilean entrepreneurs. Instead, foreign investment flowed in, and the large-scale exploitation of nitrate was begun under British control after 1880 (Pinto 1962; Cariola and Sunkel 1982).

Prior to World War I, natural nitrate was a key input in the manufacturing of explosives; it was also an important fertilizer. Thanks to the large northern deposits, with high nitrate content and easy access to the sea (the large mines were some 40 to 80 kilometers from the sea), Chile soon became the world's largest nitrate producer.

Nitrate exports made up half of Chilean exports in 1890, and nitrate production had a sustained and relatively high growth rate for forty years: from 1880 to 1920 the quantity of nitrate exports increased by 6.1 percent a year. From around 1900 to World War I, the export share was over 70 percent. In value terms, nitrate exports increased from $6.3 million in 1880 to $70 million in 1928, with a peak of $96 million just before World War I. The GDP share of nitrate exports was about 25 percent during the 1900-1920 period.

In developing countries, the government's ability to tax is usually quite limited. Therefore, the foreign sector provides a "tax handle" or a convenient mechanism for the extraction and collection of the taxable surplus. The level of nitrate export taxes increased from less than $1 million in 1880 to more than $20 million in the first part of the twentieth century, and they made up nearly 50 percent of total government taxes from 1895 to 1920. The nitrate exports also contributed to the state's budget in another way: imports, and thereby tariff income, increased with the supply of foreign exchange that was generated by the exports. Thus, taxes on the external sector made up 60-80 percent of total taxation during the nitrate boom.

As a result of the growing tax revenues, the Chilean government acquired a greater share of the economy (Mamalakis 1971; Cariola & Sunkel 1982). In relative terms, the government's share of GDP increased from 5 to 6 percent in 1880 to 12 to 14 percent between 1910 and 1920. In absolute terms, government employment expanded from 3,000 employees in 1880 to more than 27,000 by 1919. Other indicators showing the increased role of the government are related to public expenditure. In 1860, there were 18,000 students in public primary schools, and 2,200 in public high schools. By 1900, there were 157,000 and 12,600 students in public primary and high schools, respectively, and by 1920, the numbers had grown to 346,000 and 49,000.[1] Government railroad construction increased the number of public railroad kilometers from 1,106 in 1890 to 4,579 in 1920, and the public sector began to displace the private sector. Some 60 percent of the Chilean railroads were privately owned in 1890; this figure was reduced to 44 percent by 1920.

The growth of the public sector illustrates the important impact a resource export boom can have on developing countries, even though this fact has been ignored by the "Dutch disease" literature. The abundance of tax revenue generated by the export boom eroded the government's fiscal discipline; financial constraints were not binding. The government re-

---

[1] The total Chilean population in those years was: 1,635,000 (1860); 2,959,000 (1900); and 3,785,000 (1920). Therefore, the percentage of students in public schools out of the total population increased from 1.3 percent (1860) to 10.5 percent (1920). There was also an additional small percentage of students in private schools.

ceived funds through the taxation of foreigners which it used to increase expenditure. Thus, Chilean society became accustomed to low levels of taxation at the same time as government expenditure increased. While no studies have been made on how the additional fiscal resources were used, it seems that a significant share of the resources were allocated to increase the physical and human capital of the country. Yet, it is clear that there were quite a few expenditures and projects which would not have been undertaken if the government had not had access to such abundant resources.

The decline of the nitrate boom began with the production of synthetic nitrate during World War I. The final blow came during the Great Depression, when the value of nitrate exports fell to almost their 1880 pre-nitrate boom level.

The nitrate boom experience has been characterized by many Chilean analysts as a missed opportunity. The extreme version is that nitrate exports generated a large amount of resources that were wasted or taken out of the country by foreign firms, leaving nothing for Chile in the end. This corresponds to the "enclave" hypothesis: The export sector exploited by foreign investment is more connected to the developed countries than to the domestic economy since very few domestic inputs are used, and profits are sent abroad. Therefore, the host economy does not benefit at all from the enclave.

From this perspective, two different issues are often raised: Why were Chilean entrepreneurs not in control of the nitrate export business? Was the contribution of the nitrate export boom to Chilean development really so insignificant?

It is not easy to understand why Chile allowed foreign entrepreneurs to acquire a large share of the nitrate business after having fought a war to protect the rights of Chilean entrepreneurs to exploit the northern nitrate mines. Several explanations have been suggested (for a detailed discussion see Pinto 1962; Mamalakis 1971). The most relevant may be that large-scale exporting required very distinct skills. Although the production technology required for nitrate exploitation was known and available to Chilean entrepreneurs, the scale of production and export was simply so large that the specific human capital that was needed—banking and marketing expertise, organizational and diplomatic external contacts, etc.— was not available in the country.[2]

In short, foreign investment was fundamental to generate a booming

---

[2] There have been charges that corruption at various government levels helped foreign investors. However, as Pinto (1962) points out, where were the domestic entrepreneurs who should have counteracted those actions? If these Chilean entrepreneurs had existed, they would have been very powerful and would have been able to neutralize foreign investors' bribes to government officials. The question of for whom the South Pacific War was fought would have been very difficult to answer.

nitrate export business. Foreigners obtained large returns for their investment, and the Chilean government was able to get an important share of the
surplus. It has been argued that Chile should have retained a larger share of
the surplus. In this respect, it should be pointed out that the main (and
possibly only) objective of government policy with respect to the nitrate
sector was to extract Chilean surplus through the taxation of nitrate exports.
Tax revenues from nitrate exports reached about 30 percent of total nitrate
sales; compared to earlier government revenues, this percentage was quite
high. On the other hand, nitrate production was a highly profitable activity;
after-tax profits have been estimated to be over 30 percent of gross sales.[3]
Given the fact that foreign investors controlled approximately 70 percent
of nitrate exports, profit remittances out of Chile would have reached about
6 percent of GDP (Mamalakis 1971).[4] This figure is higher than the present
share of foreign debt service.

Nevertheless, a large part of the nitrate export surplus remained in
Chile. As mentioned earlier, the government used part of the nitrate tax
revenues to finance social and physical infrastructure. Some of the nitrate
surplus also stayed in the Chilean private sector. Where this occurred, there
were many examples of wasted resources through "conspicuous consumption." In fact, for several years during the nitrate boom, imports of
consumption goods such as wine, jewels, cloth, and perfumes were almost
twice as large as imports of industrial and agricultural machinery (Pinto
1962).

In all, the nitrate export experience provided a big push to the Chilean
external sector and nitrate became the engine of growth. It also generated
two fundamental structural changes in the Chilean economy. First, foreign
investors became important agents, mainly in the mineral export sector.
Second, in spite of the prevailing laissez-faire ideology, government began
to have an increasingly important role in the economy because of the large
tax revenues generated by nitrate exports.

Copper (1920-1970)

Copper was already one of the main Chilean export products during the first
half of the nineteenth century. Chilean copper production was carried out

---

[3] Nitrate export sales would be divided in the following way (Mamalakis 1971):
one-third for production costs, one-third for government taxes, and one-third for nitrate
producers' profits.

[4] Nitrate exports represented about 25 to 35 percent of GDP. Sixty to seventy
percent of nitrate production was foreign owned. It was assumed that foreign firms were
10 percent more efficient than domestic ones, and after-tax profits represented one-third
of total sales. Mamalakis (1971) adds amortization of capital which is included among
the production costs, and arrives at a figure of 7 percent of GDP for profit remittances.

Table 3.1. Share Retained by Chile of the Value of Production of Large Copper Mining, 1925–1971
(Percent)[a]

Prior to 1925	1925–40	1941–51	1952–60	1961–70	1971
Around 11	38	58	61	66	(nationalization)

[a] Percentage corresponds to the median value of the annual percent of each period.
Sources: 1925–1951: Reynolds 1965.
         1952–1970: Ffrench-Davis 1974.

by a large number of small mines, none of which produced more than 20,000 tons per year. These small mines had a very high copper content of up to 10 percent and the technology used was very rudimentary and highly labor intensive. During this time, copper was mainly used for kitchen utensils and some construction work. By the end of the nineteenth century, however, there was a sharp increase in the world demand for copper, generated by the new electrical industry and the expansion of the construction sector. Concurrently, a major technological innovation (in the U.S.) made the large-scale exploitation of ore with low copper content (1-2 percent) profitable. This new technology was highly capital intensive.

U.S. firms discovered and began investing in the world's largest underground copper mine, El Teniente, in 1904, and in the world's largest open pit copper mine, Chuquicamata, in 1911. The initial investment in Chuquicamata was around $125 million. Production in the two mines expanded rapidly. By 1924, El Teniente was producing 78,000 tons per year and Chuquicamata was producing 107,000 tons per year.[5] In other words, in ten to fifteen years, the two large copper mines were producing 80 percent of the total Chilean copper output. From that point on, the large copper mines have represented about 80 to 90 percent of Chilean copper exports.

One may again ask why foreign firms exploited the Chilean copper mines. The answer seems to be similar to the nitrate case. Although there were both Chilean copper producers and domestic investment resources generated by nitrate exports, the exploitation of copper required sizable investments and the use of modern, large-scale technology that was unknown to Chilean producers. Moreover, investment in large-scale copper mining is a slowly maturing activity, requiring many years for the return on invested capital. This was a notable difference to the known process of nitrate exploitation (Reynolds 1965). Therefore, there were no domestic entrepreneurs who were able to initiate large copper mining exploitation.

---

[5] For more detailed information on the history of Chilean copper, see references provided in Meller (1990).

Table 3.1 shows how much of the value of the production of large copper mining (LCM) was retained in Chile. Three different periods can be distinguished. Prior to 1925, a sort of laissez-faire attitude prevailed. Nitrate exports provided enough government revenues during the time when copper exports were slowly expanding. Given the large amount of investment made by U.S. firms (the Chilean share of LCM production was around 11 percent), copper taxes were kept very low, at less than one percent of total copper sales.

In the 1925-1960 period, the Chilean government increased the taxation of LCM production. During the 1950s, taxation accounted for about 60 percent of the Chilean share of LCM exports, and the average tax rate on LCM exports was close to 38 percent. At that time, Chileans controlled 61 percent of LCM exports. Another mechanism used to increase the Chilean share was related to the wage bill, but the spillover effects were minimal because less than one percent of the labor force worked in the copper mines. Moreover, because of the relatively backward technological level of Chilean industry, it was difficult to implement a "buy local inputs" policy.

A concern that U.S. firms were not expanding Chilean copper output according to Chilean goals was evident during the 1950s. Then, another element was added to the bargaining between the Chilean government and U.S. firms, namely, the increase of investment. The U.S. firms' slow rate of investment, together with the perception that foreign exchange was the main bottleneck of Chilean development and that larger copper exports could eliminate that bottleneck, suggested that Chile and the U.S. firms did not share the same objectives. Although the domestic Chilean share of LCM exports increased to 66 percent during the 1960s (the highest level up to that time), that was not considered to be enough. Copper was thought to be too important for Chilean development to be foreign controlled. Therefore, the issue of Chilean participation in production and investment decisions became fundamental in the bargaining process between the Chilean government and U.S. firms.

LCM exports gained increasing importance in the Chilean economy. Beginning with 1945, LCM exports made up over 50 percent of total exports (and even close to 60 percent in the 1955-1959 period).[6] The taxation of LCM exports was over 26 percent of total government taxation in the 1950s. This share decreased to about 20 percent in the second half of the 1960s due to an increase in the domestic tax effort (Ffrench-Davis

---

[6] As mentioned previously, LCM exports constituted about 80 to 90 percent of total copper exports. Therefore, the share of total copper exports as compared to total Chilean exports has been higher than 70 percent from 1955 on, being even close to 80 percent in some years during the 1955-1970 period.

1974). The relative importance of LCM exports in total GDP fluctuated between 6 and 9 percent between 1950 and 1970.[7]

It is interesting to look closer at Chilean policies with respect to the LCM sector.[8] As pointed out previously, taxation was the main mechanism used to extract the economic surplus from U.S. LCM firms. Direct profit taxes were the most important tool. The exchange rate was also used as a tax tool. There were different ways in which the exchange rate played this tax function. Overvaluation of the exchange rate was considered a mechanism by which foreign firms controlling the export sector would transfer resources to the domestic economy. Furthermore, a dual exchange rate system was implemented with a special (more overvalued) exchange rate for copper exports to generate a larger transfer. The operational expenditures of the LCM firms required that foreign currency be sold to the Central Bank in exchange for domestic currency, and the special copper export exchange rate was used for this purpose. Hence, the exchange rate was used for a different purpose than to provide a signal for resource allocation between tradables and non-tradables. Tradable production for the domestic economy was protected by a complex and high tariff system. This type of policy could be justified by the "Dutch disease" framework in which the highly productive export commodity is taxed and isolated from the rest of the economy. To avoid deindustrialization, subsidies are given to the other sectors producing tradables through tariff protection.[9]

There has been sharp criticism of the Chilean governments for not having a clear policy with respect to copper (Ffrench-Davis 1974). Until 1955, there was a lack of information within the country about Chilean copper and the role of copper in the world in general. In fact, it was often stated that one could learn more about Chilean copper in foreign libraries than in the national ones. Statistical information on copper was scarce, and U.S. firms restricted access to their data for reasons of confidentiality. During this time, there was little or no discussion about the most appropriate strategy of copper exploitation according to Chilean objectives. There was also a complete lack of concern about the development of domestic human capital capacity, i.e., there was no training of engineers and technicians specializing in copper. It was not until 1955 that the Copper Department was created to oversee U.S. firms' LCM operations and to collect statistics on physical production, prices, taxation, profits, and so forth. This process created a bureaucracy of Chilean professionals, engineers, economists,

---

[7] Morán (1974) has made the following analogy: Fortune 500's largest U.S. corporations have never played as important a role in the U.S. economy as the two U.S. firms exploiting LCM played in the Chilean economy during the 1950-1970 period.

[8] For a more detailed and profound discussion of this subject, see Ffrench-Davis 1974a.

[9] However, as discussed in the next section, these foreign trade policies created important distortionary problems.

accountants, and lawyers who were able to analyze and check U.S. companies' balance sheets and economic information. During the 1960s, Chilean human capital experience and competence greatly increased; even in U.S. LCM firms, most people were Chilean. For example, at Kennecott (El Teniente) only ten out of 10,000 workers were foreign, including white-collar, blue-collar, management, professionals, and technicians (Morán 1974).

In short, it took about forty years, from 1925 to 1965, to develop a domestic capacity to analyze the role of copper and to educate Chilean professionals and technicians in the management of LCM. More specifically, it took thirty years (1925-1955) for the Chilean governments to realize that Chile had to build such a capacity and about ten years to train Chilean specialists. This slow awareness process is a clear indication of underdevelopment. A laissez-faire environment maintained a situation where the government neglected to educate domestic copper specialists. The attitude was that if the U.S. firms required copper technicians, let them solve their own problem. One of the main roles of ECLA (Comisión Económica para América Latina, CEPAL) during the 1950s was to increase Latin American consciousness about the need for more active policies to pursue Latin American objectives: in this way ECLA provided an important stimulus for developing regional thinking capability.[10]

Over time, there has been a changing perception of what is a "fair distribution" of LCM surplus between U.S. companies and the Chilean government (Morán 1974). The profits and capital depreciation remittances by U.S. LCM companies represented 1-2 percent of GDP in the 1950-1970 period (Ffrench-Davis 1974), and were considered to be relatively high with respect to domestic resource availability for investment in Chile. Given that total domestic investment was about 20 percent of GDP, U.S. companies' profit remittances were close to 10 percent of gross savings. Moreover, the yields of the U.S. companies in Chile were much larger than elsewhere. During the 1950s, the rates of return of U.S. copper multinational companies were at least 19 percent per year in Chile and less than 10 percent per year worldwide. The yearly rates for the 1960-1965 period were 14.8 percent for Chile and 4.8 percent worldwide (see Table 3.2). However, it is not clear why the investment levels of the U.S. companies were lower in Chile than elsewhere. Chilean governments claimed that Chilean copper output was losing its share of world copper production. In fact, in the 1945-1970 period, there was a decline of the Chilean share of world copper output from 21 percent (1945-1949) to 15 percent (1950-1959) and to 14 percent (1960-1970). However, it should be remembered that the Cuban Revolution created an unfriendly environment for U.S. investment overall in Latin

---

[10] This fact is independent of the issue that some of ECLA's policy proposals might have generated important economic distortions.

Table 3.2. Investment and Rate of Return of U.S. Multinational Copper Companies (Anaconda and Kennecott), 1945–1965

| | Return on Assets (Annual average) (Percent) | | Investment (Total for period) (US$—millions) | |
	In Chile	Worldwide	In Chile	Worldwide
1945–1950			35	195
1950–1955	19.0	9.0	115	344
1955–1960	25.9	9.5	168	519
1960–1965	14.8	4.8	82	422

Source: Morán 1974. An average procedure has been used, giving 60 percent to Anaconda and 40 percent to Kennecott figures. Kennecott has higher rates of return in Chile and elsewhere.

Table 3.3. Comparison of the Relative Importance of Nitrate and Copper in the Chilean Economy
(Percent)

	Export Share of GDP (1)	Share of Total Exports (2)	Share of Total Taxes (3)	Foreign Profits percentage of GDP (4)
Nitrate 1900–1920	25 to 35	65 to 80	45 to 53	5 to 7
Copper (LCM) 1950–1970	7 to 9	55 to 65	15 to 30	1 to 2

Sources: Palma 1979; Reynolds 1965; Mamalakis 1971; Ffrench-Davis 1974.

America during the 1960s, which might be a partial explanation for the falling investment rates.

There seems to have been a self-fulfilling prophecy in the behavior of the U.S. copper companies in their Chilean investment pattern. Looking at the increasing share of Chilean taxes on copper rents, U.S. companies restricted investment, and tried to get out as much profits as possible while they could. This, in turn, led to heavier taxation and, finally, to the nationalization of the copper mines in 1971.

Besides the LCM nationalization experience, there are several other events related to U.S. government interference in the Chilean copper economy (Pinto 1962; Reynolds 1965; Morán 1974). During the Great Depression, World War II, and the Korean War, the U.S. government imposed either a price ceiling on Chilean copper or an excise tax on copper imports that led to important economic losses for Chile.[11] This action left

---

[11] There is a range of estimates between $100 million and $500 million. The differences are related to the use of the price of copper in the U.S. market or in the world market. In per capita terms, Chile's contribution to financing World War II would be higher than the Marshall Plan for rebuilding Europe (see Morán 1974).

many Chileans with the perception that free trade and free price systems were applied only when they were convenient to the U.S. economy, but suspended when they might benefit the Chilean economy. Chile had to absorb the costs related to depressed copper prices, but could not benefit from boom prices. This is one of the elements stressed by the Latin American dependencia social scientists.

Lessons Learned from the Nitrate and Copper Experiences

Table 3.3 provides a comparison of the relative importance of nitrate and copper in the Chilean economy during their respective peak periods. All indicators show a much larger relative importance of nitrate exports, mainly because nitrate exports represented about 30 percent of GDP, whereas LCM exports constituted about 8 percent. However, the relatively low GDP during the nitrate era overestimates the importance of nitrate as compared to LCM exports. In fact, in dollar terms of equal purchasing power, annual LCM exports during the 1950-1970 period were similar to annual nitrate exports during the 1900-1920 period.

In both cases (nitrate and copper), it has been argued that export fluctuations generated instability in the balance of payments and in government revenues. However, world prices of nitrates were quite stable (although copper prices were unstable) and export values of both commodities were stable. Moreover, considering the respective periods, it is not possible to reject the null hypothesis of no trend of the terms of trade during the nitrate era, 1885-1915, whereas the Chilean terms of trade clearly improved during the copper period 1940-1970.[12] In short, ECLA's general criticism regarding a deterioration of the terms of trade and export instability has not really described the main problems generated by the dominance of one NR commodity in the export basket in the Chilean case.

In the nitrate case, the end of the boom story is related to the appearance of synthetic nitrate produced at a relatively lower cost, which eventually displaced Chilean natural nitrate from the world market. The Chilean problem in this context is to have put most eggs of Chilean development in the nitrate export basket; the predominant role played by nitrate in the Chilean economy and the almost monoexport feature of exports generated a highly vulnerable economy. But in spite of nitrate export instability problems, and in spite of the northern ghost towns that were left after the crash of the nitrate boom, Chile was able to take an important step ahead in its development path as a result of nitrate exports.

In the copper case, the main problem is a profound discrepancy between U.S. multinational companies and the Chilean government with

---

[12] For empirical tests, see Meller 1990; for a different view, see Palma 1984.

Table 3.4. Impact of the Great Depression upon the Chilean Economy
(Percent)

	Situation at year 1932 w/r. to		Situation at year 1938 w/r. to	
	1929[a]	1927–1929[b]	1929[a]	1927–1929[b]
GDP	− 45.8	− 38.3	− 7.3	+ 5.5
Exports	− 81.4	− 78.3	− 38.4	− 28.2
Nitrate x-Prices	− 59.0	− 61.1	− 45.2	− 48.0
Nitrate x-Quantum	− 78.5	− 74.0	− 56.8	− 47.7
Copper x-Prices	− 69.3	− 63.4	− 44.8	− 34.3
Copper x-Quantum	− 71.4	− 68.6	− 10.1	− 1.2
Imports	− 86.8	− 83.5	− 68.7	− 60.7
GDP/Cap	− 48.2	− 42.0	− 16.1	− 6.0

Note: The figures shown correspond to the percent of variation with respect to the reference level, i.e., a − 45.8 percent for GDP means that GDP of 1932 fell 45.8 percent with respect to the 100 level of 1929.
[a] (1929 = 100)
[b] (Average 1925–1929 = 100)
Source: Sáez 1989 (for basic data references).

respect to investment decisions and output expansion of LCM. During the 1950-1970 period, LCM under the control of U.S. firms had an annual output growth rate of less than 2.5 percent, while after nationalization, in the 1971-1987 period, LCM exhibited an annual output growth rate of more than 4 percent.

Nitrate and LCM exploitation by foreign investors emerged mainly because of the absence of domestic entrepreneurs who could engage in large-scale operations. From the Chilean perspective, foreign investment was the best alternative available at the time. The enclave hypothesis underestimates the development effects on Chile from the foreign-controlled nitrate and copper exports.[13] However, if Chilean governments had adopted a more active attitude leading to an earlier development of domestic human capital and entrepreneurial capacity, the Chilean economy could have had a larger share of the surplus generated by the NR export sector.

Industrialization and the Role of the State, 1930-1973

The impact of the Great Depression of the 1930s on the Chilean economy was so severe that it produced a complete change in the pattern of development: "inward-oriented development" replaced "outward-oriented development." Industrialization was considered to be the formula for developing the domestic economy. Therefore, import-substitution industrialization (ISI) became the first stage of the development process, making industry the new engine of growth. Due to the relatively slow reaction of the

---

[13] There is widespread agreement on this issue in Chilean literature; see Meller 1990 for references.

private sector, and the perception that large basic industries in key energy and intermediate input sectors were a prerequisite for a successful ISI, the state took on an increasingly important role in the economic process.

The Impact of the Great Depression

A League of Nations' report stated that Chile was the country that was hardest hit by the Great Depression. Using the average of years 1927-1929 as a reference level, the economic situation in 1932 (the worst year of the Depression for the Chilean economy) can be explained as follows (see Table 3.4). GDP fell by 38.3 percent and the level of exports and imports were reduced by 78.3 percent and 83.5 percent, respectively. GDP per capita was about 60 percent of the 1927-1929 level. The quantities of nitrate exports and copper exports were at their 1929 levels, but the international prices of nitrate and copper fell by some 60 and 70 percent, respectively.

The recovery of the Chilean economy was fast, at least for the domestic variables. By 1938, GDP had recovered the level it had prior to the Depression, although GDP per capita was still 6 percent lower.[14] However, the variables related to the external sector recovered more slowly. Exports stood at 70 percent of their pre-Depression level. Import recovery was even slower, and by 1938 had reached 40 percent of the earlier level.

The severity of the Great Depression was related to the serious magnitude of the external shocks. However, domestic policy "helped" to magnify the internal effects. Economic dogmatism led Chile to maintain the gold standard and full convertibility even after it had been abolished in the United Kingdom.

The Depression led to the abrupt abandonment of both the NR export-oriented strategy and the laissez-faire policies. This was not motivated by ideology, but by the nature and gravity of economic problems generated by the Depression. Reliance on exports (like nitrate or copper) as the leading sector that could keep the domestic economy going was not a feasible alternative. Moreover, the damaging effect of the external shocks was evidence of the Chilean economy's vulnerability. Therefore, development priorities had to be oriented towards sectors producing for the domestic market in order to avoid external instability problems. While the developed countries emerged from the Great Depression with the goal to avoid high unemployment, the Latin American countries seemed to have decided to reduce their dependence on the external sector. One of the outcomes of this process was that the role of the government began to change gradually, from liberalism to restrictionism and from restrictionism to intervention-ism, so that the public sector was made into an important productive agent.

---

[14] This is equivalent to the recovery period of the Depression of the 1980s; however, the fall of GDP in the 1980s was "only" 16 percent (1982-1983).

Import-Substitution Industrialization

Let us start with a schematic overview of the ISI strategy. It should be pointed out that some Latin American countries, including Chile, implemented the ISI strategy in the 1930s, before the ECLA framework of thought and policy prescriptions was formulated in the 1950s.

The emergence and the main elements of ISI can be sketched as follows.[15] The impetus for ISI came from abroad. World War I, the Great Depression and World War II created severe shortages of imported goods, which raised their relative prices, thereby increasing the profitability of investment in ISI. Particularly during the Great Depression, the huge contraction of imports created a vacuum; although local demand decreased, it was still there, and ISI filled the void. This first stage of ISI was generated by market incentives: prices and profit differentials were the mechanisms by which resources were channeled to manufacturing.

In the second stage of ISI, the government played a more active role. The Latin American development strategies were to accomplish two objectives: (i) economic independence of world markets, and (ii) reduction of external vulnerability. ISI was the easiest way to solve these two objectives, and manufacturing industry became the engine of growth. In fact, before the 1960s, ISI was believed to be the only mechanism leading to industrialization. Infant industry was to be protected. The main tools used to promote ISI were high tariff protection, special incentives to manufacturing through cheap credit and special access to foreign exchange, and public investment in infrastructure oriented towards complementing industrial production.

The promotion of manufacturing industry was indiscriminate, i.e., there were no attempts to focus the incentives on those industries that might have had potential comparative advantages. Any domestic production that replaced imports was believed to eventually increase national welfare. This scheme led to "ISI at any cost," with benefits that were believed to come later.

There is a discussion in Chilean literature about when ISI really began in Chile, i.e., if it was before or after the Great Depression.[16] An industrial sector existed in Chile prior to 1930; manufacturing industry represented about 11 percent of GDP in 1908, and it had an average annual growth rate of 3.5 percent in the 1908-1925 period. Although a free trade regime prevailed, the average implicit import tariff during the 1880-1930 period fluctuated between 15 and 25 percent (Behrman 1976), and high transport costs were an additional barrier to rudimentary manufacturing production. As previously mentioned, the nitrate boom spending effect may also have

---

[15] For classical references on this subject, see Meller 1990.
[16] See Muñoz 1978; Palma 1984.

stimulated the production of low quality manufacturing goods. This would correspond to an ISI induced by market incentives.

During the Great Depression, the Chilean policy environment changed completely. ISI and the foreign-sector-controlled (and almost closed) economy replaced the monoexport open economy as the way to economic development. Although there existed tariffs for imports and taxes for exports before the 1930s, there were no other restrictive policies, and there existed a unified exchange rate. During the 1930s, Chile implemented the main ISI tools which most Latin American countries would implement after World War II. Restrictive policies with respect to the external sector were considered the most efficient policies to promote ISI and to maintain and allocate scarce foreign exchange. All types of restrictive tools were used in the 1932-1973 period (Behrman 1976; Ffrench-Davis 1973). Foreign exchange controls were introduced during the Great Depression and have continued to the present, although there has been some relaxation of the controls during certain periods. Other examples of restrictive tools included multiple exchange rates, high and wide dispersion of tariffs, many different taxes and surcharges on imports, licensing, quotas and prior deposits for imports, permitted and prohibited imports lists, explicit and implicit subsidies, exemptions and special regimes, direct taxes on exports and tax rebates, and special regulations concerning foreign investment and related capital movements.

However, despite the fact that Chile had an ISI policy early on, it was not possible to fulfill the objectives of such a policy because of a shortage of foreign exchange. Moreover, necessary machinery could only be imported after World War II. Up to that time, an ISI with a low technology level was the only feasible alternative (Behrman 1976). During the 1940s, industry's annual growth rate was 4.4 percent, slightly higher than in the 1908-1925 period. During the 1950-1970 period, industry showed an annual growth rate of 5.6 percent, which was higher than the 4.0 percent GDP annual rate.

The ISI strategy increased the importance of the manufacturing industry in the Chilean economy; the industrial share of GDP, which was around 13 percent in 1925, increased to more than 25 percent by 1970. However, overall GDP performance was considered to be unsatisfactory, and the increases in domestic productivity were very low. While total productivity growth during 1950-1973 was 1 to 1.5 percent per year in all of Latin America, in Chile it was less than one percent. In developed countries, total productivity increased by 2 to 3 percent during the same period. The Chilean economy had a relatively slow incorporation rate of modern technology into its productive sectors (Marshall 1984).

During the 1960s, the ISI strategy began to be criticized. There were widespread signals of inefficiency in domestic industry. ISI had not been able to make the domestic economy independent from the external sector. On the contrary, the degree of dependence seemed to be at best unchanged.

There are several reasons for the persistent vulnerability of the domestic economy to the external sector after a long period of ISI. The export share of GDP has been reduced, but the low diversification structure of the export basket is still the same: one basic NR commodity (copper) constitutes more than 65 percent of total exports. The anti-export bias policies of ISI are responsible for these results. The import coefficient of the Chilean economy has been reduced compared to the one prevailing prior to the Great Depression, but there has been an important change in the import structure. Now, imports are dominated by intermediate inputs necessary to keep production running, and capital goods imports crucial for growth. Therefore, present balance of payments crises produce a contraction of imports and in this way, a reduction of present output levels and future growth rates. Thus, after almost forty years of ISI, the rate of growth of the economy is still crucially dependent on the growth of exports that now are required to break the existing foreign exchange bottleneck. Moreover, each balance of payments crisis generates new protectionist regulations. External problems are solved by piecemeal increases of protective measures providing partial solutions, further complicating the situation.

The evolution of trade policy restrictions was a clear example of the increasing bureaucratization of the Chilean economy, which led to a complex network of regulations, extreme instability of government decisions, arbitrariness, and corruption. The policy system used to promote ISI was not flexible to changing conditions—protection, once granted, became very difficult to remove. This led to a rent-seeking society where profits were more related to having the right connection than to productive entrepreneurship. Furthermore, distorted prices and market signals generated a productive structure with a noncompetitive oligopolistic industry, protected by high tariff barriers where the opportunity cost of a (marginal) unit of foreign exchange saved by ISI activities was two to four times higher than the official exchange rate.[17]

In summary, the industrial sector was inefficient in the use of economic resources, and it was blamed for the failure to transform Chile into a developed economy. In other words, industry generated relatively little employment and did not produce enough basic goods (at low prices) to satisfy the needs of most Chileans. After a long period of preferential ISI policy incentives, industry still required a high level of protection at the beginning of the 1970s. It is difficult to explain why high protection levels were still required after forty years of ISI, i.e., why was it that the Chilean infant industry never grew up? The result of this failure was that domestic consumers had to pay relatively higher prices for relatively low quality industrial products. Also, there was an industrial sector "excessively

---

[17] For a review and analysis of the Chilean trade regime under the ISI, see Behrman 1976 and Ffrench-Davis 1973.

diversified with inefficient and underutilized industrial plants...kept afloat financially by subsidized inputs, particularly credit, and monopolistic pricing made possible by import restrictions" (World Bank Report 1979). There would seem to be a paradox: the sector that benefitted from the imposition of most economic incentives achieved a relatively higher level of inefficiency. Was this an intrinsic problem of ISI and/or of the way in which ISI was implemented?[18]

The Role of the State

To understand the role of the state in Chile, we have to examine the sociopolitical situation prior to 1940.[19] During the nineteenth century and before the nitrate boom era, the prevailing economic regime was basically the one inherited from Spanish colonial times, i.e., a mixture of landed oligarchy and mercantilism. Wheat was an important export product, and the agricultural oligarchy controlled the government. Most of the population lived in rural areas; it was not until 1940 that more than 50 percent of the Chilean population lived in urban areas. During the nitrate boom, the economic influence of agriculture began to decrease for two different reasons. On the external side, Chilean wheat exports were displaced by competitive exports from Australia and Argentina. On the internal side, the expansion of other domestic activities such as mining, commercial and financial activities, and industry created new groups with more economic power than the agricultural oligarchy. Moreover, as pointed out previously, nitrate export taxes were the fuel that increased the size and organizational capacity of the state. The government used a large part of the resources to increase the degree of urbanization of the country; this led to an increase in the middle class, especially the one related to public employment.

In 1883, an entrepreneurial organization for the industrial sector was created. This was the Sociedad de Fomento Fabril (SOFOFA), which began to use its political influence to establish specific ad hoc tariffs to protect incipient domestic industries. Some of the new industrial entrepreneurs were foreigners, either immigrants or foreign investors, related to foreign banks or commercial firms established in the country. However, most of the new entrepreneurs were domestic capitalists, whose wealth came from mining or agriculture, and who had close social relations with the agricultural oligarchy. Therefore, an adversary relationship did not exist between industrial entrepreneurs and agricultural landowners.

The existence of mining and industrial activities with a relatively large

---

[18] For a more profound discussion of these matters, see Behrman 1976, Mamalakis 1976, and Marshall 1984.

[19] For a more profound review and analysis, see Cariola and Sunkel 1982, and references provided by Meller 1990.

concentration of workers (and the concurrent urbanization) led to the emergence of political activity of a very different kind than that of the conservative landed oligarchy. The Democratic Party was created in 1887 and the Socialist Workers Party in 1912. The Radical Party (a middle class party), which existed since the 1850s, had a major shift in 1906, from economic liberalism to state socialism. Moreover, the first National Labor Union (FOCH, Federación Obrera de Chile) was created in 1909. By 1930, even though it was illegal, the National Labor Union had 200,000 workers (who belonged to 1,200 unions). Political tension between labor and capital began early in Chile, especially in the mining and industry sectors. In the 1890-1925 period, there was an average of nine strikes per year. In the 1925-1935 period, this average had increased to forty-five strikes per year (Bianchi et al. 1989). This environment led to the introduction of social issues in the political debate even prior to the Great Depression. In fact, in 1925, major institutional changes took place. Despite the opposition of the landed oligarchy, a new constitution was approved (which lasted up to the military coup of 1973), and new social laws and labor legislation were introduced.

From the start of the nitrate boom to the Great Depression, the main role of the Chilean state was to act as a mediator between foreign investors and the Chilean society. The Chilean state used its power to acquire an important share of the nitrate export surplus. Domestic groups tried to benefit as much as possible from the expenditure and investment pattern of the public sector, so part of the political game was oriented towards influencing the state's investment and expenditure decisions. Also, the state gradually became the most important source for the generation of white-collar jobs.

In 1938, a new government was elected with the support of the middle class and the workers. These new social groups viewed the state as the mechanism to balance the power of oligarchic groups. Therefore, there was political support and pressure for increasing the role of the state in the economy. There was also some consensus about a more active role for the state because of the effect of the Depression, as noted earlier. To rescue Chile from the Depression, the state had imposed restrictions and control measures related to the external sector during the 1930s. During the 1940s it went further and assumed a direct role in the productive process and in promoting development. In this context, there was a major institutional change, namely, the creation of a National Development Corporation, CORFO (Corporación de Fomento 1939). The functions of this government agency were to formulate a national development program, and to allocate resources towards productive activities included in the national development program. CORFO constituted the first explicit public institutional mechanism which had resources to finance investment activities.

It is interesting to observe the political discussion and support related to the creation of CORFO (for details, see Muñoz & Arriagada 1977). Industrial entrepreneurs (SOFOFA) agreed to a more active role of the state when it came to increasing protection of domestic production. They also agreed with state policies that formulated a national development program, as long as these policies channeled the resources towards the private sector. However, they opposed the idea of state enterprises, because that would lead to unfair competition between private and public firms. On the other hand, the landed oligarchy's main concern was the avoidance of social problems in agriculture. This led to a political compromise, where the parliamentary representatives of the landed oligarchy supported the creation of CORFO, but only in return for promises that the government would not press for the creation of unions in agriculture. The landed oligarchy would maintain its power in rural areas, while middle income groups would increase their power in urban areas. It took more than twenty-five years, i.e., not until 1965, for effective unions to be created in agriculture.

CORFO became the main mechanism for promoting growth and implementing development policies. CORFO created the main state enterprises in basic industrial intermediate sectors: ENDESA (National Electric Company, 1944), CAP (National Steel Company, 1946), ENAP (National Oil Company, 1950), and IANSA (National Sugar Beet Company, 1952). During the 1939-1973 period, CORFO dominated Chilean economic life through direct investment by its state enterprises and by credit allocation. In the 1939-1954 period, CORFO controlled 30 percent of total investment in capital goods, more than 25 percent of public investment, and 18 percent of total gross investment.[20]

In short, in the 1940-1970 period, the state began to acquire new roles in the productive process. First, it was the state-promoter that provided credit to private industrial investment; then, the state-entrepreneur that created state enterprises; and finally, the state-programmer that defined the long-term outlook of the Chilean development pattern and specified where future investment, both private and public, should be directed, using special credit, tax and subsidy incentives. During the 1960s, the forestry and fishery sectors were favored. In this way, the state played a key role in the development of basic infrastructure related to electricity and telecommunications (national and international), and in the training of professionals who acquired technological and entrepreneurial abilities, and who made up a fundamental component of the later export expansion process.

Also during the 1940-1970 period, the state became an important mechanism for the achievement of gradual, but continuous, economic growth and the implementation of many distinct social reforms. However, in 1970, a new government supported by a leftist coalition, Unidad Popular,

---

[20] Mamalakis, cited in Bianchi et al. 1989.

Table 3.5. Share of State Enterprises in Chile's GDP
(Percent)

	1965	1973
Mining	13.0	85.0
Manufacturing	3.0	40.0
Public utilities	25.0	100.0
Transport	24.3	70.0
Communications	11.1	70.0
Finance	—	85.0
All State enterprises and public administration	14.2	39.0

Source: Hachette and Lüders 1987.

was elected. Unidad Popular felt that the previous economic development pattern was too slow. This relatively slow growth was associated with the control of the economy, specifically manufacturing industry, by foreign and national monopolists. To speed up growth, deep structural changes were required, which meant that the state should have greater control of the economy and become the central planner. This was also considered a necessary condition for creating a new socialist society. Table 3.5 shows the large increase in the state's role in 1972 (compared to 1965) in the control of most productive sectors. The state enterprises' share of GDP increased from 14.2 percent in 1965 to 39 percent in 1972. The continuation of the story is well known. The socialist experiment ended with the military coup of 1973.

Liberalization and the Role of the Private Sector, 1973-1990

The economic model implemented in Chile after the 1973 military coup, which emphasizes the role of the private sector, free markets, liberalization of the external sector, and deregulation of the economy, can be considered to be an extreme version of the orthodox traditional "pure textbook recipe" recommended by multilateral organizations (the IMF and the World Bank) for developing countries. After an initial successful performance during the 1976-1981 period, when there was much talk of a "Chilean miracle," and the Chilean model implemented by the "Chicago boys" was considered to be the example to be followed by most developing countries, the Chilean economy experienced an almost complete collapse in 1982.

After a deep and prolonged recession with a high cost of adjustment[21] (GDP fell by 16 percent during 1982-1983, effective unemployment rose

---

[21] For a more complete review and analysis of adjustment policies and their distributive impact, see Meller 1989.

above 30 percent in 1983 and remained over 20 percent until 1986, and real wages were reduced by almost 20 percent and were kept close to that level for five years) most of the main features of the liberalized market model have remained the same. Although the present GDP and income per capita and the Chilean external debt situation are comparable to those observed in other Latin American countries, Chile has a relatively much better macroeconomic situation, and it has achieved a more solid structural base for the growth and development perspectives of the 1990s. However, the behavior and performance of the private sector, which is now considered to be the main economic agent of the economy, will be the fundamental factor.

In this section, a schematic description of the deep structural reform policies implemented during the 1970s will be provided. Most of the analysis will be focused on the liberalization of the trade account. Finally, the behavior and performance of the private sector will be examined.

Structural Reform Policies, (1973-1982)

From 1940 to 1973, the Chilean economy was characterized by an increasing role of the public sector, and by an ISI strategy supported by high levels of tariff and non-tariff barriers.

These characteristics where further enhanced during the 1970-1973 period, when the number and coverage of government interventions and controls reached an extremely high level. In short, in 1973, the Chilean economy switched from strong state control, almost full price control, and an almost closed economy to a free market, free prices and a fully liberalized economy, with a decreasing role played by the government and the public sector, and an increasingly predominant one played by the private sector. All the liberalization and deregulation measures were applied in the middle of a severe anti-inflation stabilization program, with three-digit inflation rates during 1973-1976. A schematic description of the reform policies implemented after 1973 is provided in Exhibit 3.1.[22]

Most of the widespread and thorough policy changes described in Exhibit 3.1 were implemented in a very short span of time (two to four years) by a group of Chilean economists trained at the University of Chicago, who became known as the "Chicago boys." The economic liberalization and privatization scheme was imposed while, at the same time, there were severe political restrictions; political parties, social organizations, and basic human rights and freedom were severely repressed. It seems paradoxical that a military dictatorship, where all power is centralized at the top, would support an economic model which is based on

---

[22] For a more detailed discussion, see Foxley 1982, Edwards and Cox 1987, and Morandé and Schmidt-Hebbel 1988; see also references provided therein.

Exhibit 3.1. Chilean Structural Reform Policies (1973-1982)

1972-1973	Post-1973

PRIVATIZATION

More than 500 firms and banks controlled by the State	In 1980, 15 firms (including one bank) remained in the public sector

PRICES

Price control system	Free prices (excluding wages & exchange rates)

TRADE REGIME

Multiple exchange system	One exchange rate
Existence of prohibition & quotas	Homogeneous flat import tariff
High tariffs	of 10 percent
Prior import deposits	No trade barriers

FISCAL REGIME

"Cascade" sales tax	VAT (20 percent)
High public employment	Reduction of public employment
High deficits	Existence of surplus (1979-1981)

DOMESTIC FINANCIAL MARKET REGIME

Control of i	Free i
Bank nationalization	Privatization of banks
Control of credits market	Liberalization of capital markets

EXTERNAL CAPITAL ACCOUNT REGIME

Total control of capital movements	Gradual liberalization of capital account
Government main borrower	Private sector main borrower

LABOR LEGISLATION REGIME

Important union role & bargaining power	No unions & no bargaining power by workers
No worker dismissals	Dismissals relaxation
Mandatory wage increases	Relaxation of wage readjustment & severe cut of real wages
High & increased non-wage labor costs (40 percent of wages)	Reduction of non-wage labor costs (3 percent of wages)

decentralization and autonomy of economic decisions. Moreover, the armed forces are a state institution and it seems contradictory to support economists who say that everything related to the state is inefficient. Many questions have been raised in this respect. What are the reasons for the high degree of affinity observed between the military regime with centralized power and the economically decentralized free market scheme? Why did the military and the Chicago economists complement each other so neatly? How were the Chicago economists able to implement such deep structural changes without any resistance from the business community? Could all the policy reforms have been implemented in a democratic regime?[23]

Liberalization of the Trade Account [24]

The protection system prevailing in Chile in 1973 had an average nominal tariff rate of 94 percent, and a maximum nominal tariff rate of 220 percent. In addition, more than 63 percent of all imports were subject to quantitative restrictions (QRs). There were two types of QRs: (i) a 90-day, non-interest-bearing prior deposit of 10,000 percent of the imported good's CIF value, and (ii) a ban on imports of more than 300 goods. QRs and non-tariff barriers were practically eliminated by 1976. The tariff reductions occurred very quickly during the first few years. By 1976, the average nominal tariff was 36 percent and the maximum nominal tariff was 66 percent, i.e., they had been reduced to about one-third the level they had been in 1973. In 1979 (June), Chile introduced a uniform nominal tariff of 10 percent for all imports (except cars). As noted, QRs, prohibitions, and antidumping and countervailing duties had also been abolished. Hence, in a relatively short span of time, Chile implemented a drastic liberalization of the commercial account.

Several development topics have been raised in relation to the drastic external sector reform. Two of these topics will briefly be reviewed here. The first is related to the industrial sector. If ISI policies generated a highly inefficient Chilean industrial sector, how has domestic manufacturing adjusted to face import competition? How severe has the deindustrialization process been? The second issue is related to exports. What is the composition of the export basket going to be? Is there going to be a return to the monoexport, basic commodity pattern? Can exports become the new engine of growth?

Industry was the sector most affected by the liberalization of the

---

[23] For a review of these issues, see Moulián and Vergara 1980, Foxley 1982, and Meller 1989; see also references provided therein.

[24] For a review and analysis of previous Chilean trade liberalization experiences, see Behrman 1970. For a more detailed review of the trade liberalization policies, see de la Cuadra and Hachette 1988, and the World Bank Report 1979.

commercial account. In fact, during the 1970s, trade liberalization corresponded largely to industrial import liberalization. There was also a sort of "Dutch disease" phenomenon related to the large inflow of external credit, which put pressure on an appreciation of the real exchange rate.[25] In this case, there was no domestic "booming" sector, but the effect was the same because there was a decrease of the relative price of tradables versus nontradables, leading to stagnation in the levels of tradable production.

There are two different channels through which imports affect the level of the domestic production of tradables. The first is the direct substitution of domestic goods and inputs by imported ones. The second is related to the use of imported intermediate inputs in the production process, where some stages of domestic production are eliminated, i.e., imported inputs are substituted for domestic value added.[26]

There has been some degree of deindustrialization in the Chilean economy. During the import boom years, 1977-1981, while (real) imports increased at 19 percent per year, industry exhibited a 3.5 percent annual growth rate. The industrial share of GDP decreased from over 25 percent at the end of the 1960s, to around 20 percent during the 1980s. The industrial sector generated employment at a rate of 2.9 percent per year during the 1960s; during the trade liberalization process, in contrast, there was an annual rate of industrial "job destruction" of almost 2 percent.

The role of exports in the Chilean economy changed notably after the deep structural reform policies of 1973. There are several reasons for this. The external trade reforms eliminated the anti-export bias policies of the ISI regime. Especially during the 1980s, a relatively sustained undervalued real exchange rate provided clear and stable incentives to exporters. LCM exports under state enterprises' control have significantly expanded output: the share of Chilean copper in total world output (excluding centrally planned economies) increased from 14 percent at the end of the 1960s to more than 20 percent during the 1980s. The prevailing economic environment with free market prices, free trade, deregulation, and debureaucratization has increased the overall efficiency of the economy.

The export share of GDP has increased from 12 percent in the 1960s, to more than 27 percent during the 1980s. In spite of the important increase of copper exports, the share of copper of total exports has declined, from

---

[25] There is still a discussion in Chile with respect to the type of relationship existing between the deficit of the commercial account and the surplus of the capital account, i.e., which was the initial cause and which is the effect. For different views on this issue, see Edwards and Cox 1987, Morandé and Schmidt-Hebbel 1988, and Meller 1989.

[26] The usual procedure used in Latin America to measure industrial GDP through the use of physical output indicators does not capture this substitution mechanism, and official figures may show increasing figures of industrial output while, in fact, there may be a decrease in the value-added of the industrial sector.

more than 75 percent to less than 45 percent over the same period.

The composition of total Chilean exports during the 1980s was the following: mining, 56 percent; agriculture, 12 percent; forestry and wood products, 11 percent; and fish and sea products, 10 percent. There has been an increase of industrial exports and the current composition of industrial exports is the following: paper, wood, and wood products, 31 percent; fish meal and food products, 30 percent; and basic metal products, 9 percent. In other words, 70 percent of industrial exports are related to existing NR commodities.

The present Chilean comparative advantages are structurally the same as in the past, i.e., close to 90 percent of the export basket depends on the Chilean NR endowment. However, there are two important differences from the past. First , there is a clear diversification of the distinct NR goods in the export basket. If the fluctuations in the world prices of basic NR commodities are not highly correlated, the Chilean economy will be exposed to relatively smaller external shocks than those observed in the past. Even more importantly, the collapse of one commodity market will not have as damaging an effect as the appearance of synthetic nitrate did in the 1920s. Second, most of the Chilean exports are produced by Chilean-owned enterprises. Therefore, most of the surplus generated by the exports can potentially be reinvested in the country.

The Role of the Private Sector

Let us examine the elements that have been influential in the transformation of the domestic private sector into the main agent of the development process.

First, during the ISI period, domestic private entrepreneurs were quite passive. Before 1970, industrial entrepreneurs did not perceive the state as a threat, but were instead pessimistic about being able to survive and expand without state support. The highly protected Chilean economy and the rent seeking society environment reinforced the passive attitude of domestic entrepreneurs, which stimulated an even more active role by the public sector.

During the 1980s, several factors are behind the transformation of passive and state-dependent domestic private entrepreneurs into active and autonomous ones (Muñoz 1988). One is related to the implementation of free prices and an open economy, which forces the private sector to be more autonomous and active. The increasing competition also stimulates increases in efficiency, at least on average, since passive entrepreneurs are eventually displaced from the market. Furthermore, entrepreneurs are highly sensitive to incentives. The maintenance of adequate and stable incentives provides a clear signal for resource allocation. In addition, through the reprivatization and privatization processes, there has been an important transfer of resources to the domestic private sector. In the 1974-1989 period, Chile has had two reprivatization and two privatization processes, and the amount of subsidies provided in the divestiture processes has been important.[27] During this period, the main domestic private entrepreneurs seem to have operated under a moral hazard principle, where all private profits have been privatized, while most private losses have been socialized.

A fourth factor behind the rise of active entrepreneurs is related to the availability of domestic managerial capacity. In this respect, it should be pointed out that the type of entrepreneur really required in a Latin American economy is not the innovative Schumpeterian one, but a person who is able to coordinate and manage all the distinct and complex features of modern enterprises. A manager with organizational abilities is required, who selects responsible and qualified personnel, and who is well informed about the latest technologies and developments of industrial countries. In semi-industrialized economies it is more important to do these things well than to be an innovator—incompetence and inefficiency in entrepreneurship ability are the bottlenecks of a firm's expansion (Ray 1988).

It is premature to provide a critical judgment about the future success or failure of the private sector in guiding the Chilean economy toward a high and stable growth pattern. Looking at the experience of the 1970s, it is observed that the Chilean private sector has proved that it can grow and go bankrupt. Things could be different at the end of the 1980s, given the fact that almost 4,000 entrepreneurs are now engaged in the export business, whereas, at the end of the 1970s, most entrepreneurs were engaged in speculation. In short, the Chilean economy will develop only when domestic entrepreneurs have a long-term outlook.

Final Observations

It is easy to be too severe in an evaluation of past behavior. However, in our opinion, the initial stage of the modern Chilean economy started in 1880, when the country was quite backwards. Not much could be done and no faster growth was possible, given the initial conditions. Foreign investment in nitrate and copper played an important role, connecting the domestic economy to the international world. In spite of the fact that foreign investors remitted relatively high profits, Chile had, at that time, no better alternatives. Moreover, Chilean governments did their best to retain as much export surplus as possible. Their main fault was related to not knowing how to change the actual situation and to identify the bottlenecks in order to

---

[27] For a discussion of this, see Larrain 1988, and Marcel 1989.

improve future development performance and future relations with foreign investors.

The "great contradiction" of the Chilean development process (Pinto 1962), meaning the fast political evolution and the slow economic improvement of the majority of the population, stimulated the intervention of the state in the productive process to speed up growth and to improve the unequal distribution of income. Again, given the prevailing conditions, the outcome was satisfactory in terms of growth and reducing inequality. However, the economic measures that were appropriate for the 1930s through the 1950s became inappropriate in the 1960s. Once more, the fault was related to not perceiving when and how to change the actual situation. Also, ideological political competition generated unrealistic economic expectations. More of the same old policies were implemented, increasing the role of controls and of the public sector, which produced full economic chaos in the end.

The deep economic chaos of 1973 was used as a benchmark for a complete reversal of development policies. In this process, the "pendulum" law was applied, and in less than ten years Chile went from one extreme to the other. The implementation of the free market open economy is appropriate for the small Chilean economy in the highly interdependent world economy of today. However, the implementation has indeed been a costly one. Now, the domestic private sector has the responsibility of showing that it can do what its counterparts have done in industrial and East Asian countries. The final test will be whether the Chilean majority shares the benefits of an eventual successful export development. Stable long-term development and a long-run time horizon for private investors require, in a democratic regime, a more equal income distribution pattern.

REFERENCES

Behrman, J. 1976. *Foreign Trade Regimes and Economic Development: Chile.* New York: Columbia University Press.

Bianchi, A., E. Lahera, and O. Muñoz. 1989. "The Role of the State in the Economic Development of Latin America, Argentina and Chile." *Joint Research Programme, Series 77*, Tokyo: Institute of Developing Economies.

Cariola, C. and O. Sunkel. 1982. *La historia económica de Chile, 1830-1930.* Madrid: Instituto de Cooperación Iberoamericana.

De La Cuadra, S. and D. Hachette. 1988. "The Timing and Sequencing of a Trade Liberalization Policy: The Case of Chile." Documentos de Trabajo, 113. Santiago: Instituto de Economía, Universidad Católica.

Edwards, S. and A. Cox. 1987. *Monetarism and Liberalization.* Cambridge, Mass.: Ballinger.

Ffrench-Davis, R. 1973. *Políticas económicas en Chile, 1952-1970.* Santiago: Editorial Nueva Universidad.

_____ and E. Tironi, eds. 1974. "La importancia del cobre en la economía Chilena." In *El Cobre en el Desarrollo Nacional.* Santiago: Ediciones Nueva Universidad, CIEPLAN.

Foxley, A. 1982. *Latin American Experiments in Neoconservative Economics.* Berkeley: University of California Press.

Hachette, D. and R. Lüders. 1987. "El proceso de privatización de empresas en chile, 1974-1982." *Boletín Económico 22.* Santiago: Instituto de Economía, Universidad Católica.

Larrain, F. 1988. "Public Sector Behavior in a Highly Indebted Country: The Contrasting Chilean Experience." Santiago: Catholic University. Mimeo.

Mamalakis, M. 1971. "The Role of Government in the Resource Transfer and Resource Allocation Processes: The Chilean Nitrate Case." In *Government and Economic Development*, edited by G. Ranis. New Haven: Yale University Press.

_____. 1976. *The Growth and Structure of the Chilean Economy: From Independence to Allende.* New Haven: Yale University Press.

Marcel, M. 1989. "Privatización y Finanzas Públicas: El Caso de Chile, 1985-1988." *Colección Estudios CIEPLAN.* Santiago: CIEPLAN.

Marshall, J.R. 1984. "Economics of Stagnation. Analysis of the Chilean Experience 1914-1970." Ph.D dissertation, Harvard University.

Meller, P. 1986. "Un enfoque analítico-empírico de las causas del actual endeudamiento externo." *Colección Estudios CIEPLAN.* Santiago: CIEPLAN.

_____. 1989. "Economic Adjustment and its Distributive Impact: Chile in the 1980s." Paris: OECD. Mimeo.

_____. 1990. "110 Años de desarrollo económico chileno (1880-1990)." Santiago: CIEPLAN. Mimeo.

Morán, T. 1974. *Multinational Corporations and the Politics of Dependence. Copper in Chile.* New Jersey: Princeton University Press.

Morande, F. and K. Schmidt-Hebbel. 1988. *Del auge a la crisis de 1982.* Santiago: ILADES.

Moulián, T. and P. Vergara. 1980. "Estado, ideología y políticas económicas en Chile: 1973-1978." *Colección Estudios CIEPLAN.* Santiago: CIEPLAN.

Muñoz, O. 1968. *Crecimiento Industrial de Chile, 1914-1965.* Santiago: Instituto de Economía.

_____. 1986. *Chile y su industrialización. Pasado, crisis y opciones.* Santiago: CIEPLAN.

_____. 1988. "El Estado y los empresarios: Experiencias comparadas y sus implicaciones para Chile." *Colección Estudios CIEPLAN.* Santiago: CIEPLAN.

_____ and A.M. Arriagada. 1977. "Orígenes políticos y económicos del estado empresarial en Chile." *Colección Estudios CIEPLAN.* Santiago: CIEPLAN.

Palma, G. 1979. "Growth and Structure of Chilean Manufacturing." Ph.D dissertation, Oxford University.

_____. 1984. "Chile 1914-1935: De Economía Exportadora a Sustitutiva de Importaciones." *Colección Estudios CIEPLAN.* Santiago: CIEPLAN.

Pinto, A. 1962. *Chile, un caso de desarrollo frustrado.* Santiago: Editorial Universitaria.

_____. 1985. "Estado y gran empresa: De la pre-crisis hasta el gobierno de Jorge Alessandri." *Colección Estudios CIEPLAN.* Santiago: CIEPLAN.

Ray, D. 1988. "The Role of Entrepreneurship in Economic Development." *Journal of Development Planning 18.*

Reynolds, C. 1965. "Development Problems of an Export Economy: The Case of Chile and Copper." In *Essays on the Chilean Economy*, M. Mamalakis and C. Reynolds. Illinois: Irwin.

Sáez, S. 1989. "La economía política de una crisis: Chile, 1929-1939." *Notas Técnicas 130.* Santiago: CIEPLAN.

World Bank. 1979. *Chile: An Economy in Transition, Report 2390.* Washington, D.C.: World Bank.

CHAPTER FOUR

THE DEVELOPMENT OF
THE RICH WELFARE STATE
OF DENMARK

*Martin Paldam**

Introduction

An attempt will be made in this chapter to interpret the economic history of Denmark since the middle of the nineteenth century. Obviously, such an undertaking has to be rather broad and incomplete. Little emphasis will be placed on formal modeling. Instead, generalizations will be made even when many details could be presented to make this historical review much more complex. Special attention will be paid to the "kinks" in Denmark's history and the experiences that shed the most interesting light on the development problems confronting middle-income countries today.

The three most well-known facts about the Danish economy probably are that Denmark is a rich, socialist welfare state with a relatively large agricultural sector. The least debatable fact is the country's wealth. Denmark has been on the top twenty list as regards GDP per capita for longer than the period covered.

Regarding the second well-known fact, Denmark has one of the third or fourth highest levels of transfer payments in the world. No less than 30 percent of GDP is transferred to make income distribution more equal. Correspondingly, Denmark has a very high tax burden. There are two other important points to note regarding Denmark's socialist welfare state. The first is that the welfare state is a very recent creation. Although the key welfare programs were created in the 1930s, they did not become significant relative to the average OECD country until the late 1960s, i.e., the programs have only been of consequence for twenty years. The second important point is that the large transfer payments are almost exclusively between individuals—90 percent of all taxes are on personal income and

* This paper has greatly benefitted from discussions within the project and from comments of Niels Geert Bolwig, Jørgen H. Gelting, Ruth Klinov, Peter Nannestad, Conni Paldam, Peder J. Pedersen, and Shlomo Yitzhaki. Flemming Nielsen and Jesper Iwersen have provided research assistance. To prevent misunderstanding when an English translation is ambiguous, square brackets [ ] have been used to contain the Danish word.

consumption and 90 percent of all domestic transfers are to individuals. Denmark has an unusually small, nationalized state-owned production sector, and the smallest transfers (per capita) to trade and industry in the European Community. In addition, Denmark has a strong tradition for free trade and a high degree of integration in the world market. Danish (Scandinavian) socialism is built upon a big compromise: redistribution socialism goes hand-in-hand with an open economy liberalism when it comes to property rights and production.

With respect to the agricultural sector, it is interesting to note that the main agricultural production unit throughout the period considered has been the family farm. It became the dominant economic unit early in the nineteenth century, but did not achieve political power until 1901. Since then, agriculture has lost such power. Today, agriculture accounts for a mere 5 percent of GDP. The Farmers' Party, Venstre, only receives about 10 percent of the vote. Even though agriculture exports two-thirds of its value added, this only accounts for 20 percent of Danish exports.

An important fact to note is that Denmark has no natural resources apart from arable and moderately fertile land. The only "natural resource" of the country is its fortunate geographical location. It sits above one of the richest and most heavily populated areas in the world, and forms a bridge to the large, thinly-populated areas of the Scandinavian peninsula. The main sea lanes between Eastern and Western Europe are the Danish straits. Perhaps Denmark's location is the main reason why it has been a relatively wealthy country for the last four to five centuries. Denmark was certainly richer than the other Scandinavian countries until quite recently (see Chapter One). It can be argued that the other Scandinavian countries are "peripheral" countries in Europe, while Denmark belongs to the "center."

One less fortunate consequence of Denmark's geographical location must be mentioned. The Danish king was also the Duke of Schleswig and Holstein, a double role which eventually led to the two Schleswig Wars. Thus, one history of Denmark could be the one that describes the political decay leading to a gradual reduction in the power and size of the country. However, another way to describe Denmark's history is to relate the story of a country's remarkable economic success, in spite of everything. The latter is the story told here.

A simple way to tell this story is to look at Figure 4.1, which shows real GDP for as long as data exist. The data are also shown on a per capita basis, and the size of the population is given for selected years. Two interesting kinks are visible on the two curves: the kinks in 1880-1890 and those around 1960 (the second kink is perhaps obscured by the GDP loss between 1930 and 1945, and the reconstruction that took place between 1945 and 1950). These kinks correspond to the most important periods of rapid economic growth in Danish history:

Figure 4.1 Real GDP of Denmark, 1820 to 1990, Drawn on a Logarithmic Scale

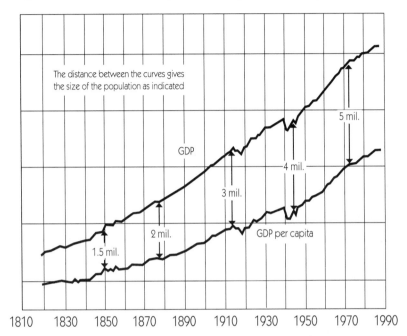

The distance between the curves gives
the size of the population as indicated

GDP

5 mil.

4 mil.

3 mil.

2 mil.

1.5 mil.

GDP per capita

1810   1830   1850   1870   1890   1910   1930   1950   1970   1990

Notes: Constructed by chaining together the long historical series in S.A.Hansen (1972) from
1818 to 1948 (using 1929 weights and chaining over the changes of territory in 1864 and 1920)
and ADAMBk (see references) for 1948-1985 (using 1980 weights). The curve rises 85 times, or,
as the population has risen 5 times, 17 times per capita. Disregarding all problems comparing
over long periods and across countries this corresponds to the difference today between
Denmark and Peru or Morocco.

(1) The first period, from 1870 to 1900, propelled Denmark to the list
of the twenty richest countries in the world. In this period, growth was based
on agricultural exports from family-owned farms employing two to five
farm hands. Here the country may best be described as a politically
paralyzed laissez-faire economy, i.e., an open economy with a very small
public sector.

(2) The second period, from 1958 to 1974, gave Denmark one of the
fastest growth rates in the developed world and propelled it to the top ten
list. Here the driving force of growth was the rapid expansion of public
consumption and transfer payments, as well as a large-scale residential
building boom which was also a result of public policies.

It is a bit of a paradox that the two growth periods are so different
regarding the role of the state. Future historians will probably conclude that
the first period led to a more sustainable increase in the income level than
the second one.

The Early History of Resource Based Growth, 1870-1900

During the eighteenth century, feudalism was extremely widespread in Denmark. The country was an absolute kingdom, with no Parliament or voting rights. Virtually all land was owned by a few thousand noble families (0.8 percent of the population earning probably about 35 percent of total incomes), having large estates with the land tilled by tenants/serfs (about 55 percent of the population) who, de facto, belonged to the land [stavnsbundne], so that they could be "sold" with the land. The income distribution was probably more skewed than in any LDC today, with noblemen earning incomes many hundred times that of the illiterate serfs[1]. Yet despite all this, the country was not poor compared to other countries. The export share of agricultural output was high (about 20 percent in 1800), and there was a significant shipping sector (about 2 percent of the population). The story to be told in this section can be briefly summarized in six points:

(1) The basis for growth was a new middle class of family farmers who emerged after the land reforms between 1784 and 1814 that dramatically changed land ownership. The land reforms were followed by the school reform of 1814 which introduced universal primary enrollment.

(2) Growth was based upon agricultural export (to the United Kingdom) of new products produced by this new class. New family farms producing goods with more value added (such as butter, bacon and cheese) replaced the large estates producing grain and live cattle.

(3) Ownership of land was strictly private, but the support sector was built up by the farmers themselves on a cooperative basis. The support sector had a three-legged structure: credit and trading, adult education, and processing.

(4) In spite of the rapid growth, the income distribution became much more equal during the period 1850-1900. This was partly due to the character of the technical progress achieved in this period.

(5) Through a strange twist of history, this was a time when the political decision-making process in the country was paralyzed, and the Farmers' Party was excluded from power. The entire development of the country was unplanned and unsupported by the government. The public sector was small and very few regulations and restrictions existed.

(6) The new wealth led to rapid industrialization, with a lag of ten to twenty years.

---

[1] It is also interesting to note that corruption in public affairs was as widespread then as it is in any LDC today. Corruption gradually disappeared during the nineteenth century through a dynamic process that is not entirely understood. This is no doubt an important part of economic history, but it will not be discussed in this chapter.

From Land Reforms to the New Production Structure

The change in the ownership structure of land was a very thorough process, affecting about half of the agricultural population. The laws affecting this change were (1) the abolition of serfdom [stavnsbåndsløsningen] in 1788, allowing tenants/serfs to move, and (2) those allowing the tenants/serfs to buy the land they tilled (cheaply) from the noblemen. It is remarkable that of the 60,000 tenant farmers, 40,000 managed to buy their farms between 1790 and 1820, but then the purchase of land stopped due to the severe depression after the Napoleonic Wars. The depression followed high inflation [statsbankerotten]—the last bout of high inflation Denmark has experienced. It wiped out the debt of the new owners. After 1860, the last third of the tenant farmers quickly bought their farms. The other half of the landless rural population did not benefit from this process until later.

Another crucial reform was the School Law of 1814 promising universal primary enrollment. It followed a century of piecemeal school reforms, but by the time the law was enacted, about 50 percent of the population could read simple texts and sign their names. This crude rate of minimum literacy grew to at least 90 percent in the mid-nineteenth century, and has gradually led to a more meaningful literacy.

The land reform laws and school law were proposed to the (fairly unenlightened, but still absolute) King by a small group of enlightened noble landowners, so the laws were very moderate. Though it is possible to argue that these reformers believed they were acting in their own long-term interests, this is certainly not the impression given by the historians who have read their letters. They were, by and large, idealists trying to make a better society for everybody (with hindsight, we can say that for once, idealism succeeded).

As a result, a sizable new class of family-owned farms existed between 1860 and 1870. During this time, however, grain exports were severely affected by cheap (and better) grain from Russia and the United States. To maintain their incomes, the farmers had to change production, which is, in fact, what happened in the 1870s and the 1880s (see Figure 4.2). This process took place under very adverse political conditions.

Political Paralysis during Agricultural Change

During the period of the great agricultural changes, political power was in the hands of the enemies of the emerging middle class of farmers. The politico-economic history of the period of rapid agricultural growth is a history of a politically paralyzed laissez-faire economy. A brief summary of the political history follows.

After a short round of peaceful demonstrations in 1848, the King approved a democratic constitution. Figure 4.2 outlines the party structure

Figure 4.2. The Political Structure of the Population since Elections Were Introduced in 1849

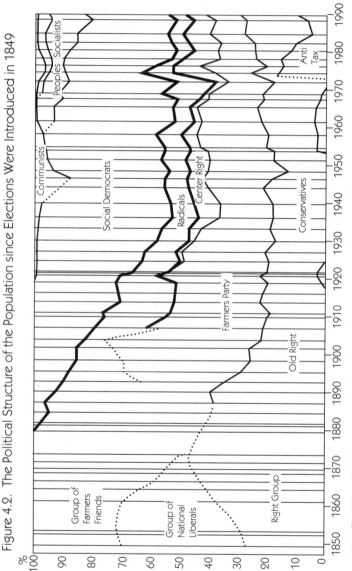

Note: The thin vertical lines are the elections. The parties are drawn cumulatively from the right (bottom) to left (top). The dividing line is either between the "socialist/labor" parties including the Social Democratic Party (SDP) and the "bourgeois" parties, or it includes the Radicals as the historical ally of the SDP - hence the two bold lines. The parties to the left of the SDP are termed the "Left Wing". They include four to five small parties sometimes in and sometimes out of the parliament - such as the Communists.

In addition, the Left Wing includes the Peoples Socialists that is becoming gradually a left Social Democratic Party. The Center Right is 3-4 parties, sometimes in the parliament and sometimes outside. The Old Right is dissolved in 1915 and replaced by the Conservatives - under a new group of leaders. To the right of the Conservatives is normally only one party, but not the same one. Note that the formal parties did not exist before the 1870s. However, there were some groups, see Nannestad (1972).

in the Parliament [Folketinget] since that time. Power first fell to the group of National Liberals [Nationalliberale], which was dominated by a small, educated group of lawyers, clergymen, merchants, and a small group of "Farmers' Friends." The old noble class of the large landowners formed the "Right Party" [Højre] in opposition. However, the National Liberal Party led the country into the Second Schleswig War of 1864, which was lost to the combined forces of Prussia and Austria. The futility and loss of human life that resulted from heroically fighting much larger armies loomed large in the minds of many Danes after the war.

As a result, the National Liberal Party was discredited in the eyes of most voters and the party soon faded away. The old Right grew in size and the farmers developed their own party—the Farmers' Party—termed Left [Venstre], even when it was never a leftist party. In the meantime, the King appointed a Right government, and observed the situation in Prussia, where the King kept a tough Junker, Otto von Bismarck, as Prime Minister, against the majority of the Parliament. It was not clear that the new Danish Constitution required the King to appoint the majority leader, the Prime Minister, so even though the Farmers' Party grew to gain the majority, the King retained the Right party in power from the defeat in 1864 until 1901. The Prime Ministership gravitated to the toughest and most conservative Junker, J.B.S. Estrup, who ruled from 1875 to 1894.

In order to remove Estrup peacefully, the Farmers' Party followed a policy termed the withering policy [Visnepolitikken], which essentially consisted of voting down anything proposed by the government, including the budget—thereby forcing the government to enact emergency budgets that could only finance existing projects. At the same time, the government refused to implement any of Parliament's demands. Thus, there was a long period of political paralysis. This was a period when total public expenditures were about 7 to 10 percent of GDP, with defense taking more than half of the state funds.[2] The largest public project was the fortification of Copenhagen, where a forty kilometer-long "Maginot-line" was built at great cost. As time has shown, the line came to serve no military purpose. The amount of total state funds spent on assisting the new agricultural sector was certainly never above one percent of GDP, although something was spent on schools and infrastructure (harbors and railroads). It is clear that the farmers firmly believed that they paid more in taxes than they received from the state. Instead of obtaining help from the state, the farmers developed a support system among themselves which had three "legs."

---

[2] The public sector was small throughout the western world during that period; but in most countries it was about twice as large as the Danish one. The main reason was that Denmark never acquired large expensive colonies and it maintained a relatively small army even then.

The Origin and Development of the Three-Legged Self-Help Package

The three legs of the self-help support system were: credit and trading, adult education, and processing. In all three cases, most of the institutions were based on cooperatives.

The first leg to grow was credit via the cooperative savings bank [sparekasse]. [3] The first savings bank was imported by a nobleman of the land reform group in 1810 from southern Germany (Rhineland). A few more savings banks were also opened at that time. But it was not until twenty or thirty years later that savings banks began to lend money and expand. Then, a whole system of savings banks rapidly emerged. They were small, local institutions—typically the schoolteacher, who was the son of one of the farmers, kept the records. All the leading farmers sat on the board, and everybody in the village provided the savings. Loans were given at low interest, but at high security. It was difficult for anyone to continue living in the village if they defaulted on a loan.

Almost parallel with the development of the savings banks came the development of the second leg: education. The primary schools were run locally by the municipalities, which gradually were taken over by the Farmers' Party. In addition to these schools, came the development of a unique adult school system [Folkehøjskolen], in the form of boarding schools for young farm boys and girls. For a moderate tuition fee the farm children could spend three to six months in school during the lean season. The main curriculum emphasized cultural and general knowledge, but there were agricultural subjects, too. The first adult school was established in 1844 by a group of associates of one extraordinary clergyman, N.F.S. Grundtvig (a prophet, reformer, and prolific writer who also became a bishop). The next dozen adult schools were opened during the 1850s. They initially received a small subsidy, but during the next two decades, and with the establishment of many of these schools, the subsidies were removed and the schools were organized locally. By the 1870s, the great majority of all farmers had received seven years of schooling (every second day), and had spent about half a year in an adult school. At this time most farmers subscribed to a daily newspaper. Once more, the landless segment of the rural population caught up with a lag.

In the 1850s and 1860s it was also the large landowners who imported, from Prussia, another important type of cooperative credit—the Mortgage

---

[3] Savings banks have always coexisted with commercial banks. Even when savings banks were more important than the commercial banks in the period discussed, they lost out gradually during this century when, to hold their own, they merged into federations. During the last few decades, they have gradually turned into ordinary banks. They still maintain about 25 percent of the total banking sector balances.

Bond Unions [Kreditforeninger].[4] Under this system the owner of property traded in a mortgage on his property to the Union. After a thorough check by the local representative (elected by the community), he received a corresponding amount of anonymous bonds that were easy to sell in the open market. The capital market was so developed that the cooperative mortgage unions became the main source of long-term financing in agriculture from the 1870s onwards.

Finally, it was a few large landowners who "discovered" the export of butter and bacon, and who built the first small dairies on their estates. Until the 1870s, it was well known that estate butter was superior to farm butter. Then the quality of farm butter improved and it soon exceeded estate butter in quantity. The first cooperative dairy was not opened until 1882, but after this time the number of dairies increased rapidly. Cooperative slaughter houses soon followed, and by 1890, these two kinds of cooperative production units accounted for two-thirds of the agricultural exports, which were about 75 percent of all exports.

In conclusion, about 100 years after the major land reforms, a new class of family farmers dominated Danish exports, selling new products. It is quite clear that the development that took place could not have happened without land reform. Without such a reform, a very different kind of development would have occurred. The result would probably have been a much more socially painful industrialization process.

Agricultural Growth Instead of Rent Seeking

In principle, there are two ways for an individual to obtain wealth and power:

(1) By starting new firms, organizing old firms better, inventing new techniques, increasing sales domestically or abroad, and by normal entrepreneurship. With various, well-known qualifications, this is the path to economic growth for all of society and, hence, it is a socially desirable method.

(2) By rent seeking, defined as the (more or less legal) activities of an agent aimed at obtaining public regulation, generating monopoly profits to

---

[4]The non-profit bond issuing mortgage institutions are still the financing agent for all real estate in the country, but today they have merged into a few giant institutions, where the local control is almost a formality (with predictable results). The turnover in mortgage bonds is still the dominating trade at the Danish Stock Exchange. Open market operations are in these bonds. Pension and insurance funds are in such bonds.

the agent in excess of the costs involved in obtaining the regulation.[5] This is, of course, a much less socially desirable method, and the result is loss of income and future growth.

If the socio-political conditions in a country are "right," it might appear much more promising for the most enterprising and dynamic part of the population to engage in rent seeking, rather than in normal entrepreneurship. After successful rent seeking by old firms, enough regulations are obtained to close the domestic markets to new firms. The result is high production costs which can only be maintained through continuous political support—support that has to be constantly bought from politicians who come to rely on these payments. Middle-income countries normally grow relatively fast (Laursen and Paldam 1982); but some middle-income countries (such as the ones on the Southern Cone in Latin America) are low growth economies. It is arguable that historical chance has caused these countries to develop into rent seeking societies.[6]

It is a fact that the new class of family farmers knew they had to develop their business without any support or protection from the state, which was in the hands of their enemies. The farmers would surely have fared much worse if they themselves had not developed the three-legged self-help package. The rapid expansion and great success of all three legs in the package was probably the result of the strong desire of the farmers to control their environment in a hostile world. There are many examples where such institutions have failed miserably, even when they were actively supported by the government. Perhaps it helps if the government is the enemy? It is difficult to imagine what would have happened if the farmers had gained (as they should have) political power in the 1870s.[7] Further, it is probably not very profitable to speculate about the relative role of each of the three legs of the self-help package in creating the agricultural

---

[5] The concept of rent seeking has a strange history as it was first introduced by Tullock in 1967, but then forgotten. It was reinvented and elegantly modeled by Krueger in 1974. Now it has been generalized and expanded in many ways (see Rawley, Tollison and Tullock 1988). It is interesting to note that everyone involved in the concept dislikes the term "rent seeking," but it has caught on.

[6] Often rent seeking emerges as a way of life as a result of an alliance between: (1) the left, fearing the exploitation of the capitalist world system (or in cruder terms, the populists exploiting racist feelings); (2) established old industry, wanting protection; (3) unions, wanting secure employment for their insiders; and (4) politicians, who see this mixture of nationalism, racism and interests as the promised land of votes and money.

[7] If the farmers had been in power when the grain prices fell in the late 1860s, they would probably have demanded and obtained compensation from the state for the loss suffered. They would further have demanded and obtained protection against the unfair competition of farmers in countries with much more and better land. The result would surely have been less structural change in agriculture and a slower industrialization.

boom. However, it is clear that the great agricultural change, which did not occur until 100 years after major land reform, was the result of increased exports and the self-help package. In addition , the fact that education came before the establishment of the cooperative movement, and that price stability existed during the period, also contributed to agricultural growth.

Industrialization and the Emergence of the Social Democrats

During the same period, but one to two decades later, an industrial boom occurred. The first major "Gründer-bank" was founded in 1856, with two more established during the following twenty-five years. For centuries, there had been considerable trading and shipping interests concentrated in Copenhagen as well as in a few other shipping towns.

The timing of the industrial revolution and its causal relation to the "old" trading and shipping interests, the new banks, and the agricultural boom has been extensively examined. Causality in complex historical processes is always very hard to establish. But it appears that at least half of the production, and maybe as much as three-quarters of the industrialization boom in the 1880s and 1890s, was somehow connected to the agricultural boom.

Many of the entrepreneurs involved in the earlier, much smaller and less successful "industrial" attempts had been foreigners. But this time, the great majority of the new entrepreneurs were Danes of varying backgrounds—though perhaps mostly from the old trading and shipping middle and upper class. Foreign entrepreneurs and multinationals played a small role in the industrialization process at its peak. The new industry became export oriented and developed without protection.

By the turn of the century there were as many employed in industry as in agriculture; but industrial exports did not overtake agricultural exports before the 1950s. By the time the Farmers' Party finally obtained political power in 1901, known as the Regime Shift [Systemskiftet], the Social Democratic Party was already rapidly growing. The period of the political domination of the farmers, therefore, proved to be of short duration. When the Farmers' Party finally gained power, the dominant farm group behind the party had already become quite wealthy, and the party had turned sharply to the right. As a result, the party became divided. The more left wing broke away to form the Radical Party—a moderate center party, with a strong tradition of neutral foreign policy. It was a strange coalition of small landholders and town intelligentsia. The Radicals quickly formed an alliance with the Social Democrats, and together they ruled from the mid-1920s until recently, when the Radicals made a major change to support the Conservatives (the new Right), who are now the allies of the Farmers' Party.

While Danish politics will not be extensively discussed here, it must be noted that the Social Democratic Party, as shown in Figure 4.2, only obtained between 40 and 44 percent of the vote during the long period it was the dominant party. In fact, there has rarely been a really stable and secure majority in the Danish Parliament. Furthermore, the Radical Party was never a very obedient ally. Thus, the Social Democrats sometimes ruled alone as a minority government, and sometimes the Radicals supported a coalition of the Farmers' Party and the Conservatives.

Towards Equal Income Distribution

Income distribution is a complex phenomenon with many groups moving relative to each other. When Danish income distribution is viewed in the short term, it is easy to interpret the data differently; but when viewed in a long-term perspective, a picture of a strong trend towards equality emerges. Systematic data exist after World War I, but from scattered observations, it is known that the trend towards more equality was strong throughout the nineteenth century.

The distribution was, as already noted, extremely skewed around 1800, when a group of large landowners constituted about 0.8 percent of the population and earned 25 to 40 percent of total incomes. The first half of the nineteenth century saw the creation of the new middle class of family farms. This class constituted about one-third of the population around 1870, when farm incomes started to increase rapidly. This changed the distribution dramatically towards equality even when the other one-third (landless) of the rural population was not, at first, affected. But contrary to the development in many countries, the technical changes in the countryside were labor intensive. In addition, there was emigration to the U.S.,[8] and inflow to the cities where a proletariat appeared in the last three decades of the nineteenth century[9] while the farmers grew wealthy. As industrialization and unionization progressed, incomes also increased rapidly in the cities.

Long statistical series for certain aspects of the income distribution exist since 1920. But it is worth noting that the salary structure as late as the 1880s was similar to what it is today in many middle income countries, with skilled workers earning about two times the income of unskilled workers, and an engineer earning four or five times the wages of an unskilled worker.

---

[8] Emigration from Denmark was much less than from the other Scandinavian countries, and there was some immigration from Sweden and Poland. Thus, the net number were marginal—adding up to, at most, 5 percent of the labor force over a seventy-year span.

[9] It appears that the soldiers were drafted with a bias towards the poor. Information exists regarding the average height of drafted soldiers. If height is an indication of the living standard of the poor, then it is noteworthy that it decreased temporarily by two to three centimeters during the industrial revolution between 1870 and 1900.

These ratios have now decreased to 1.2 and 1.7 times in Denmark—or, if after-tax income is considered, probably about 1.1 and 1.25.

The wage distribution between major groups of workers over time is shown in Figure 4.3. The distribution is calculated based on pretax data for hourly earnings. Taking into account taxes and transfers would result in even more equally distributed incomes. The compression of the income structure for all wage and salary earners has been considerably stronger than the one shown for the workers; but there are gaps in the statistics.

Figure 4.4 gives the long-term trends in the functional distribution. Obviously, there has been a fairly strong, though uneven, development towards a smaller share for capital. This development reached a crisis-like profit squeeze in 1975 and 1980, but has led to some recuperation of profits since that time.

External Openness: A Free Trade Nation

The foreign economic policies pursued by Denmark are evidence of the country's rather strong tradition of free trade. Three points are crucial in understanding this tradition:

(1) The lack of most resources, such as all minerals, most wood and paper, all tropical and subtropical fruits and vegetables and, until recently, most forms of energy, has made the country totally dependent upon trade. It has never been seriously proposed as a worthwhile goal that Denmark should be self-sufficient and not rely upon the world market.

(2) An early tradition of free trade, due to the historical circumstances as further discussed below.

(3) The unusual fact that the Danish people have managed to live rather well, until recently, with permanent balance of payments difficulties, as will be discussed later.

Trade Shares

Figure 4.5 shows the history of Denmark's export share, h_X. It is defined as: $h_X = X/Y$, where X is exports of goods and services, while Y is GDP. It is difficult to provide numbers for trade in services from the beginning, but a backward prediction from the figures available can be made by adding about 5 percent (of GDP) to the trade shares for the goods given back to 1900. The corresponding import share h_m can be derived from Figure 4.5a and b. The resulting pattern can be summarized as follows:

(1) Around the turn of the century, the trade shares (h_m and h_X) were almost at the same level (35 percent of GDP) as they are today; but there were major swings around World War I, and a fall during the Great Depression in the 1930s and during World War II. The rise of the export

Figure 4.3
The Wage Distribution between Major Groups of Workers, 1921-1987

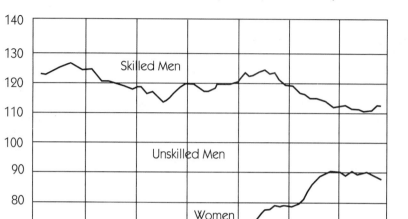

Note: The distribution is calculated by setting the average wage for unskilled men equal to 100, see Pederson (1978b). The series is updated by the author. The results for the three main groups are representative. Most skilled women are salaried, so most women in the data shown are unskilled.

Figure 4.4. The Wage Share, 1922-1987

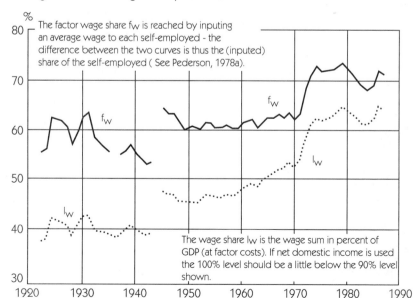

share during the last decade includes the effects of joining the EEC in 1972.

(2) The agricultural revolution between 1860 and 1900 (as already discussed) roughly doubled the shares; but even 150 years ago, the Danish trade shares were higher than they are in most middle-income countries today.

(3) The share of agriculture in exports has fallen since 1900. However, if the absolute size of real agricultural exports is considered, it is higher now than it ever was. Therefore, agricultural exports have not been replaced with industrial exports. Industrial exports have been added to agricultural ones.

It is well known that it is difficult to tax, especially if people cannot read, write, or keep accounts, and tax collectors are unreliable. Therefore, in order to generate revenue, the government must find taxes that are easy to collect, such as those collected at the borders. Therefore, a sure sign of underdevelopment is high taxes on foreign trade. For the complex political reasons discussed earlier, Denmark was slow in making large public expenditures and when it did, a land tax was used to finance most of these expenditures. Thus, there was no need for heavy taxes on foreign trade between 1820 and 1920. The total tax burden on foreign trade stood at approximately 2 percent of GDP, corresponding to about 3 to 4 percent of the value of imports and exports together.

It is also worth mentioning that Denmark never had multiple exchange rates. Instead, Denmark's policy has been remarkably consistent over the last 200 years: to have one, fixed, convertible exchange rate, with as few restrictions on capital flows as possible. Deviations from this policy, in the form of exchange controls, have only occurred during, and immediately after, the two World Wars, and during the Great Depression of the 1930s. These controls were seen as emergency measures to be abolished as soon as possible.

A Small but Almost Permanent Balance of Payments Deficit

Figure 4.5b shows the trade balance and the goods and services balance since 1843. Throughout the period covered, Denmark has had a large trade balance deficit; but at the same time there has been a fairly large surplus on the services balance which has covered most of the trade balance deficit. The main source of the services surplus has been shipping. However, there has been a permanent deficit in the total goods and services balance every year since 1870, a fact worthy of a few comments.

The key point to note is that for most of the time a small balance of payments deficit was not threatening. Denmark was able to borrow to finance the deficit at an interest rate r that was considerably lower than the growth rate y. It can be shown (Paldam 1988) that the debt burden d = D/

Figure 4.5 a. Foreign Trade of Denmark, 1820-1988
The Share of Export in GDP and some Components

The top (thin) line gives goods and services export. The series goes back to 1948 only the net series exists, see figure b. The next (bold) line gives the goods export alone. Before 1835 there are gaps in the data so the rapid increase between 1820 and 1835 is probably not genuine. The dotted line gives total agricultural exports i.e., between the bold and the dotted line is the industrial export. The bottom (thin) line gives the agricultural export of vegetable origin (mainly grain). Between the dotted and the bottom thin line is the agricultural export of animal origin: butter, bacon, cheese, etc.

4.5 b. The Trade and Goods and Services Balance in Percent of GDP

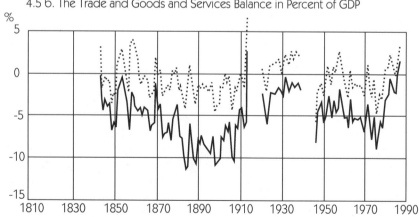

The dotted lin gives the goods and services balance, and the full (bold) line gives the goods balance. The only large post not illustrated is the interest payments on the foreign debt.

Y, where D is the foreign debt and Y is the GDP, converges to:
$$d \to d^* = h/[r\text{-}y], \text{ where } h = (X\text{-}M)/Y$$
As the average size of the "deficit margin" $[r\text{-}y]$[10] for the two main deficit periods 1870 to 1914 and 1948 to 1980 was no less than 3.5 percent, and h was about one percent, this caused the debt burden to remain between 20 and 30 percent during most of that period. So it appeared to most Danish policy makers that the balance of payments deficit was a small problem, as long as the deficit was kept within certain bounds. However, both periods ended with a fairly large debt burden as interest rates caught up with growth rates. But twice Denmark was extremely fortunate. In 1914, Denmark remained neutral during the war and had very large balance of payments surpluses (not shown, as the data are somewhat problematic) that alleviated most of the debt. World inflation during the war also helped. Similar good fortune occurred at the beginning of the oil crisis.

When Denmark was hit by the oil crisis in October 1973, it already had a permanent balance of payments deficit, which it did not take seriously. It had also just received a political shock during the elections, which saw the number of parties doubled (see Figure 4.2). Therefore, the first reaction to the increase in the balance of payments deficit, from an annual rate of 1.5 percent (of GDP) to 5 percent, was to do nothing. But international interest rates reacted slowly to the large jump in world inflation in 1974-1975. Therefore, much of the old debt was wiped out in real terms during these years, although it was rapidly replaced by new debt.

At the end of the 1970s, the debt problem suddenly emerged—and it emerged with a vengeance. After many years of comfortably coexisting with a balance of payments deficit (while listening to the dire predictions of economists), it was difficult for the population and the governments to believe that trouble had finally arrived. Growth rates declined, and interest rates rose—more than doubling in real terms. Suddenly the debt burden soared. From 1978 to 1985 the Danish debt burden increased from 28 percent of GDP to 47 percent (almost as large as in Brazil), i.e., from being a minor problem to becoming an explosive and threatening problem. However, while the development of the debt is the same as it is in many LDCs, the Danish debt problem does not seem quite so formidable, thanks to the much larger trade shares.

For the last four years, the balance of payments has been a priority while employment has suffered, with unemployment around 10 percent. The goods and services balance has improved, climbing from -5 to +3 percent, so that the surplus in 1990 finally covers two-thirds of the interest burden. As a result, the debt burden has begun to fall. There are predictions that the debt burden may continue to fall in the 1990s.

---

[10] The golden age result in optimal growth theory says that the deficit margin $[r\text{-}y]$ should be zero. That happens when the savings rate is so determined that steady state consumption is maximized.

The Industrial Structure and the Peaceful, Centralized Labor Market

When compared with most developed countries, industrial Denmark has three unique characteristics:

(1) It has always had a relatively small industrial sector and a large tertiary sector.

(2) There are a few large firms that are conglomerates dominated by trading firms, while the industrial sector is made up of relatively small firms.

(3) The labor market is highly centralized and very peaceful.

The Industrial Sector: Truncated Development and the Fragmented Structure

Between 1910 and 1920, employment in the industrial sector reached 20 percent of the labor force, a number which has remained fairly stable until now. Similarly, the industrial sector has never reached more than 22 percent of GDP, which it did in the early 1950s. The share of the industrial sector has, therefore, been almost constant for about sixty years, even when industrial exports overtook agricultural exports in the 1950s. The apparent stability hides significant changes in the combination of subsectors and a dramatic change in the "surrounding" sectors, where the primary sector has fallen (as already discussed) and the tertiary sector (in particular, the public sector) has grown, as discussed in the following section. When compared with other developed countries, Denmark's industrial sector growth has generally been below 5 percent (compare Chenery and Syrquin 1975).

Another characteristic of the industrial sector is the absence of large firms and the lack of sectoral concentration. Since so little of the industrial sector was built around any particular raw material or product, light industry has always dominated. The firms are small to medium-sized, with no reason for their location except chance. In the 124 sector input-output table used as the basis for national accounting, the largest sector is the "machine" industry, employing about 200,000 people. The largest firm in that sector, Danfoss, which makes thermostats, employs about 10,000 people, mostly in the remote village where the founder was born. The cement processing equipment (and cement) company of F.L. Smith is almost as large. There is some concentration in the ownership of the agro-based industries, but the largest single plant does not employ more than a few thousand people. The key phenomenon is the amount of diversification. In value-added terms, the largest industrial firm is LEGO, which produces plastic bricks for children. It is a high-tech firm, exporting 97 percent of its production. LEGO is located in a small village in central

Jutland where the original inventor/salesman was born almost eighty years ago.

It has often been asked why industrialization in Denmark has not progressed further. Industry has never been the main sector, and even now, when industrial growth has been resumed, growth is clearly stronger in the tertiary sector. The tertiary sector has even less concentration, since it consists of many kinds of high-skilled, high-tech occupations, where the material production (if any) takes place in other countries (such as the newly industrialized countries of the Far East). There are two explanations for Denmark's "stunted" industrialization:

(1) From 1964 onward, the public sector grew at such a rapid pace that it squeezed the industrial sector of manpower. The reason industrial growth has recently returned is that the public sector has stopped growing, for the moment.

(2) The trade union movement made Denmark a high wage country very early.

The first explanation will be discussed in the next section since this mechanism occurred relatively late. The second explanation is, however, very questionable since there are two sides to consider. On the one hand, there is the unquestionable fact that a strong, central union came to dominate the labor market since the early 1920s and, on the other hand, there is the remarkable stability that the union has given the labor market.

On occasion, discussions have centered on whether the economy could benefit from more central planning or the nationalization of key industries. Three arguments seem to speak decisively against such actions:

(1) The few state firms and cooperatives that have been established by the trade unions (in the 1920s and the 1930s) have not performed well. The union firms have almost all closed down.

(2) It is difficult to point out "key" industries to nationalize.

(3) Most of the fast growing industries, such as LEGO, were the creation of one entrepreneur and would never have been established by a bureaucrat.[11]

---

[11] At one time in the mid-1960s, the Social Democratic Party created a Capital Market Council to better direct investments as an election platform; but even when they won the election, and established such a council with a membership of top civil servants, the party never managed to formulate explicit guidelines for the council. It died in silence after a dozen meetings. From the discussions at that time, it appears that the type of project such a council would have favored would have been the production of substantial goods, such as ships, but not frivolous and superfluous goods. What would not have been supported was the production of another brand of something already produced, such as plastic bricks for children.

On the other hand, it is clear that the agricultural cooperatives in the processing and banking sectors have done well, so the evidence is not conclusive.

The Anti-Subsidy Tradition

The organizations of the industrial sector have strongly opposed subsidies. For many of the smaller branches of manufacturing and trade there have been instances of rent seeking, where the sector obtains a special certificate allowing the extraction of some rent (e.g., taxis are licensed so they are classified as new luxury cars which are expensive to transport); but the central organizations have been strongly against subsidies, state interference, and protection.

The main reason why the Central Union of Manufacturers [DA, Dansk Arbejdsgiverforening and Industrirådet]—referred to below as CUM—has vigorously fought subsidies and rent seeking is its belief that a social democratic country runs considerable risk of public sector encroachment once it gives up the strictest standards of property rights. As a result, there is relatively little industrial policy and very little public ownership within the manufacturing sector.

The Development of the United SDP-CTU Labor Movement

There has been significant unionization of the labor force in Denmark for a long time. Already in 1917, about 40 percent of all blue and white-collar workers were members of a union (Pedersen 1982). The degree of unionization reached 70 percent in 1960 and 80 percent in 1980, and there are no signs that the unions are decreasing in popularity as they are in the United States, the United Kingdom and many other countries.

The union movement consists of two kinds of unions: industrial and skill unions. Since the union movement has never had a logical structure, there have been interunion tensions. However, most unions have always belonged to the Central Trade Unions—the CTU [LO, Landsorganisationen, De Samvirkende Fagforbund]—which has some power to make the member unions work together. The CTU has a strong interest in internal peace, i.e., that the member unions maintain internal peace and work together to improve the incomes of all members of the CTU vis-à-vis outsiders.

The growth of the union movement corresponds to the growth of the Social Democratic Party (SDP). The SDP has always had a clear majority on the CTU board. At the annual congresses of both the CTU and the SDP, many consider the CTU and the SDP as the political and labor market arm of the labor movement. Since the mid-1920s, the labor movement has been the strongest single political force in the country. However, it is important to keep two qualifications in mind: first, that the SDP itself never had a majority, but always had to work with non-socialist parties to rule, and second, that the industrial sector was always relatively small and highly diversified. Two consequences emerged from these qualifications:

(1) The traditional socialist goal of central control of the industrial sector did not appear to make sense, as already discussed.

(2) The labor movement had to be very moderate in the ideological field. A strong socialist ideology (not to speak of a Marxian tradition) within the labor movement was never developed.

The more revolutionary wing broke with the labor movement around the time of the Communist Revolution in Russia (and the three to four unsuccessful revolutions in Germany) after World War I. The years 1918-1922 were actually very dramatic years for the labor movement, with many strikes and lock-outs which caused wild movements in nominal and real wages. It is difficult to imagine, from today's perspective, that the Danish labor market was one of the most unruly during these years, and that real wages rose by 40 percent in 1919, and fell again the next year.[12]

Figure 4.2 shows that a non-SDP-CTU left wing has gradually emerged since the 1920s and especially since the early 1970s. The existence of a growing left wing has made it very difficult for the SDP to formulate policies since 1970. For now, it is important to note that the left wing has somewhat influenced the trade union movement, but it has always had very few votes on the CTU board since the board is elected by the majorities in each union.

Even with qualifications, the labor movement of the SDP-CTU became the central political power in Denmark beginning in the mid-1920s. Since central planning and nationalizations were never seriously considered, the main goal of the movement became the creation of the welfare state. Protectionism was never really a policy issue for the labor movement. In connection with the labor market, the movement led to centralized wage setting and the gradual demise of strikes from the late 1920s to the mid-1950s.

The Centralized Three-Part Wage Setting System and the Incomes Policy Tradition

Every second year, the CTU and the much weaker CUM meet to agree on the central component of wage raises. The key meetings often take place at the Arbitration Institution, normally with a judge as the chief arbitrator.

---

[12] Much the same story of large-scale labor unrest and wild fluctuations in real wages occurred in Norway, Sweden and Germany. However, while the three Scandinavian countries managed to obtain stable and moderate social democratic governments and gradually more and more stable labor markets during the 1920s, Germany became less and less stable until the final disaster in the early 1930s.

That central component of the wage raise is about half of all wage increases, and the public labor market and most other wage agreements are somehow coordinated with the "big" negotiations. The rules of the game change from one round to the next, but the central element is always important. The negotiations take at least half a year, and the last few months are quite dramatic.

The government—which has the responsibility for steering the rate of unemployment, the balance of payments, and the general level of demand, as well as being employer to many people—always participates, if only indirectly. The government has frequently interfered and enacted into law the final agreement based upon an arbitration proposal even though one or both participants (the CTU and the CUM) has rejected the proposal. It is a tradition to call the way in which the government interferes, its "incomes policy." However, the interference has the character of a game, where everybody knows in advance that the government might interfere, and this knowledge influences the draws of the other players.[13] Before the possible effects of this policy game are discussed, it is appropriate to consider the plain facts of the levels of wage raises, w, and unemployment, u, in the three most recent periods:

(1) 1948-1958—a decade with w stable, at 5-7 percent, and u stable around 4.5 percent.

(2) 1960-1974—fifteen years with w accelerating from 6 to 20 percent, and u stable around 1.5 percent.

(3) 1976-1989—fifteen years with w falling from 20 to 4 percent, and u rising to and remaining around 10 percent.

When wage costs are calculated, relative to international competitors (Paldam 1989), it appears that relative wage costs fell gradually in the first period, but then rose steadily during the second and most of the third period, as already mentioned.

This scenario seems far removed from the one predicted by standard wage relation in modern economic theory: the Phillips curve augmented with rational expectations—assuming a fairly stable natural rate of unemployment. The main prediction of the theory is that when the rate of unemployment is kept at an extremely low level, such as 1.5 percent, wage raises should quickly explode—not rise gently over fifteen years. To make the theory fit, it would appear that a strong braking mechanism is needed. Possible braking mechanisms are the CTU and the incomes policies.

Hence, it is arguable that the centralized system of wage bargaining had

---

[13] It is hard to formalize the whole of the negotiation process, especially as the rules keep changing; but it is quite clearly a key element in policy making in Denmark and the other Scandinavian countries as well (Calmfors 1990 and Andersen and Risager 1990). An attempt to analyze the game has been made by Holler and Paldam (1987) where the few assessments following are further substantiated (but proof is hard to provide).

the effect of keeping the unemployment rate very low for fifteen years during the second period. On the other hand, the same system had the effect of making the adjustments to a new international situation very slow in the third period, prolonging the crisis dramatically.

The incomes policies have undoubtedly played a role in this set-up. However, nobody has been able to show that the net effect has been to keep wage raises down, except in the short run (notably in 1963). But the incomes policies have certainly led to strong tensions within the labor movement, and have probably played a role in the rise of the left wing. In the end, it proved to be too difficult for the SDP to convince its brothers in the CTU to show wage restraint. For example, it was the conservative government in 1982 that finally, after many years of advice from independent economists, abolished the automatic cost of living adjustment, COLA [Pristalsregulering]. This was done over the forceful objections of the SDP (then in opposition). But the interesting fact is that the SDP did not—even when greatly prompted by the left wing—promise to reinstall the COLA.

Peaceful Labor Market

One important effect of the centralization of the labor market was the gradual demise of strikes from the late 1920s to the mid-1950s. Denmark has never had the level of industrial conflict known to the Anglo-Saxon and Latin countries (Paldam and Pedersen 1984). At first, this was because the industrial sector in Denmark lagged behind in size. By the time the sector really grew, the CTU-SDP-movement also grew, so while there was a tendency to reach the "standard level" of conflict of the Anglo-Saxon countries in the early 1920s, as it did in Norway and Sweden, this did not happen in Denmark. Instead, the labor market quickly turned peaceful, and there are at least two explanations for this occurrence.

First, there is the "alternative road" explanation put forward by Hibbs (1978) which suggests that the inclusion of the CTU in the labor movement opened up other "roads" to improving the lot of the workers. Therefore, the workers came to rely less on the strike measure. What supports this theory is that the workers did get relatively high wage increases, an internationally high wage share, plus a very developed welfare state. So, why strike?

The second explanation is the wage structure internalization theory in Paldam (1989). It appears that most strikes are not to change the wage share, but to improve the position of the members of one group vis-à-vis other groups, i.e., it is changes in the wage structure that generate industrial unrest. The growth of a CTU internalizes more and more of the wage structure and coordinates more and more of the wage raises and, hence, decreases the relevant wage structure changes.

The stable and peaceful labor market has no doubt helped Danish industrialization. On the other hand, a number of studies (discussed in

Figure 4.6. The Share of the Public Sector in Denmark

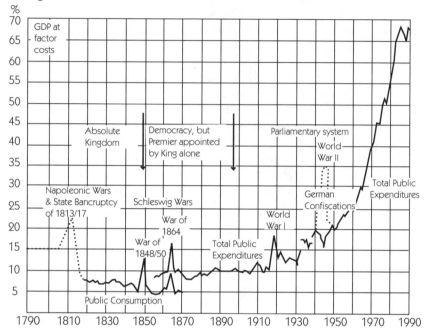

Data constructed as in figure 4.1. The finances of the municipalities are much more integrated into the state budget from the early 1970's. The dotted line for expenditures during World War II are German confiscations, paid for by (worthless) proscriptions on the Central Bank, Main source Norstrand (1975).

Paldam and Pedersen 1984) have demonstrated that strikes have little effect on production—strikes can help explain wage raises (and vice versa), but not production.

The Second High Growth Period: The Push of the Public Sector and the Development of the Big Compromise

The Danish public sector, which, relatively speaking, was well below average size for OECD countries as late as the mid-1950s, is now the second largest in that group, only slightly smaller than Sweden's. If more detailed comparisons are made (Lybeck and Henrekson 1988), it appears that the Danish public sector is relatively small in defense and, as mentioned, in subsidies to industry. Furthermore, it is not really above average in education and health. However, it is relatively large in transfer payments or redistribution.

The development of the public sector is depicted in Figure 4.6. It shows two things: (1) how late the development of the welfare state occurred, and (2) the incredible speed and smoothness by which the public sector expanded, once it got underway. Returning to Figure 4.1, it appears that the second period of high growth in Denmark was the period 1958-1974, a period when economic growth was higher in Denmark than in nearly all other OECD countries. In the previous decade, the country struggled with a balance of payments deficit and a relatively high rate of unemployment; but a change to a more expansive policy was made in 1958. This is not easy to see on the very aggregate Figure 4.6, but it is obvious in more disaggregated data.

The Policy Shift in 1958

It is far from clear why policy changed in 1958,[14] but perhaps it became clear to some key decision makers that Danish international competitiveness had improved so much that some expansion could be allowed without a significant balance of payments deficit. In any case, it was then decided that welfare could be expanded. The two most rapidly expanding sectors were the public sector, as is illustrated in Figure 4.6, and home building, where Denmark, between 1960 and 1973, held the world record as measured in m^2 housing area per capita. In the two-sector open macromodel, known as the Scandinavian Model,[15] this amounts to an expansion of the sheltered S-sector, and in the light of the model, it is easy to explain why Denmark has experienced serious balance of payments difficulties from the early 1960s.

The Great Expansion: 1958 Until the Early 1980s

The explosive development in the public sector raises many interesting issues (Paldam and Zeuthen 1988). The following six points must be mentioned:

(1) The extraordinarily smooth path of public expansion, in which political changes and other seemingly important factors fail to disrupt the

---

[14] One explanation that many Danish economists favor is that there was a small terms of trade change in 1958. This is, however, an unlikely explanation, because there have been larger changes in the terms of trade with no such effect. Another more likely economic explanation is that foreign competitiveness was at a peak in 1958 (Gelting 1976 and Paldam 1989a). Finally, it should be noted that 1958 was also the year when Viggo Kampmann became Minister of Finance, and the key economic policy maker.

[15] This model originated from various Norwegian White papers from the mid-1960s, with Odd Aukrust as the key author. It was then taken up by Edgren, Faxén and Odhner in 1968 (and by R. Courbis in France). The main point in the model is the distinction between the competitive C-sector, producing tradables, and the sheltered S-sector, producing non-tradables. The Anglo-Saxon literature has been dominated by the Fleming-Mundell tradition, where both the domestic and the foreign goods are tradables, but of a limited substitutionality.

curve, raises the following question: To what extent is the development shown in Figure 4.6 deliberate? In other words, is the development the result of a strategy chosen by the government and supported by the population, or a result of forces too big for any government to control? This is a difficult question to answer since it may depend on how the terms "deliberate" and "strategy" are defined. One aspect of the answer is given by the demand model.

It is often argued that the welfare state developed as a reaction of the political and economic system to the demand of the population, i.e., social security is seen as a "luxury good" with a high income elasticity. Evidence for this view appears to be weak, except in the circular sense that the share of the public sector and average incomes have both risen in many countries. When Figures 4.1 and 4.6 are compared in more detail and divided into subperiods, it becomes clear that the connection is extremely weak (Paldam and Zeuthen 1988). However, if the argument is accepted, the causal relation runs from the real growth to the expansion of the public sector.

There is much less doubt about the reverse causality: the rapid expansion of the S-sector brought about a rather fast growth of the rest of the economy. Many studies of the short and long-run multipliers of a balanced and unbalanced public expansion (notably the experiments with the two macromodels: ADAM and SMEC) have shown that such policies are expansionary. It is clear that the significant expansion of the public and related sectors is the main explanation for the rapid growth between 1958 and 1974.

(2) In the beginning, the expansion of the public sector was very helpful in stabilizing employment, as it absorbed the large outflow of manpower from the agricultural sector. However, as the expansion continued, and full employment resulted, the C-sector (the tradables sector) was squeezed. This explains the lack of growth of the private sector after 1966 and, in particular, why the renewed (relative) growth of the industrial sector from the mid-1950s ceased in the mid-1960s.

(3) The Danish economic profession since the 1940s has been dominated by Keynesianism.[16] The same applies to everybody else engaged in economic policy making. In this light, it should be noted that throughout the full employment period until 1974, the expansion took place with continuous budget surpluses. As a result, the domestic public debt vanished. This changed after the external shock of 1973, and large budget deficits resulted. However, since 1985, the deficits have been curbed (by raising taxes), so that the domestic public debt is, once more, under control and actually

---

[16] The belief in Keynes was, as in Sweden and Norway, often combined with a SDP orientation. The most popular SDP/Keynes model was the one where only fiscal policy matters. Money is just a veil. SDP/ Keynesianism is now receding among economists, even in Sweden, where it used to be strongest.

falling. It is surely not because of the lack of a balanced budget constraint that the Danish public sector has grown.

(4) The drawing in Figure 4.6 looks like a logistic curve, rising from an old, low level of about 9 percent of GDP to a new high level. This new level is not yet established, but if the curve is extended symmetrically, the new level appears to be a little above 100 percent, or at least too high to be sustainable. Thus, there is clearly a problem of finding a level that is compatible with long-run growth. No mechanisms seem visible by which agreement can be reached on that level, and even if everybody could somehow agree, it is hard to see how a constant level for the public sector could be kept.

(5) The result of increased public spending has been rather dramatic taxes. The taxes are, as mentioned, on personal incomes and consumption, so the average citizen pays more than half of his income in taxes. Marginally, people typically pay between 50 and 68 percent in direct taxes and around one-third in indirect taxes on the non-savings part of the rest. This has led to several rounds of "tax revolts" in the form of increased support for the Anti-Tax Party (to be discussed). It is now a very strong political wish to halt further tax increases, and to substantially cut the marginal tax rate.

(6) The national accounts include no productivity increases in the public sector. However, this is surely incorrect, even though it is hard to measure productivity in the public sector. It has often been discussed whether a gap exists between productivity in the public and the private sector. There probably is a gap, but it appears that it is small.

Forces Behind the Great Expansion

Much could be said about the mechanisms behind the build-up of the welfare state. From the politico-economic history that was told before, it is clear that the development was generated after the change of power from the Farmers' Party to the SDP-CTU. In other words, the growth of the welfare system was strongly connected to the growth of the labor movement as the key political power. However, the true workers were always a fairly small minority of the population (20 to 30 percent), so in order to convince the great majority to support this policy, the labor movement needed the big compromise:[17] the combination of the welfare state with the economic efficiency of a liberal economy. Furthermore, it should be added that it sustained the big compromise for three decades.

---

[17] It is interesting to compare the Scandinavian tradition of moderate left-center coalitions, with the southern European/Latin American tradition of much more radical workers' parties and, as a result, a more or less permanent right-center majority. Perhaps, it was just historical chance in the years following the First World War that set into motion the path that has led to the big compromise and the Scandinavian Model.

The right wing governments that actually ruled during the great build-up of the welfare state, notably the "VKR-government" (1968-1970) of the Conservatives, the Farmers' Party, and the Radicals, are invisible in the time series data for the expansion of the public sector. They were powerless (or uninterested) in stopping the growth of the public sector. The internal dynamics proved to be very strong: once some people are provided with a certain service, the political process works so that the service—and many related services—have to be provided to everybody. Once compensation is given for one social event, it must be given for many related events.

The Braking Process: Is it Permanent?

There is still overwhelming support for the welfare state in Denmark. Although many people (about half of the voters) want to curb it, nearly everybody wants the welfare state. Nevertheless, it is clear to most economists that in order to return to a reasonable growth rate, a more manageable foreign debt, and a lower unemployment rate, some reduction in the public sector is necessary.

In addition to the pressures from the balance of payments and the foreign debt, the tax revolt has been a main factor in curbing public sector expansion. This revolt began in the mid-1970s when a new, extreme right wing, anti-tax protest party was formed and entered the Parliament with 14 percent of the votes. The party surprisingly received votes from the whole political spectrum thereby having a significant impact, although the other parties tried to ignore it.

In the 1990s a new factor is entering into the braking process—the plans of the EEC to harmonize taxes. The combined pressures from the EEC, the anti-tax protest party and economic logic will perhaps be enough to resist strong pressure for renewed public sector expansion.

Concluding Remarks

It appears that at least three lessons can be learned from this chapter:

(1) A high degree of integration into the world market is an efficient way to curb rent seeking (and many other inefficiencies) and, hence, an important engine of growth.

(2) It is possible to develop a considerable redistribution/welfare system after a country has acquired a high level of efficiency, without losing the dynamism of the economy.

(3) It appears that redistribution has the smallest impact on the efficiency of the economy if it is confined to personal incomes and consumption, while property rights and production decisions are left to the market.

The first lesson is probably the least problematic. The key advantage of an open economy is the ability of the world market to control rent seeking. If the only loss of an autarkic economic development was a loss of scale or comparative advantage, it would be limited; but the problem is that lack of foreign competition may propel a country into becoming a stagnating rent seeking society.

The second lesson is more debatable. There are two main problems. The first problem is that there appears to be limits to the amount of redistribution that can take place in any case, i.e., the 30 percent of GDP now redistributed in Sweden and Denmark is clearly problematic, although 20 percent would probably be fully compatible with efficiency. The main problem is that redistribution is made by an administrative-political system that has its own interests in mind, in addition to the ideal of making income distribution more equal. A second problem is that to have a system of taxation/redistribution that generates the desired result, one has to have an administration capable of efficiently monitoring all incomes in the society. It is hard to imagine that the tax administration could work as a small island of high efficiency in an underdeveloped economy.

The third lesson appears to be a natural outcome. It appears that the main decisions of the households are much more robust (labor supply functions are almost vertical, and the consumption set depends upon incomes in a very stable way so that redistribution has little effect in the aggregate), while the decisions of the firms react much stronger to incentives. In other words, it is easy to become less efficient once a system of taxes and subsidies to the firms is introduced.

Despite all these qualifications, it seems that we are still left with some positive lessons that apply to the middle-income countries of today.

REFERENCES*

ADAMbk. [The dataset for the official macroeconomic model, on disk from The Danish Central Bureau of Statistics].

Andersen, T.M. and O. Risager. 1990. "A Wage Bargaining Model for Denmark." Calmfors, L. ed.

Calmfors, L. ed 1990. *Wage Formation in the Nordic Countries*. London: Basil Blackwell.

Chenery, H.B. and M. Syrquin. 1975. *Patterns of Development, 1950-1970*. London: World Bank and Oxford University Press.

Dansk Socialhistorie. 1983-1985. Copenhagen: Gyldendal. [Broad survey of Danish demography, social laws and conditions, income distribution and living conditions].

Edgren, G., C.O. Faxén, and C.E. Odhner. 1973. *Wage Formation and the Economy*. London: MacMillan.

Gelting, J.H. 1976. "Skraimmebillede." *Nationaløkonomisk Tidsskrift* 114: 210-213.

Hansen, S.Å. 1972-1973. *Økonomisk vaikst i* Danmark. Copenhagen: Gad. [An Economic History of Denmark].

Henriksen, O.B. and A. Ølgaard. 1969. *Danmarks udenrigshandel 1874-1958*. Copenhagen: Gad.

Hibbs, D.A. Jr. 1978. "On the Political Economy of Long-Run Trends in Strike Activity." *British Journal of Political Science*. 8: 153-176.

Kislev, Y. and W. Peterson. 1982. "Prices, Technology, and Farm Size." *Journal of Political Economy 90*: 578-595.

Krueger, A.O. 1974. "The Political Economy of the Rent Seeking Society." *American Economic Review 64*: 291-303.

Kaergaard, N. 1982. "CLEO." Memo. Økonomisk Institut, University of Copenhagen. [An Econometric Long-Run Model of the Danish Economy].

Laursen K. and M. Paldam 1982. "The Dynamics of the World's Income Distribution 1955-2000." In *Economic Essays in Honor of Jørgen H. Gelting. Nationaløkonomisk Tidsskrift* 120.

Lindbeck, A. 1986. *Hur mycket politik tål ekonomin? Högskattesamhällets problem*. Stockholm: Bonniers.

Lybeck, J.A. and M. Henrekson, eds. 1988. *Explaining the Growth of Governments*. Amsterdam: North-Holland.

Mogensen, G. Viby. 1985. "Forskning i sort økonomi - en oversigt." *Nationaløkonomisk Tidsskrift* 123: 1-19.

_____ 1987. "Nyere Forskning i dansk økonomisk historie - en oversigt." *Nationaløkonomisk Tidsskrift* 125: 153-170.

---

*Translations of some Danish titles and comments in English are written in brackets [ ].

Nannestad, P. 1972. "At the Cradle of a Party System: Voting Patterns and Voting Groups in the Danish Constitutional Convention 1848-1949." *Scandinavian Political Studies* 7: 119-135.

_____ 1989. *Reactive Voting in Danish General Elections 1971-1979.* Aarhus: Universitetsforlaget.

Nordstrand, R. 1975. "De offentlige udgifters vaeksti Danmark", memo nr. 41, Econ. Dept., Copenhagen University.

Olsen, E. 1970. *Dansk økonomisk historie*, 1970. Copenhagen: Gad. [Concise survey of the economic history, 1800-1970].

Paldam, M. 1977. "Bliver verdens indkomstfordeling skaevere?" *Nationaløkonomisk Tidsskrift* 115: 276-299.

_____. 1979. "Towards the Wage-Earner State. A Comparative Study of Wage Shares 1948-1875." *International Journal of Social Economics* 4: 45-62.

_____, and P.J. Pedersen. 1984. "The Large Pattern of Industrial Conflict - A Comparative Study of 18 Countries 1919-1979." *International Journal of Social Economics* 10: 3-28.

_____, and M. Holler. 1987. "Overenskomster og indkomstpolitik. Aspekter af det Danske spil." *Økonomi og Politik* 60: 35-52.

_____. 1988. "An Essay on the Power of National Banks." *Geld und Währung/Monetary Affairs* 4: 5-30.

_____, and H.E. Zeuthen. 1988. "The Expansion of the Public Sector in Denmark - a Post Festum?" In Lybeck and Henrekson, *Explaining the Growth of Governments*. Amsterdam: North-Holland.

_____ a. 1989. "Den reale Danske valutakurs. Overfor DMk, FMk, NKr, SKr, FF, UK£, US$ og Yen, 1950-1987." In Paldam and Sørensen.

_____ b. 1989. "A Wage Structure Theory of Inflation, Industrial Conflicts and Trade Unions." *Scandinavian Journal of Economics* 91: 61-81.

_____, and N.K. Sørensen, eds. 1989. *Valutakursteori og - politik.* Århus: Skrifter fraøkonomisk Institut.

Pedersen, P.J. 1978a. "Den funktionelle indkomstfordeling i Danmark i mellemkrigsårene." *Økonomi og Politik* 51: 197-219.

_____. 1978b. "Langtidstendenserne i den faglige og geografiske lønstruktur i Danmark." *Nationaløkonomisk Tidsskrift* 116: 303-322.

_____. 1982. "Union Growth in Denmark, 1911-1939." *Scandinavian Journal of Economics* 84: 583-592.

_____. 1983. "Lønudviklingen i Danmark, 1911-1976. Stabilitet og specifikation." *Nationaløkonomisk Tidsskrift* 121: 102-129.

Phillip, K. 1947. *Staten og fattigdommen.* Copenhagen: Gjellerup.

Politikens Danmarks Historie. Copenhagen: Politiken. [Standard political history with many references—new revised edition every decade].

Rawley, C.K., R.D. Tollison and G. Tullock, eds. 1988. *The Political Economy of Rent-Seeking.* Boston: Kluwer.

Statistik Årbog. [Annual Yearbook of Statistics from the Central Bureau of
    Statistics since 1895].
Tullock, G. 1967. "The Welfare Costs of Tariffs, Monopolies and Theft."
    Western Economic Journal 5: 224-232.

CHAPTER FIVE

ECONOMIC GROWTH AND STAGNATION IN URUGUAY

*Martin Rama**

Introduction

By the middle of this century, Uruguay was known worldwide for its high level of development. Demographic transition was already achieved and the population (less than 3 million people) was homogeneous. Labor legislation, social security, and public education were the most advanced in Latin America and there was a democratic political system, based on a large urban middle class. By the 1950s, Uruguay could, in some sense, be seen as a "Scandinavian model" in the far south.

The Uruguayan welfare state was partly attained due to the efforts of Batlle y Ordóñez, President during 1903-1907 and 1911-1915 (Vanger 1963 and 1980). He confronted the last armed uprising in 1904, thereby consolidating both democratic forms of government and political parties. Inspired by a secular, humanitarian philosophy, he promoted social legislation, which even anticipated the claims of trade unions, and which was deeply influenced at that time by anarchist immigrants. Moreover, he built a strong central authority, characterized by financial equilibrium and active economic policies.

From a purely economic point of view, Uruguay reached a high welfare level even with respect to industrialized countries. If dollars are adjusted to have the same purchasing power as in the United States, the Uruguayan GDP per capita was similar to that of some of the wealthiest European countries by the middle of the century. Indeed, GDP per capita in Uruguay amounted to $2,973 (in 1975 prices) in 1955, whereas it reached $2,757 in Belgium, and $3,023 in Denmark (Kravis et al. 1981).

However, fifteen years later, real GDP per capita of Belgium and Denmark had increased some 75 percent; meanwhile, GDP per capita in Uruguay was lower than in 1955. Such an economic failure was accompanied by a social and political crisis that was almost as extreme as the national complacency of the 1950s. Important sectors of the society, both right-wing and left-wing, despised the virtues of democracy, while human rights

---

* Carlos Grau provided efficient research assistance.

Figure 5.1
Output Trends (1935-1988)
Per Capita GDP in 1975 dollars

Source : Based on data from Banco Central del Uruguay and Dirección General de Estadística y Censos.

activists were outraged by the conflict between the army and the police and a well-known guerrilla movement (the Tupamaros). Finally, in 1973, Uruguay was governed by a military dictatorship that would have been inconceivable some years before.

The aim of this paper is to analyze the reasons behind the rise and fall of the Uruguayan economy. Was it caused by policies guiding the use of natural resources? What were the effects of trade policies on economic growth and stagnation? What effects have the interactions between social partners and the state had on policy choices, and what are the reverse effects? These questions are particularly relevant today since Uruguay has once again returned to democratic rule.

The first section identifies the main stages of Uruguayan economic growth since the Great Depression (the choice of the starting point is based on data availability). It also gives a brief description of policy choices, economic structure, and social developments during these stages to familiarize the reader with Uruguay. The second section discusses the conventional explanation for Uruguayan stagnation, which is based on the bias against natural resources arising from highly distortive trade policies. This section also analyzes the role played by natural resources in each of the stages, particularly through their direct and indirect share of foreign exchange earnings. The third section stresses the importance of institutional arrangements in explaining Uruguayan growth and stagnation, by showing that the interaction between some relevant social partners changed dramatically from one period to another. The final section is a chapter summary.

Growth Patterns

Main Trends Since the Great Depression

A long-term view of Uruguayan economic growth is provided in Figure 5.1, which shows (in a logarithmic scale) real GDP per capita between 1935 and 1988. Clearly, there are four distinct periods. These periods will be referred to throughout the chapter: Period 1, until 1956; Period 2, between 1957 and 1967; Period 3, between 1968 and 1981; and Period 4, 1982 and onwards.[1]

Up to 1956 and between 1968 and 1981, real GDP per capita increased significantly. If we exclude 1935 to 1939, which was strongly influenced by the Great Depression, growth rates were strikingly similar between Period 1 (2.87 percent) and Period 3 (2.82 percent).[2] The resemblance is emphasized in Figure 5.1 by the bold upward lines, which represent the values corresponding to the estimated trends.

Between these two growth periods, however, real GDP per capita declined; the estimated annual trend (statistically significant) for Period 2 was -0.50 percent. Also Period 4 is characterized by stagnation, but here it is difficult to assess the underlying trend.

It is worth stressing that the differences in growth rates between the four periods can neither be explained by changes in the international environment, nor by external shocks. For instance, although the average level of the Uruguayan terms of trade was lower during Period 2 than Period 1, it was even lower during Period 3, which was characterized by growth rates as high as during Period 1.

In a more rigorous manner, a set of causality tests was performed in order to check whether or not the terms of trade level preceded the output growth rate. The results led to the rejection of both the Granger-causality and

---

[1] These years were chosen in the following way. First, it was assumed that real GDP per capita grew at a constant rate within each stage. Therefore, an exponential time-trend equation was estimated for each of them, with changing turning points (say 1954 to 1957, 1965 to 1972, etc.). Finally, these points were chosen so as to maximize the adjusted coefficient of determination of the estimated equations.

[2] In estimating the first of these time trends, a dummy variable was used to account for the droughts of 1942 and 1943.

causality in the sense of Haugh and Pierce. The experiment was repeated with the international real interest rate instead of the terms of trade, with similar results.[3] Therefore, changes in the world environment do not seem to explain the long-run output trends in Uruguay, and an examination of the domestic events is warranted.

Period 1: Import-Substitution Industrialization (until 1956)

By the end of the 1920s, an important share of Uruguay's economic activity was still associated with cattle raising (particularly beef, wool, and hide production), which was undoubtedly the country's most competitive sector. This activity was carried out on natural greenlands, thereby leading to a slow, thriving process. The only outstanding technological improvements were more selective breeding and increased use of wire enclosures.

In addition, some important services were provided, either by the government or by British investors. The former administered many financial institutions, port facilities, and electricity and telephone services. The latter owned the railway network (the largest by land area in South America) and some of Montevideo's public utilities, such as gas, water, and tramways.

Concerning manufactures, protection had been adopted as a policy principle since the last quarter of the nineteenth century. In 1888, a general tariff of 31 percent was introduced. However, exceptions were made for several goods, for which tariffs were allowed in the 6 to 51 percent range. A free import regime was also established for machinery and some industrial inputs; the latter was generalized in 1912. As a result, the manufacturing sector accounted for a significant share of total output in 1930 (13 percent), the third largest share in Latin America, after Argentina and Mexico. However, only 158 out of the 10,549 establishments recorded in 1936 had more than fifty employees. Moreover, four slaughterhouses accounted for 20 percent of industrial output.

The impact of the Great Depression on the Uruguayan economy was severe: available estimates suggest that real GDP per capita fell by about 10 percent between 1930 and 1935 (Millot et al. 1973). This slump was due to the sharp fall in foreign demand for livestock products, and to world deflation, which implied that tariffs ceased to be an efficient protective barrier for the manufacturing sector.[4] The fact that Uruguay was governed by a so-called "mild dictatorship" in 1933 is probably related to the extent of this crisis.

---

[3] The estimation of the real interest rate was based on British treasury bills and the consumption price index for the United Kingdom. The growth in the 1970s cannot be attributed to credit availability since Uruguay was a net creditor by the end of that period.

[4] Protection was still far from being prohibitive in the 1930s, except for some alcoholic beverages and matches (Finch 1981). Concerning exports, they fell from $100 million in 1930 to $58 million in 1932.

The economic policy response was to strengthen import substitution in both public and private sectors. A state enterprise (ANCAP) was created in 1931, monopolizing both production and the sale of refined petroleum, alcohol, and cement. The argument for this was that Uruguay was (and still is) completely dependent on fuel imports.

The private sector was encouraged by the stepwise erection of new protective barriers. The general tariff rose from 31 to 48 percent in 1931, multiple exchange rates were established in 1933-1934, and import licenses in 1938. But the main instrument for import substitution was the Contralor de Exportaciones e Importaciones, a central bureau created in 1941, which had authority to allocate foreign exchange, approve import licenses, and ban imports that were considered to compete with domestic production.

Such policies led to a significant expansion of manufacturing output, which grew at an annual rate of 6 percent between 1940 and 1956. Industrial employment, in turn, rose from 85,000 in 1942, to 190,000 in 1958.[5] Manufacturing production was almost completely devoted to domestic sales, and exports continued to consist basically of beef, wool, and hides. Given the long-lasting stagnation of cattle-raising production that began in the 1930s, there was a substantial increase in the manufacturing share of GDP, which reached 20 percent in 1956.

From the point of view of institutional arrangements, the most important event was the creation in 1943 of a wage bargaining mechanism, the Wage Councils. These councils operated at the sectoral level, with the state as a mediator. By that time, there was a revitalization of the trade union movement, whose strength had been sharply reduced by the Great Depression and by conflicts between Marxists and anarchists. However, the initiative for creating the Wage Councils came from a parliamentary committee investigating the living conditions of the working class.

Period 2: Stagflation (1957-1967)

Economic growth would probably have stopped before 1956 had it not been for the high export earnings associated with the Korean War (1950-1953) which led to a significant rise in international wool prices. Import-substitution industrialization was already exhausted by that time. The size of the domestic market prevented the development of a capital goods industry and the production of many durable consumption goods, such as automobiles.

The mid-1950s also marked the beginning of some specific economic problems in Uruguay. First, inflation started to rise and reached an impressive 36.8 percent a year in Period 2. Second, the balance of payments became a

---

[5] In sharp contrast with other import-substituting Latin American countries, foreign investment did not play an important role in the Uruguayan industrialization process (Pascale 1980).

Table 5.1. Openness Coefficient

| | Total exports + imports as a share of GDP | | Manufacturing exports as a share of industry sales | |
	Goods only	Goods and services	In domestic prices	In world prices
1930	n.a.	n.a.	25.8	n.a.
1935	35.5	n.a.	n.a.	n.a.
1942–45	34.1	n.a.	13.0	18.6
1946–56	28.9	34.7	8.2	11.7
1957–67	20.9	27.4	6.3	8.9
1968–81	23.0	31.5	12.8	18.2
1986	28.7	40.4	29.1	41.5

Source: Based on L. Macadar 1986, J. Millot *et al.* 1973, and data from *Banco Central del Uruguay*.

bottleneck of economic activity. Imports were increasingly oriented towards goods for which there was no domestic production, such as machinery, fuel, and raw materials. Despite the outstanding growth of world trade, exports continued to center on beef, wool, and hides, and rose only from $136 million in 1957 to $159 million in 1967. As a result, the openness coefficient of the economy during this stagnation period was about 40 percent below that of the 1930s (see Table 5.1).

One of the most stunning features of this period was the rapid growth of the state bureaucracy. A well-known novelist wrote: "Uruguay is the only office in the world that has reached the status of a Republic" (Benedetti 1960). However, despite the large number of public sector jobs, international emigration continued to grow. In the following decade, after the military coup,[6] emigration increased even more.

During the stagnation period, there was also an unquestionable strengthening of the labor movement, which attained its heyday in the first half of the 1960s with the establishment of a central organization (the CNT). Although trade unions had a somewhat Marxist rhetoric, they aimed basically to protect the economic interests of their members. The apogee of the labor movement lasted until the beginning of authoritarian rule.

Period 3: Back to Growth (1968-1981)

Period 3 was characterized by a dramatic change in labor market institutions. In 1968, after annual inflation had reached 180 percent, a stabilization policy was established, which included a temporary freeze of wages and prices and the abolition of the Wage Councils. After the 1973 military coup, repressive measures were sharply reinforced, and trade union activities forbidden.

The fact that the economy started to grow again in such a context of political and social disorder is surprising. However, the recovery might have

---

[6] About 192,000 people left Uruguay between 1963 and 1975, and 156,000 emigrated between 1975 and 1985. The sum represents almost 12 percent of the 1985 population.

been based on solid grounds, since all during this third period there was almost no decline in total GDP (except in 1971-1972), despite the significant real shocks suffered by the economy. Indeed, the impact of increasing oil prices was particularly severe since Uruguay produces no petroleum. Moreover, there was a dramatic slump in foreign demand for beef in 1974 as a result of European agricultural policy.

The foreign exchange shortage arising from this balance of payments crisis resulted in the launching of a set of measures aimed at opening the economy. In the very short run, exports were heavily subsidized and important trade agreements were signed with Argentina and Brazil. In addition, financial and commercial exchange rates were unified and exchange rate controls abolished. In a somewhat longer perspective, the dismantling of protective barriers was undertaken.

Another economic policy change during this period was related to budget expenditures. The size of the public sector (government consumption and public employment) had been almost frozen since the end of the 1960s. But the dramatic decline in real wages that began in the early 1970s allowed for a substantial increase in public investment, particularly after 1975. Such a shift was probably in accordance with the military ideology, for which ruling also meant building.

Finally, it is worth stressing some similarities between the 1968-1981 period and the two earlier periods. First, as in the 1940-1956 period, there was a sustained growth of the manufacturing sector after 1968 (except at the beginning of the 1970s), but with the difference being that industrial sales during the latter period were increasingly oriented towards the foreign market (see Table 5.1). This led to a significant expansion and diversification of exports. Second, there was a resemblance in inflation rates between Period 2 and Period 3; the average annual inflation rate between 1968 and 1981 was 57 percent, even above the 1957-1967 level.

Period 4: And Now?

For almost all Latin American countries, the 1980s represent a "lost decade" in terms of economic growth. In Uruguay, real GDP fell by 14.7 percent in just two years (1982-1983). This was partly due to an unsound exchange rate policy adopted in 1978, which was intended to slow down inflation by means of a decreasing devaluation rate. This policy became unsustainable in 1982. The extent of the economic crisis might have hastened the democratic transition, which had already begun in 1980 when a constitutional amendment, submitted to referendum by the military regime, was massively rejected. This, finally, led to an elected government in 1985.

Under the democratic rule, the financial liberalization which characterized the military regime was preserved, while gradual tariff reduction was pursued. Further, the Wage Councils were reestablished and there was a labor movement revival, with trade unions having almost the same features as in the 1960s. Concerning economic performance, a significant recovery resulted in real GDP per capital levels similar to those attained at the beginning of the 1980s. Meanwhile, real wages rose enough to outweigh the 1982-1983 decline.

Because of the sharp economic fluctuations during the 1980s, it is difficult to foresee what path Uruguay will take in the future. Will it recover growth rates like those of the earlier days, or will it once again stagnate? Any serious attempt to answer this question should be based on a better understanding of the main differences between the four periods discussed here.

The Conventional Approach

Natural Resources

The main natural resource in Uruguay is land. About 90 percent of the country's 43 million acres are arable. This is why agriculture, particularly cattle raising, has played such an important role in the Uruguayan economy. According to conventional wisdom, this endowment should explain the high welfare level attained by Uruguay in the earlier periods. Along the same lines of thought, the subsequent bias against agriculture, especially because of trade policies, could account for the economic decline. However, before accepting this conventional wisdom, it is worth taking a closer look at the role of natural resources in the Uruguayan economy.

In fact, in contrast to conventional wisdom, the share of agriculture and cattle raising in GDP was already low in the 1930s—about 20 percent. These sectors also provided little employment, since Uruguayan cattle raising is not very labor-intensive. In addition, the role of agriculture and cattle raising declined both in output and employment creation after the 1930s.

Patterns were different for export shares, at least until the end of the stagflation period. Indeed, so-called traditional products (wool, beef, and hides) represented, on average, more than 80 percent of total foreign sales before 1967, as indicated by the upper line (called e_t) in Figure 5.2. But the share fell dramatically during Period 3 identified above, to finally stabilize below 40 percent during the 1980s.

Such a decline, due to the expansion of manufactured exports, casts some doubts on the conventional view of the Uruguayan economy. If land-based activities neither play the main role in output, nor in employment or exports, why should we then accept that Uruguay is still a "cattle raising country"? However, nontraditional exports correspond basically to light industries, like leather products, textiles, milled rice, and dairy products, and since these industries have strong backward linkages to agriculture, it has been argued that foreign sales continue to rest heavily on natural resources (Barbato et al. 1984).

An appropriate way to measure the importance of natural resources in Uruguayan exports is provided by the use of input-output tables. Let us consider the one of 1961, which corresponds approximately to the middle of the studied period. This table includes twenty activity sectors, the first one being agriculture, and the second cattle raising. Strictly speaking, exports directly based on natural resources are just $E_{1,t} + E_{2,t}$ with $E_{i,t}$ representing the exports of sector "i" in year "t."[7] However, in order to test the "agroindustrial" hypothesis, it is necessary to take into account total production requirements of agriculture and cattle raising embodied in Uruguayan exports. Let us call $N_{i,t}$ ($N_{2,t}$) the agriculture (cattle raising) requirements embodied in total merchandise exports in year t. In a similar way, $S_{1,t}$ and $S_{2,t}$ are the corresponding requirements when all exports of goods and services, including freight, tourism, etc., are considered.

Now, define n_t as the share of $N_{1,t} + N_{2,t}$ in total merchandise exports, and s_t as the share of $S_{1,t} + S_{2,t}$ in total exports of goods and services.[8] If economic growth was associated with an intensive use of natural resources, and stagnation to a bias against agriculture and cattle raising, the n_t and s_t ratios should be high both during Period 1 and Period 3, defined above, but low during Period 2. According to Figure 5.2, this is obviously only partially true. Indeed, n_t and s_t declined during Period 2, first as a result of lower agricultural exports, then when wool production was substituted by beef and tanned hides (both with a higher degree of industrialization). But the decline continued during Period 3 due to the expansion and diversification of industrial exports. In the case of s_t, it also accelerated as a result of the sustained increase of tourism after the end of the 1960s. Tourism represented about 15 percent of total foreign exchange earnings during Period 4.

In fact, the export share of natural resources is low enough to question the conventional explanation of Uruguayan international competitiveness.[9]

---

[7] Note that $E_{1,t} + E_{2,t}$ is less than traditional exports because beef sales are included in manufacturing as are industrialized wool and tanned hides.

[8] In analytical terms, $N_t = (I - A)^{-1}. E_t$ and $S_t = (I - A)^{-1}. B_t$ with N_t, S_t and E_t being the vectors $(N_{1,t}, N_{2,t}, ..., N_{20,t})$, $(S_{1,t}, S_{2,t}, ..., S_{20,t})$ and $(E_{1,t}, E_{2,t}, ..., E_{20,t})$, respectively. Concerning vector E_t, it is equal to B_t, except for $E_{17,t}, ... E_{20,t}$, which are replaced by zeroes since they do not correspond to merchandise exports, but to freight, tourism, etc. As regards A, it represents the (20x20) matrix of technical coefficients arising from the 1961 input-output table, whereas I is a (20x20) unit matrix. Therefore, the relationships $S_{1,t} > N_{1,t} > E_{1,t}$ and $S_{2,t} > N_{2,t} > E_{2,t}$ are always fulfilled. Finally, ratios n_t and s_t are defined in the following way: $n_t = (N_{1,t} + N_{2,t})/(E_{1,t} + ... + E_{16,t})$ and $s_t = (S_{1,t} + S_{2,t})/(E_{1,t} + ... + E_{20,t})$.

[9] A similar doubt arises from the study by Vaillant (1988), which is based on a different approach. The study shows the increase in competitive manufacturing sectors which basically process nonagricultural inputs.

Figure 5.2
Natural Resources in Uruguayan Exports
(Percent of Total Exports)

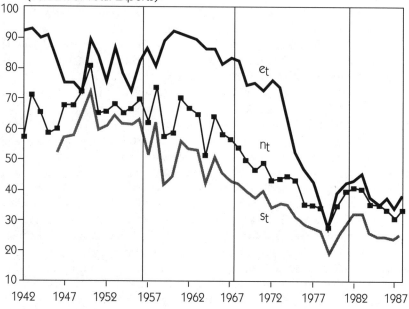

——— Beef, wool and hides in merchandise exports (e_t)

—■— Agriculture and cattle raising requirements in merchandise exports (n_t)

▓▓▓ Agriculture and cattle raising requirements in exports of goods and services (s_t)

Source: Based on data from Banco Central del Uruguay and CINVE.

Table 5.2. Nominal Protection (1975–1986)
(In percentages)

	1975[a]	1976[a]	1977[a]	1978	1979	1980	1981	1982	1985	1986[b]
FORMAL										
Domestic market	287.0	—	—	86.5	—	49.1	46.0	60.1	49.6	48.8
Exports	17.0	—	—	16.2	—	16.0	11.6	22.8	5.8	6.8
Total	158.0	119.3	90.1	74.8	52.8	43.5	39.9	53.3	34.1	33.2
IMPLICIT										
Domestic market	52.0	—	—	24.7	—	35.7	38.6	41.5	27.2	36.7
Total	23.3	37.2	35.6	23.3	35.4	32.4	19.6	38.1	25.6	—
REDUNDANT										
Domestic market	60.7	—	—	23.1	—	5.9	1.1	8.6	10.4	2.7

[a] Non-weighted averages by products.
[b] In March.
Source: M. Rama 1982, CINVE 1987, and L. Macadar 1988.

One could even be tempted to conclude that import-substitution policies provided the basis for dynamic comparative advantages. Nevertheless, according to Figure 5.2, the role of natural resources in total exports was different in Period 1 and Period 3, despite the fact that growth rates were almost the same in both cases. Therefore, economic growth does not seem to depend directly on the sectoral structure of foreign sales.

Trade Policies

A related explanation for the rise and fall of Uruguay is provided by its trade policies. Again, according to conventional wisdom, the ten years of economic stagnation after 1957 is associated with the perseverance on import-substitution policies in a country with a domestic market of less than 3 million people. And conversely, the recovery observed during Period 3 would be the result of an increasingly open economy.

This commonly held view is based on the theory of comparative advantage. Import substitution results in factor transfers from sectors where the country has comparative advantages (agriculture and cattle raising) to others in which it does not (manufacturing). This transfer would also explain why the livestock production stagnated after the 1930s.

This kind of approach has been widely accepted in Uruguay since the 1960s, from the left-wing intelligentsia to the government's economic advisors. For the latter group, it provided the rationale for export subsidies and the gradual tariff reduction which was undertaken after 1974 (Bensión and Caumont 1981); the subsequent steps of the process are reported in Table 5.2. The left-wing intelligentsia, on the other hand, drew more pessimistic conclusions regarding social progress prospects (Instituto de Economía 1968). Within capitalist structures, the only possible choice they foresaw was between stagnation associated with import-substitution policies, and the dismantling of protective barriers claimed by landlords. Since manufacturing production factors were specific, the second possibility would necessarily lead to high social costs.

A closer examination of what really happened in Uruguay during these years casts some doubts on the relevance of the conventional view. The main criticism of it is that it does not fit the data very well. First, high protective barriers were raised during Period 1, and dismantled during Period 3. But despite this opposite sign of trade policies, the average growth rate was almost the same during both periods. Second, the trade liberalization process that began in 1974 cannot explain how growth rates became positive in the end of the 1960s. Finally, for many years, tariff reductions only affected redundant protection, not the spread between domestic prices and international prices (see Table 5.2). In fact, the higher openness coefficient of the Uruguayan economy during Period 3 arose from larger exports and higher import prices, rather than from increased purchases abroad. And it was not until the beginning of the 1980s that manufacturers had to face import competition (Rama 1982; CINVE 1987).[10]

In sum, the dismantling of protective barriers could account, at best, for the extent of the economic crisis during the beginning of Period 4, but it cannot be made responsible for economic growth during Period 3. Thus, the main difference between the periods has to be found elsewhere.

Distributional Activities

Autonomy of the State

President Batlle y Ordóñez could hardly have undertaken the radical social and economic changes he did had it not been for the high degree of autonomy of the Uruguayan state at the beginning of the century (Barrán and Nahum 1983). Indeed, politics did not fit any simple model of domination by the economically powerful, represented at that time by the landlords. Such an outcome was probably due to mass immigration, since the foreigners identified the traditional party groupings with the civil wars and anarchy of the premodernization period (Finch 1981).[11]

Whatever the reason, the political system was able to carry out its own "innovation" project, despite the opposition of large factions of the dominant class. The project was led by a technocratic elite who directed the public enterprises and institutes for technological development (in chemistry, fishing, agriculture, etc.) created by Batlle y Ordóñez during his second presidency (Cheroni 1986). Such a technocratic feature was partially preserved by the "mild dictatorship" of President Terra (1933-1938), in which a significant public investment was made to build the first hydroelectric dam.

It is worth stressing the role of formal education in this process. Many important members of the elite referred to above were graduates from the School of Mathematics, which had been created in 1887. The innovation project included, in turn, the establishment of new colleges: agronomy and veterinary science in 1907, chemistry and pharmacy in 1929, and business in 1932. Concerning the arts and crafts education, the reform under Terra allowed the development of skills which until then had been imported with the immigrants.

The hypothesis we want to discuss is that the economic decline was related to a progressive weakening of the Uruguayan state, with the conse-

---

[10] The latter was particularly severe because of the overvaluation of the peso which resulted from the stabilization policy described above.

[11] In 1889, 78 percent of Montevideo's adult men were foreigners.

quential loss of autonomy for relevant policy decisions. Such a loss was not for the benefit of the landlords, whose revenge for import substitution was long expected by the left-wing intelligentsia. Although ruralistas won the 1958 elections, the only significant changes they made were a reorganization of protective barriers and a sharp devaluation. Actually, the loss of autonomy was for the benefit of social groups developed as a result of the state's own innovation project.

During Period 1, the growth period up to 1956, growth was based on industrialization for the domestic market and on the development of a large variety of public utilities. Therefore, civil servants, manufacturers, and wage earners became relevant social partners who had to be taken into account by the political system, which was much more receptive to these groups' demands than it had been to the landlords' claims.[12] This became particularly true by the end of this period, since the relative affluence attained by the Uruguayan economy significantly enlarged the pie that could be allocated by the political system.

The state's weakening lasted until the end of the 1960s. At this time, it started to recover some of its lost autonomy, not as a result of a new "technocratic" project, but as the outcome of rising authoritarianism. From then on, and particularly after the 1973 military coup, the main purpose of successive governments was to "discipline" the country. In fact, the choice of market-oriented policies probably pointed at such a goal, and not only at promoting economic efficiency. As a result, collective action by the three groups mentioned above was neutralized, and many of their demands neglected.[13]

The relationship between distributional activities and economic decline is suggested by the fact that the three identified social partners seem strong enough to have had an effect on economic equilibrium, but not sufficiently strong to bear a significant fraction of the social costs resulting from their actions. However, the main point remains to be proved, i.e., that collective action by civil servants, manufacturers, and salaried workers could have accounted, at least partly, for the social and economic decline during the stagflation second period, 1957-1967. Since this is undoubtedly a polemic assertion, the role of these three social groups will be discussed separately.

---

[12] This could be due to a widely accepted solidarity principle for which producers' failure and workers' unemployment had to be avoided at all cost. More generally, some widespread beliefs characterizing the Uruguayan society may have played an important role in preventing the political system from facing economic decline (G. Rama 1988).

[13] The same happened with the landlords' claims, so that the rise of the authoritarian rule was not for their benefit either, as would have been expected by the left-wing intelligentsia.

Table 5.3. Civil Servants and Pensioners

| | In thousands | | | As a percentage of total population | | |
| | Civil Servants | | | Civil Servants | | |
	Central administration	Whole public sector	Pensioners	Central administration	Whole public sector	Pensioners
1901	19.0	—	—	2.08	—	—
1905	20.0	—	—	1.99	—	—
1925	30.1	—	—	1.95	—	—
1932	33.0	52.0	—	1.88	2.96	—
1937	39.4	—	69.3	2.09	—	3.68
1938	43.2	57.5	73.3	2.27	3.02	3.85
1941	—	58.1	—	—	2.95	—
1945	—	—	106.0	—	—	5.16
1948	—	—	142.0	—	—	6.65
1955	95.5	168.5	207.7	4.04	7.12	8.78
1961	—	193.8	298.5	—	7.52	11.59
1969	112.7	230.0	454.7	4.15	8.46	16.73
1975	—	235.8	—	—	8.46	—
1980	—	233.6	620.3	—	8.24	21.63
1981	144.3	236.1	—	5.00	8.18	—
1985	148.9	248.7	707.0	5.04	8.42	23.92
1987	166.1	272.0	743.3	5.56	9.11	24.88

Source: Based on H. Davrieux 1987, H. Finch 1981, M. Vanger 1963, 1980, and data from Dirección General de Estadística y Censo.

Civil Servants

Although the innovation project of President Batlle y Ordóñez accorded a significant role to the public sector, it was not at all based on a large bureaucracy. Table 5.3 reports the number of civil servants, as well as their share in total population, since 1901.[14] As can be seen, that share did not experience any significant change until the beginning of the 1940s.

However, the number of civil servants increased dramatically between 1941 and 1969, from 58,000 to 230,000 people, i.e., from less than 3 percent of total population to almost 8.5 percent (see Table 5.3). The main expansion occurred before 1955. This was partly due to a significant development of public high schools, starting by the mid-1940s. Furthermore, between 1948 and 1952, a number of public utilities belonging to British investors (including railways, water supply, and public transportation) were nationalized. With the exception of these two reasons, the growth of public employment between 1941 and 1955 mainly reflects an enlargement of the bureaucracy.

Some of the institutional arrangements allowing such an outcome had already existed in the 1919 Constitution, in which co-participation had been introduced as a government device. This meant that the minority party

---

[14] It would have been better to compare public employment to the labor force, instead of total population. Unfortunately, the data required for such a calculation are available only since the 1960s. Something similar happens with the disaggregation of public employment in bureaucracy, education, health care, etc.

received a share of total appointments in the public sector.[15] However, co-participation was temporarily reversed by President Terra, whose political campaign pointed to the "corruption" of government by the bi-party collegiate executive established by the 1919 Constitution. The latter was replaced in 1934 by a new Constitution, which set up the need for explicit rules for admission, promotion, and suspension in the civil service. In addition, during the Terra government a law was passed which even denied the right of public enterprises to establish legal monopolies like the one granted to ANCAP in 1931 (see above).

In fact, the grounds for the observed bureaucratic expansion can be found in the wave of populism, which characterized Uruguay by the middle of the century. The constitutional amendment of 1951 restored the collegiate executive, this time in such an extreme version that the presidency was directly abolished. The new Constitution also set in its own text the sharing of public administration between the two main parties (the adopted rule was: three for the winner, two for the loser). Finally, it interdicted the dismissal of civil servants.

Additional institutional arrangements reduced public sector efficiency even more. In 1953, a law was enacted in order to encourage civil servants to retire before the required age so that additional jobs could be available for cliental allocation. In 1956, the firing interdiction was extended to state enterprises and local governments. In addition, the permanent filling of vacancies was forbidden before seven months, so that politicians could allocate temporary jobs. Finally, in 1957, it was decided that promotions had to be based on seniority.

Measures were similar concerning retirement. In the 1940s, almost all social groups, including rural workers and charwomen, were supposed to have the right to retire. Moreover, there were family allowances for workers in the private sector. However, in 1951, the management of social security was shared by the main political parties according to the "three-and-two rule." From then on, a wide variety of social benefits were approved, even permitting women to retire at the age of 40! By 1967, there were about fifty different social security administrations. The share of pensioners in the total population, in turn, almost doubled between 1955 and 1969 (see Table 5.3).

Arrangements of this kind were obviously far from the "technocratic" idea of the state, implicit in the innovation project of Batlle y Ordóñez. Furthermore, they were likely to have important consequences on economic growth. The average productivity of the public sector was probably lowered by the inefficient rules adopted for hiring, promoting, and (not) firing (Rama

---

[15] Co-participation, which was the basis of peace between the two main parties in the late nineteenth century, was strongly rejected by Batlle y Ordóñez, in favor of party government. Its reintroduction in 1919 was associated with the adoption of universal suffrage as a way to reward or secure political loyalties.

1989b). Also, the impact on the average productivity of the whole economy had to be significant given the high share of public sector jobs in total employment.

A complementary aspect is related to the impact of these institutional arrangements on investment in human capital and infrastructure. Concerning human capital, the enlargement of the state bureaucracy had an impact on formal education. By the middle of the century, high school training became the key to access to the public sector. Technical education, on the contrary, was progressively neglected; almost no new university schools were created. The only exceptions were the development of the humanities and establishment of a set of minor schools (fine arts, music, library, etc.).

Investment in infrastructure was progressively crowded out by current budget expenditures. Since civil servants became an important partner for the political system, the institutional arrangements set up in the 1950s were kept in spite of the decline of export earnings after the Korean War. Moreover, a strong labor movement developed within the public sector, which had a significant role in some of the main conflicts during the 1960s. As a result of both clientlinks and distributional activities, capital accumulation fell from 23 percent of public expenditures by the mid-1950s, to less than 13 percent by the end of the stagflation period. One can expect such a cut in infrastructure development to reduce the private investment rate, thereby adding to the economic decline (Rama 1989a).

If this is correct, causality is exactly the opposite as in the conventional explanation of the development process in Uruguay. According to the conventional view, expansion of the bureaucracy was a device created by the political system to face stagnation. It was a way to absorb the labor surplus at a time when the private sector was not creating enough jobs. Our analysis, on the contrary, suggests that the expansion of the bureaucracy preceded the stagnation because it basically occurred between 1951 and 1957. In fact, it represented an unsound device created by the political system to channel the affluence resulting from temporarily high export earnings. Further, it was one of the main causes underlying stagnation.

The reversion of the reported institutional arrangements began by the end of the 1960s. The 1967 Constitution restored the presidency and put an end to the sharing of public administration.[16] The size of the public employment, in turn, was almost frozen in 1969, and remained below 8.5 percent of total population during the authoritarian rule.[17] Finally, public investment had risen from the end of the 1960s, and reached an impressive 39 percent of government expenditures in 1979.

---

[16] However, the dismissal interdiction still remains while the seniority-based promotion rule was not removed until 1987.

[17] However, by the mid-1970s, both employment and wage payments were restructured by the military regime in favor of the army and the police.

Manufacturers

Because of the small dimensions of the Uruguayan domestic market, the manufacturers' group is not very large. At first glance, the number of establishments producing industrial goods appears to be significant, reaching a maximum of almost 30,000 by the end of the 1960s (Macadar 1986). However, only a few of these establishments have more than a hundred employees: there were about 210 in 1960, 270 in 1968, and 310 in 1978. Actually, high concentration is one of the main features of the Uruguayan manufacturing sector. As shown in Table 5.4, there were twenty-one sectors in 1978 in which the four largest firms provided more than 60 percent of total production.

Since the incentive for distributional activities increases as group size diminishes, concentration is likely to favor lobbying by manufacturers. Indeed, the smaller the number of firms that benefit from a specific action, the larger the share of the gains that accrue to each firm that undertakes the action (Olson 1982). In the Uruguayan case, lobbying was traditionally aimed at increasing the effective protection rate (Macadar 1981). This was achieved either by increasing tariffs or subsidies on final goods, or by preventing the establishment of tariffs on input imports (in this case, as the result of actions undertaken by others). The results were impressive: even after seven years of trade liberalization, some of the sectors reported in Table 5.4 still enjoyed effective protection rates as high as 700 percent.[18]

Distributional activities shed a different light on the distortive effects of trade policies. The main problem of import-substitution strategies would not be the high level of effective protection rates itself, but rather the use of a scarce entrepreneurial capacity to raise such rates. In the first case, import substitution is a source of static inefficiencies. In the second one, it leads to a negative-sum game in which profits are maximized through distribution rather than by means of productivity gains.

However, one should not expect the relationship between rent seeking and the slowdown of economic growth to be strictly contemporary. Instead, it might include some time-lag. On the one hand, lobbying firms must engage some investment in order to benefit from the potential rents created by their own distributional activities; therefore, the growth rate should not decline immediately. On the other hand, once protection becomes prohibitive, rent seeking might cease to be profitable, so that the slowdown should not last indefinitely.

---

[18] Besides, the average rate for the twenty-one most concentrated sectors was higher than for the rest of manufacturing activities for which the effective protection rate was estimated (145 percent, instead of 134 percent). The spread would probably be larger if the estimation had been done for all sectors.

Table 5.4. Concentration in the Manufacturing Sector
(Percentages, in 1978)

ISIC code	Sector	The 4 largest firms in sector's production	The sector in manufacturing output	Effective protection rate[a]
3118	Sugar	100.0	0.9	220.3
3133	Beer	100.0	1.2	−27.5
3692	Cement	100.0	0.4	47.5
3411	Paper, pulp and cardboard	95.3	0.8	126.1
3419	Paper products	94.0	0.7	150.4
3610	China	92.6	0.7	n.a.
3551	Rubber wheels	91.2	1.8	592.7
3140	Cigarettes	89.3	4.0	3.5
3112	Dairy products	84.2	1.6	57.1
3512	Fertilizers	83.9	0.4	−2.9
3134	Soft beverages	82.7	3.0	−17.5
3844	Motorcycles	70.4	0.7	n.a.
3710	Basic metals	66.8	0.7	130.6
3131	Alcoholic beverages	66.3	1.5	122.4
3833	Electric appliances	66.3	1.0	185.9
3620	Glass	65.9	1.0	36.8
3114	Fish	65.7	0.6	n.a.
3115	Edible oils	64.7	0.9	[b]
3559	Other rubber products	63.0	0.8	−6.0
3832	Radios and TVs	62.4	0.9	699.9
3119	Chocolate	61.1	0.6	n.a.
Total			24.2	

[a] Based on the Corden's method. Corresponds to 1981.
[b] Sector with negative value-added at international prices.
Source: M. Buxedes *et al.* 1987, L. Macadar 1984, and Industrial Census of 1978.

Table 5.5. Lobbying by Manufacturers

	Rent-seeking actions concerning					Number of rent-seeking actions (1)	Output level (1978 = 100.0) (2)	Actions-to-Output ratio (1)/(2)
	Tariff Rate[a]	Item's position	Reference price[c]	Exchange rate[d]	Other measures			
1925	2	2	8	0	0	12	n.a.	n.a.
1930	3	7	6	0	1	17	42.2	0.4
1935	16	25	8	1	9	59	38.0	1.5
1940	2	37	9	18	0	66	39.5	1.6
1945	9	21	6	34	4	74	44.6	1.6
1950	1	38	13	28	4	84	57.9	1.4
1955	3	33	5	9	0	50	71.4	0.7
1960	50	19	9	0	0	78	71.2	1.1
1965	52	29	5	0	6	92	74.2	1.2
1970	25	19	25	0	19	88	83.0	1.0
1975	181	46	20	0	4	251	88.7	2.8
1980	40	17	0	0	5	62	113.5	0.5
1983	41	14	13	0	1	69	98.7	0.7

[a] Or subsidy rate, in the case of exports.
[b] Since different groups of products pay different tariffs, changing the item's position aims at modifying the tariff rate.
[c] In many cases, tariffs (or subsidies) are calculated on a reference price, instead of the actual international price.
[d] From 1933 to 1959, there are multiple exchange rates.
Source: Based on laws, decrees and administrative measures.

Table 5.5 measures the distributional activities by manufacturers through the number of specific protective measures adopted in selected years. The underlying hypothesis is that general protective measures (such as a rise or a diminution of the maximum tariff) usually reflect economic policy decisions, whereas specific measures (such as a higher tariff for a particular good) arise necessarily from rent seeking. Hence, Table 5.5 does not include measures concerning ten or more different goods simultaneously.[19]

Data after 1983 are not reported in Table 5.5 because that was the last year for which the whole set of laws, decrees, and administrative decisions was published. Years prior to 1925 are not considered because rent seeking did not seem so intensive at that time. Indeed, the import-substitution measures adopted in 1888 derived from the state, and were prior to the birth of any pressure group representing manufacturers (Jacob 1985). Concerning the 1912 regime of preferential tariffs on industrial inputs, one of its grounds was "to put an end to the system which consists in passing a special law for each industry starting its activities in the country" (Anichini et al. 1977).

As regards 1925 to 1983, two interesting conclusions can be drawn. First, Table 5.5 shows that the structure of protective measures kept changing. During Period 1, a significant share of distributional activities were aimed at obtaining special exchange rates. These were abolished in 1959 and rent seeking was reoriented towards the adoption of higher nominal protection rates. Finally, when the trade liberalization process that began in 1974 regrouped all rates into just a few levels, raising the reference prices on which tariffs and subsidies were calculated became an important lobbying goal.

The second conclusion is related to the intensity of the distributional activities. Clearly, 1975 was an unusual year, characterized by numerous measures. This was because of the generalization of export subsidies in 1974 which were designed to face the balance of payments crisis generated by the oil shock and the European agricultural policy. But if such an outlier is set aside, Table 5.5 suggests that distributional activities by manufacturers reached their peak by the middle of the century: the absolute number of actions was very significant in 1950, whereas the highest ratio between actions and real output corresponded to 1940.

From then on, even though rent seeking was far from disappearing, the number of actions stabilized in absolute terms, and declined quite steadily when compared to real output. The reaching of prohibitive protection levels first, and the rising of the authoritarian rule later on, could account for such an outcome. But whatever the causes, the state's weakening seems to have preceded economic decline.

---

[19] It also sets aside measures related to equipment imports by the public sector, as well as import facilities adopted to face temporary shortages (resulting, for instance, from adverse climate conditions).

Trade Unions

Import-substitution strategies indirectly represent an incentive to collective action by workers. Indeed, an organization having the monopoly of labor supply is able to capture, by means of higher wages, some of the rent enjoyed by firms as a result of protection. Therefore, after some time lag, the building up of protective barriers should lead to the development of a strong trade union movement in the manufacturing sector. The description of social developments in the second section suggests that the latter might have been able to raise wages from 1957 until the end of the 1960s or the early 1970s.

From a theoretical point of view, one can suspect such an ability to have had an effect on growth patterns. Uruguayan trade unions only manage a small share of national income. Total wage earnings, including those of civil servants and nonunionized workers, represent about a third of GDP. The incentives faced by an organization that represents only a narrow segment of society are dramatically different from those of an encompassing organization (Olson 1982; Calmfors and Drifill 1988). The latter can serve its members only by enlarging the pie society produces, so that members can recieve large slices even with the same shares as before. The former, on the contrary, finds it easier to struggle for large slices of the same pie, without caring much about the social costs of collective action. This feature would be in accordance with the Marxist rhetoric of the trade unions.

Beyond this simple conjecture, the main point is to determine if prevailing real wages were above the maximum level compatible with per capita GDP growth. Unfortunately, such a level is not directly observable; it must be inferred from available macroeconomic data by means of a simple econometric model that tries to capture some of the distinctive features of the Uruguayan economy. Although the model is not shown here, it is worth stressing its underlying behavioral assumptions.[20]

Suppose that there are a limited number of firms in the economy, each operating at increasing returns to scale and facing a downward-sloping demand curve for the goods it produces. Suppose also that aggregate demand depends on the domestic output level. If labor and imported goods are used as inputs for production, both output and profits decrease alongside with the "real" level of wages and import prices.

Assume now that investors can choose between owning the domestic firms or placing their savings abroad. Their portfolio equilibrium determines the market value of the already existing capital goods, which increases with profits and decreases with the interest rate on foreign assets. Finally, capital accumulation depends on profitability, defined as the ratio between the

---

[20] To economize on space, a description of the model was excluded. It is available from the author.

market value of a new capital unit and its cost. Under the assumptions of the model, it can be shown that such a ratio is an upward function of the market value of already existing capital goods.[21]

Therefore, since higher wages, lower terms of trade, or higher world interest rates reduce the real market value of already existing capital goods, they also lead to a lower capital accumulation rate. Furthermore, because of the increasing returns-to-scale assumption, profitability is higher the larger the capital stock, so that shifts from equilibrium may have cumulative effects. Consider, for instance, a situation in which the investment rate exactly outweighs depreciation. If terms of trade fell, but real wages remained unchanged, there would be a lower profitability and the investment rate would fall below replacement requirements. Hence, the capital stock would be reduced, leading to an even lower profitability, and so on. This implies that the real wage drop required in order to stop economic decline would be larger, the later the adjustment.

For a given capital stock, and a given level of terms of trade and the world interest rate, there is only one wage level for which the investment rate ensures a GDP growth of 1 percent a year. Consequently, there is only one wage level such that capital accumulation copes with population growth. Let us call it the "stagnation" wage. Figure 5.3 represents actual and "stagnation" wages according to the values of the model's parameters. The latter were estimated for the 1946-1981 period. The choice of the starting year was based on data availability. Concerning years corresponding to Period 4 (1982-1988), their inclusion seriously downgraded the fit. This suggests that the recession of the early 1980s could not have arisen only from shocks on real wages, terms of trade, or real interest rates.[22]

For all the points along the upward line in Figure 5.3, actual and "stagnation" wages coincide, so that the GDP growth rate should be roughly equal to the population growth rate. This is the case, for instance, in 1956. At the upper-left side of the line, in turn, actual wages are above "stagnation" wages, thereby leading to a low accumulation rate and a decline of real GDP per capital. Not surprisingly, with the only exceptions of 1964-1966, all the years corresponding to the stagflation stage are on this side of the line. Notice that years 1967-1969 are particularly far from the line (20 percent above, on average), partly as a result of a decreasing capital stock. Concerning the points at the lower-right side of the line, they correspond to high profitability

---

[21] Low investment rates during the stagnation period could also be explained as a result of a low savings rate instead of low profitability. However, the Uruguayan economy was characterized by capital flight during most of this period, thus, suggesting that savings were not a binding constraint on investment.

[22] Instead, it might be associated with net worth becoming negative for a large number of firms. Such an outcome was due to the sharp devaluation required to face the external constraint in a context of dollar-denominated liabilities (see Rama 1987).

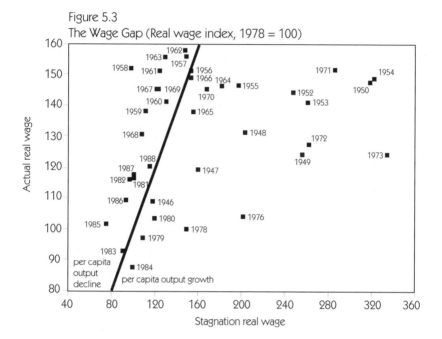

Figure 5.3
The Wage Gap (Real wage index, 1978 = 100)

levels, so that GDP grows faster than population. This is the case for all the years before 1956, and between 1970 and 1980.

Figure 5.3 suggests that stagnation partly arose from the actions of strong trade unions avoiding a real wage drop, despite the sharp terms of trade decline that took place in the second half of the 1950s. From then on, the economy followed a divergent path, characterized by low profitability, low investment, decreasing capital stock, even lower profitability, etc.[23] Since the required drop in real wages became very large by the end of the 1960s, so did the harshness of social conflicts.

The suppression of the Wage Councils and the subsequent interdiction of trade union activities undoubtedly restored investment profitability. However, Figure 5.3 also suggests that the real wage cuts during the 1970s were unnecessary from the point of view of economic growth. Indeed,

---

[23] This process may not be evident in 1964-1966 because of a temporary improvement in the terms of trade.

because of low world real interest rates, capital accumulation became highly profitable, as is shown by the sharp increase of stagnation wages.[24] Hence, as in the 1960s, there was a clear maladjustment between external conditions and factor payments, but now with the opposite sign.

The Sources of Distribution

The period of Uruguayan economic history studied in this chapter is characterized by significant transfers between economic sectors and social groups. The common feature of such transfers is that they are not at all based on explicit taxes on individuals. But depending on which period we are looking at, they sharply differ by the nature of what is being distributed.

The first growth stage (up to 1956), associated with import-substitution industrialization, can be characterized as a transfer of land rents to urban groups. Such a transfer was done by means of trade barriers, which probably depressed the real exchange rate. The stagflation period (1957-1967), on the contrary, was characterized by the distribution of accumulated stocks rather than surplus. This is where the pecuniary externality of the chosen transfers lay. The involved stocks were real balances, social security reserves, and productive capital.

Concerning real balances, the inflation process which characterized this period can be seen as a by-product of the distributional activities. Until 1961, money growth was associated with credits granted at negative real interest rates (in fact, for the benefit of some firms). From then on, money growth financed budget deficits generated by three important social partners, each of whom refused to adjust to a less favorable international environment. Civil servants were able to prevent wage or employment cuts in the public sector. Manufacturers and wage earners, in turn, were strong enough to avoid significant taxes on both profits and personal income.[25]

It is worth noting that social conflicts underlying inflation during the stagflation period were not restricted to the traditional class struggle between wage earners and capital owners. In addition, losers did not belong to any of these distributional coalitions. Indeed, the inflationary tax burden is higher for the poorest, for whom currency represents a larger share of total wealth. In Uruguay, this was likely to be the case for rural migrants to Montevideo, who were a large social group during the 1950s and 1960s.

Inflation was also the device to generate income transfers from social security reserves. At the beginning of the stagflation period, the reserves were invested in nonindexed public bonds, so that their fall in real value

---

[24] Figure 5.3 does not include 1974 and 1977 since they are located too far to the right.

[25] The fact that the main social partners refused to "pay the bill" could be seen as one of the reasons accounting for the little importance accorded to budget deficits in the economic debate of the 1960s.

avoided higher budget deficits. In addition, reserves were lent to social security employees at a nominal rate of 2 percent a year, in spite of high inflation. As a result, the average pension lost 52 percent of its purchasing power between 1963 and 1967, i.e., in a period in which real wages were spiraling downward (Mesa-Lago 1985).

Finally, as regards productive capital, the mechanism allowing its distribution during the stagflation stage was the squeeze on investment, in both the private and the public sector. As discussed earlier, such a mechanism depended on the government budget being restructured in favor of current expenditures, as well as on low profitability levels resulting from high real wages in the private sector.

The change in the sources of distribution was also important from a political standpoint. Transfers based on land rent were carried out by the state by means of economic policy decisions, which often preceded the claims of the favored social groups. Transfers based on stocks, on the contrary, were impelled by private coalitions. More generally, the state's weakening represented an incentive for a distributional struggle, while it encouraged the dominance of politics. What in other circumstances could be seen as vitality of the civilian society became nothing but gang fighting in Uruguay.

Nevertheless, there are some social groups, such as rural migrants and retired citizens, which are seldom organized in distributional coalitions. They belong to the "silent majorities." In Uruguay, not surprisingly, this group provided most of the political support for authoritarian rule. In its very beginning, such authoritarian rule was associated with the 1968 wage and price freeze that slowed down inflation for almost two years.

However, the authoritarian rule was not for the benefit of such a "silent majority" either, since inflation remained at high levels during the 1970s. But this was not the result of social partners refusing to "pay the bill" anymore. Instead, budget deficits represented an economic policy device allowing changes in relative prices in a context in which repression ensured a less than full-indexation scheme for income payments.

Concluding Remarks

If our analysis proves to be correct, the key to understanding the rise and fall of the Uruguayan welfare state is not found in natural resources, or in trade policies, but rather in the relationship between relevant social partners and the political system. The dramatic change of such a relationship in the 1940s and 1950s gave rise to stagnation and increasing violence. Its reversal by the end of the 1960s, in turn, led to a new growth stage, but also to extremely high social costs, including the end of democracy. The main question, now that military rule has been banished, concerns future prospects for this relationship. There are different answers depending on the social partners involved.

Concerning manufacturers who produce for the domestic market, their lobbying ability might have been reduced because of the emergence of a competing pressure group during the 1970s, i.e., manufacturers who sell abroad. Of course, distributive actions by the latter group could also represent a source of dynamic inefficiency. However, there is an institutional arrangement which sharply reduces their lobbying possibilities—namely, Uruguay's subscription to the GATT's subsidies code in 1979. In fact, as shown in Table 5.2, nominal protection on exports was already very low by 1985-1986.

As regards wage bargaining, it was characterized by two important features during the stagflation period. On the one hand, it did not take into account the international environment, so that changes in the terms of trade did not have any impact on real wage levels. On the other hand, trade unions only managed a limited share of national income; therefore, they faced strong incentives to adopt "class struggle" strategies.

Of these two features, the second one remains almost unchanged today. The Uruguayan economy is still characterized by a wide variety of "independent" activities, and there is no attempt to gradually "formalize" the labor market. The first feature, on the contrary, has changed as a result of a higher share of exports in industry sales. It remains to be seen if this change is important enough to modify the outcome of wage bargaining.[26]

Finally, the answer is more dubious as regards the relationship between the political system and the state bureaucracy. Although the number of civil servants has not risen significantly since 1985, there have not been any serious attempts to improve the public sector efficiency, nor to reform social security. Instead, there is some debate on privatizations, which probably misses the point, since most of the bureaucracy corresponds to a central administration and local governments (there are only twelve public enterprises in Uruguay). Meanwhile, the main social conflicts since the return to democratic rule have concerned civil servants.

A more general conclusion could be drawn from the impact of institutional arrangements on economic performance. Indeed, democratic recovery is seen as a tool allowing for the return of the welfare state of the past. However, there are two different models (or two different pasts) to choose. The one represented by the innovation project of Batlle y Ordóñez, which was made possible by the high degree of autonomy of the Uruguayan state, provided the grounds for the first growth period. The other model, based on the distribution of accumulated stocks by powerful coalitions, soon led to stagflation and political disaggregation. Consequently, depending on the chosen model, growth prospects should be significantly different.

---

[26] According to Figure 5.3, four years after democratic recovery, real wages are close to the stagnation frontier. However, these results could be misleading since the estimation of the production and investment functions did not include years 1982-1988, which did not fit the data well.

REFERENCES

Anichini, J.J., J. Caumont and L. Sjaastad. 1977. *La política comercial y la protección en el Uruguay.* Montevideo: Banco Central del Uruguay.

Barbato, D., L. Macadar and O. Rodríguez. 1984. "La crisis y el problema nacional." In *La crisis uruguaya y el problema nacional.* Montevideo: CINVE-Ediciones de la Banda Oriental.

Barrán, J.P. and B. Nahum. 1983. *Batlle, los estancieros y el imperio británico.* Montevideo: Ediciones de la Banda Oriental.

Benedetti, M. 1960. *El país de la cola de paja.* Montevideo: Arca.

Bensión, A. and J. Caumont. 1981. "Uruguay: Alternative Trade Strategies and Employment Implications." *In Trade and Employment in Developing Countries,* edited by A. Krueger. Chicago: NBER-University of Chicago Press.

Buxedas, M., J. Rocca, and L. Stolovich. 1987. *La estructura de la industria uruguaya.* Montevideo: CIEDUR-Fundación de Cultura Universitaria.

Calmfors, L. and J. Drifill. 1988. "Bargaining Structure, Corporatism and Macroeconomic Performance." *Economic Policy.* April: 14-61.

Cheroni, A. 1986. "El pensamiento conservador en el Uruguay." Serie Investigaciones 49. Montevideo: CLAEH.

CINVE. 1987. *La Industria frente a la competencia extranjera.* Montevideo: CINVE-Ediciones de la Banda Oriental.

Davrieux, H. 1987. *Papel de los gastos públicos en el Uruguay, 1955-1984.* Montevideo: CINVE-Ediciones de la Banda Oriental.

Finch, H. 1981. *A Political Economy of Uruguay Since 1870.* London: Macmillan.

Instituto de Economía. 1968. *El proceso económico del Uruguay: contribución al estudio de su evolución y perspectivas.* Montevideo: Fundación de Cultura Universitaria.

————. 1973. *Un reajuste conservador.* Montevideo: Fundación de Cultura Universitaria.

Jacob, R. 1985. "Política industrializadora y grupos de presión." *Documentos de Trabajo 24.* Montevideo: CIEDUR.

Kravis, I., A. Heston and R. Summers. 1981. "New Insights into the Structure of the World Economy." *Review of Income and Wealth 27(4):* 339-355.

Macadar, L. 1981. "La industria del cuero: un análisis de la política económica y el cambio técnico." In *CINVE-CIESU, El problema tecnológico en el Uruguay actual.* Montevideo: Ediciones de la Banda Oriental.

————. 1986. "Industrialización, apertura externa y reestructura productiva: una reseña del proceso de industrialización en el Uruguay durante los años setenta." Montevideo: CINVE. Mimeo.

—————. 1988. "Protección, ventajas comparadas y eficiencia industrial." *Suma 3 (5):* 7-59.

Mesa-Lago, C. 1985. "El desarrollo de la seguridad social en América Latina." *Estudios 1985*: 43. Santiago de Chile: CEPAL.

Millot, J., C. Silva and L. Silva. 1973. *El desarrollo industrial del Uruguay: de la crisis de 1929 a la posguerra.* Montevideo: Universidad de la República.

Olson, M. 1982. *The Rise and Decline of Nations: Economic Growth, Stagflation and Social Rigidities.* New Haven: Yale University Press.

Pascale, R. 1980. *La empresa manufacturera extranjera en Uruguay: aspectos cuantitativos.* Buenos Aires: BID-INTAL.

Rama, G. 1988. *La democracia en Uruguay.* Buenos Aires: Cuadernos del RIAL.

Rama, M. 1982. *Protección y crecimiento industrial 1975-1980.* Montevideo: CINVE-Ediciones de la Banda Oriental.

—————. 1987. "Uruguay: la politique économique dans la transition démocratique." *Problèmes d'Amérique Latine 85*: 31-54. Paris: La Documentation Française.

—————. 1989a. "Empirical Investment Equations in LDCs." Washington, D.C.: The World Bank. Mimeo.

—————. 1989b. "El esfuerzo de los empleados públicos: un análisis en términos de salario de eficiencia." *Suma 4 (7)*: 7-25.

Vaillant, M. 1988. "Exportación y maduración industrial: manufacturas basadas en materias primas no agropecuarias uruguayas." Montevideo: CEPAL. Mimeo.

Vanger, M. 1963. *José Batlle y Ordóñez, the Creator of his Times (1902-1907).* Cambridge, Mass.: Harvard University Press.

—————. 1980. *The Model Country: José Batlle y Ordóñez, 1907-1915.* Hanover: University Press of New England.

CHAPTER SIX

DEVELOPING AN OPEN ECONOMY: NORWAY'S TRANSFORMATION, 1845-1975

Helge Hveem

Introduction

In the course of some 100 years, Norway has developed from a poor, agricultural society to an industrialized welfare state. This development spans periods of industrial restructuring, significant fluctuations in foreign markets, and periods of economic growth interrupted or caused by external shocks. Because of the many disparate influences on Norwegian development, it will be necessary to adopt an approach that is both eclectic and dynamic.

This chapter will discuss Norway's development by focusing on four broad groups of factors related to institutions, policies, and the organization of the external sector. First, an examination will be made of the evolution of social structures and political institutions and how they transformed Norway from a society of relatively independent, self-sufficient agrarian communities, with few and weak linkages to the urban sector, to a highly organized society with complex bargaining between state and private institutions. Second, the rate and extent of adaptation to technical change (or the failure to adapt), innovative reactions to competition from abroad, the role of entrepreneurs, and the introduction of industrial policies (or lack thereof) will be discussed. Third, an analysis will be made of the way and extent to which the country has been able to adapt to changes in foreign markets, i.e., its ability to organize and reorganize the foreign economic sector to defend domestic stability against external shocks. Fourth, the extent to which export income or foreign capital inflows have been linked to cross-sectoral and cross-regional development, the gradual raising of processing levels, and the development of the domestic market will be examined.[1]

The choice of theoretical perspective may, for the present purposes, be reduced to a choice between two schools. On the one hand, there is the externally induced or export-led development hypothesis (Norman 1984; Bergh et al. 1980). On the other hand, there is the domestic institutions and

---

[1] A number of other issues, such as the effects of geopolitics, have also been important but will not be discussed in detail here.

policy school, which places more emphasis on domestic socioeconomic and industrial organization and on industrial policy (Katzenstein 1985). One branch of this second school attaches particular importance to the role of local communities and the political power of the primary sectors (Brox 1966). Other schools take a position in between the export-led growth and the domestic politics explanations and emphasize the way in which factors highlighted by the two schools interact (Liebermann 1970; Senghaas 1982; Maddison 1982). As these introductory comments have revealed, this chapter will take on the views of the latter group, i.e., that distinct historical epochs are characterized by different combinations of explanatory factors, and that there is an interesting new perspective to be explored in the political-economic organization of a country—i.e., the way in which domestic and foreign economic policies are merged, and what institutions are built to support the strategy. This approach appears particularly appropriate in a comparatively open economy (Gourevitch 1978 and 1986).

The Long-term Perspective: The Formative Years Until the 1890s

Being a small and for a long time a relatively open economy, Norway has been sensitive to external forces. It appears at the same time to have been able to adjust to such forces. Its vulnerability to them has, however, been dominant at times and has led to temporary stagnation or recession.[2]

Trade and preindustrial development apparently first joined forces decisively when the introduction of the water-powered saw created the basis for increased exports of wood in the 1520s. For 300 years this basis was vital for the development of a precapitalist, merchant economy in Norway, and it was vital for foreign trade.

Until well into the nineteenth century, Norway bore the characteristics of a colonized economy. Export marketing was dominated by foreign traders (Hanseatic, Dutch, etc). Production remained undeveloped and largely under the control of the colonizer, the Danish king and state. A more truly nationally based export economy started to develop at the end of the eighteenth century. Norwegian merchant capital demanded that the mercantilist privileges and monopolies established by the Danish be loosened as their own businesses improved.

Then the Danish King pledged his support for Napoleon and geopolitics took over. For Norway, it meant loss of markets in England. The vulnerability

---

[2]See Keohane and Nye 1977 for the distinction between two aspects of economic interdependence among nations: sensitivity means that a country is influenced by external events, but is able to cope (carrying whatever costs are inferred on it without changing policy); vulnerability refers to a situation where the country concerned is not coping in the short run, but has to carry costs even after having attempted to change policy.

inherent in the typically colonial division of labor between Denmark and Norway became apparent. In 1814, Norway was transferred as a colony to Sweden by the great powers that had defeated Napoleon. As a result, Norway lost important markets on the continent of Europe.

For most of the first two-thirds of the nineteenth century, Norway's economy remained relatively undeveloped or underdeveloped. In 1820, its GDP per capita is estimated to have been one of the lowest in Western Europe. It was only about two-thirds that of the previous colonial master, Denmark.[3] Norway was a clear example of a monocultural, raw material-based economy, with mostly unskilled labor.

It was only around the middle of the nineteenth century that economic activity gained speed and became more diversified. A combination of external and internal changes, some of them coming abruptly, others building up more gradually, integrated the Norwegian economy into the mainstream of European industrial capitalism. By 1870, Norway still trailed behind most of Northern Europe in gross economic terms. However, in several respects Norway had begun a process of fundamental change. It was admittedly still one of uneven development, but it meant the beginning of the end of the agriculture-based society. This is why this period may be referred to as the formation period.

Several factors have had important effects on this process in the nineteenth century. The first was a demographic explosion that imploded finally through migration. Around the 1840s, "the children of the post-1814 era" entered the labor market in large numbers, pressing wages down and leaving parents behind with more to spend in the market. When the international economic crisis occurred in the 1870s, migration to North America "solved" the political and social crisis that could no longer be controlled by a growing economy. During the period 1865 to 1910, almost two-thirds of all the population increase left the country.[4]

Two other factors that helped the Norwegian economy grow were the change in economic policy from a contractive, almost laissez-faire policy to an expansive monetary and credit policy, and the emergence of an entrepreneurial industrial capitalism. While these occurrences did not result in large-scale industrial growth that could absorb the rapid population growth, especially in agriculture,[5] they created important new reservoirs of manu-

---

[3]Maddison 1982, 161, based on estimations by Bairoch 1976b.

[4]Liebermann 1970; the figure is derived from calculating the percentage of excess births over deaths. The migration rate (number of migrants per annum per 1,000 inhabitants) during 1895-1910 was 6.44 compared to 4.21 for Sweden, and 2.55 for Denmark. Among the Western European countries, only Ireland and Italy showed higher migration rates during the period (Bairoch 1976b, 250).

[5]Liebermann is correct in pointing out that Norway did not copy the patterns of industrial expansion some decades earlier and, thus, did not confirm the mainstream economic historian's assumption that acceleration of the rate of population growth is usually concomitant with a rapid enlargement of the industrial sector, cf., e.g., Cipolla 1962.

facturing potential, including competence and "linkage industries." Textile and later mechanical industries grew up in waves by copying the front-runner nation, England. As a "latecomer" or "second wave"[6] nation, Norway could profit from the British experiences. A conscious and comparatively large-scale import of skills and technology was initiated after the English Parliament liberalized technology exports in 1842. Imports often took the form of "packaging" or product-in-hand transfers.[7] Imports of financial capital were not a necessity for this early industrialization, except in the construction of the first railways.[8] Norway completed the construction of its first railway in 1855 before the more advanced Sweden, a fact that may be explained largely by a fourth factor—favorable international market access and terms of trade. The wood industry needed to speed up transportation of timber from the inland to the sea to meet increasing foreign demand assisted by the lowering of English tariffs on wood imports in 1851.[9] Norwegian shipowners were ready to exploit the conditions opened up by the abolition of the Navigation Act in the 1840s.

Many analysts hold that Norwegian agriculture during this period did not really link up with industry as the "balanced growth" theories envisioned. But the self-owning, peasant-based economy quadrupled food production between 1809 and 1855, and important rationalizations through technical improvements took place, especially in areas close to the towns (Valen-Sendstad 1962). The agricultural society also contributed considerably to the fifth factor of importance, political institutionalization. Feudal elements were few or non-existent, largely because nobility privileges were abolished after 1814. Norwegian farmers were, in comparison with their Nordic brethren, economically and politically independent. Their power, along with cultural and political mobilization against the alien king, played an important role in stabilizing society.[10]

These stabilizing factors were particularly important during the so-called "Long Depression" of the 1870s and 1880s. The crisis apparently hit Norway later but in many ways harder than most other European countries.

---

[6]Gerschenkron 1962 for the first, Sejersted 1985 for the second expression.

[7]The latter is referring to the way by which Norwegian entrepreneurs sought out English textile firms or firms specializing in related technology, purchasing not only the production equipment, but production skills to the last detail, sometimes even buying English foremen, engineers or other skilled persons. For an author arguing the case for an explanation of Norwegian industrialization to be sought at the level of firms and their behavior, see Bruland 1988.

[8]In fact, Norway exported capital from 1865 on, when regular and reliable national accounts were registered.

[9]It meant a relative advantage for Norway vis-à-vis Canadian exporters who had so far benefitted greatly from Imperial privileges.

[10]Sweden, incidentally, was a relatively "mild" imperial power by historical and international standards, allowing Norway considerable autonomy over economic and sociocultural affairs.

Political mobilization resulted in the introduction of the party system, parliamentary rule (1884), and a change in government (from Conservative to a Liberal-Farmer coalition). Together with massive migration, these changes took away much of the effect of the economic decline, which was particularly prominent during the 1879-1883 period.

To a considerable extent, the decline was caused by decreasing foreign demand for traditional Norwegian export products. No new export industries were developed to replace the declining raw materials-based branches and the non-expanding domestic market (Bjerke 1966). Further, the shipowners did not respond until very late to the international change from sails to steam engine. They therefore lost important market shares.

The 1875-1895 crisis was in several respects a typical Schumpeterian crisis. Shipowners faced dramatic losses in market shares because foreign competitors were faster shifting to steam. But in the course of some two decades, the Norwegians organized a turnaround from sail to steam. In 1905, the steam-powered tonnage overtook sail-powered tonnage. Norway's position as the third largest shipping nation in the world was restored.

Since then, shipping incomes have accounted for roughly 40 percent of total foreign incomes of Norway. But shipping never became a major engine of industrialization. The impetus for change towards the end of the nineteenth century came instead from the introduction of a new techno-economic paradigm[11] that was associated with a strong belief in general progress. This was represented by innovations like the steam engine and electricity, which was particularly important for the Norwegian case.

Norwegian entrepreneurs appear to have been almost uncritical believers in "the gospel of communication," i.e., that with the construction of railways, roads, and other infrastructure, industrialization and economic growth would automatically follow (Collett and Andersen 1989).

During the 1880s and 1890s, there was a wave of investments in infrastructure and in new productive facilities. Much of it appears to have been associated with the kind of imports of technology from abroad that characterized the first wave in the 1840s and 1850s. But there were also Norwegian inventions and innovations. Norwegian engineers graduated abroad and brought home skills which were put into innovation.[12] Risk-taking entrepreneurs led the development.

The state had set up a Ministry of the Interior (1845) in order to assist industry, notably with roads and railways. But it had no role in the booming shipping sector, simply because shipowners did not want it to. It was only

---

[11]Freeman and Soete 1987.

[12]Examples are the gas turbine, invented by Elling in 1884, a new technique for producing oil from cod liver (Møller), and a series of innovations in the paper and chemical industries by Størmer. The latter graduated as an engineer from the Karlsruhe Technical University in 1860, an illustration of the fact that the Norwegian entrepreneurs were mostly engineers and almost always educated abroad, either in England or in Germany.

after the turn of the century, when the safety level of Norwegian ships had deteriorated dramatically and large numbers of seamen's lives were lost, that a public control body was established (Collett and Andersen 1989).

Norway was no laissez-faire economy, but followed the Rechtsstaat pattern described by Habermas (1962). The Norwegian state was still probably less active in economic affairs at the time than the state in most other European countries, including Sweden and Denmark. The fact that Norway, following England, turned to a more protectionist policy later than other European nations may also have retarded its transformation.

From Industrial Breakthrough to the Formation of the Bargaining Economy

The development of Norway in the twentieth century can roughly be divided into four periods, with different events characterizing each stage. In brief summary, the periods are the following: .

Entrepreneur-Led Industrial Breakthrough, 1890-1920

The period was characterized by Norwegian entrepreneurial spirit that led to important innovations by heavy imports of capital and by rapid industrialization linked to an exponential build-up of hydropower capacity.

Ultra-Orthodox Monetary Policy, Class Conflict, and Reemergence of the Domestic Market, 1920s-1935

The effects of an unstable international economic and political environment were much aggravated by an ill-conceived economic policy that brought high unemployment and increasing social conflict. Entrepreneurial initiative and decentralization of production by small firms producing for the domestic market greatly contributed to solving the crisis. Also contributing was the coming to political power of the Social Democratic Party and its compromise with the farming community and industrial leaders.

Emergence of the State in a Mixed Economy, 1935-1950s

The compromise constituted the foundation of the mixed economy with the state assuming a planning and orchestrating role, arranging for transfers of income to farmers and fishermen, taking the main responsibility for the infrastructure, and leaving most of industry and the services to the private sector.

Permanent Economic Growth, the Welfare State, and the Bargaining Economy, 1950s-1975

The last period was one of rapid economic growth. Surplus was invested in continued natural resource-based specialization, in a welfare state, and in a system of political alliances. That system established networks of consultation and coordination with the main social actors, between them, and between the regions and the national decision-making centers. The state assumed responsibility for compensating or protecting those sectors and groups which were injured as a result of a more open economy.

Keeping this periodization in mind, we will now leave the strict chronological description and continue by looking at five sets of factors which have influenced development during the entire 1890-1975 period, although the impact of these factors has varied over time. These factors are:

- the role of natural resources and the evolution of Norway's industrial organization;
- technological transformation and industrial policy;
- economic policies and the role of the state;
- trade policy and the organization of the foreign sector;
- the transition of Norway from a capitalist, to a mixed, and finally to a bargaining economy.

The Role of Natural Resources and the Evolution of Norway's Industrial Organization

The extraction and export of natural resources played a dominant part in Norway's early industrialization. Timber, fish, and to a diminishing extent, metal ores made up most commodity exports. This structure continued well into the twentieth century and is still rather predominant. Its content has changed with technological transformation towards higher processing levels and structural diversification leading to more varied production.

The major part of the industrial system was based on domestic natural resources. With the introduction of hydroelectricity, a growing part of the industry became an entrepôt sector. Much of the equipment and the ores and metals used in the metallurgical industry were imported. Norway has, in some sense, been an "industrial power station," importing base metals, applying hydroelectric power and exporting the resulting processed metals. This is the case both for the ferrous and non-ferrous industry (see Table 6.1).

In terms of employment, the primary sector decreased to less than half of total employment only around 1890 and to about 40 percent in 1910. The fall of primary sector employment occurred later in Norway than in several other Western European countries. The two spurts of increase in the relative share of manufacturing employment occurred in the 1890s and 1930s, that is, at the end of the two economic depressions. Some industries, in particular

Table 6.1. The Commodity Structure of Norwegian Foreign Trade, 1866-1975
(Percent)

	1866-70		1901-05		1920		1939		1955		1975	
	Ex	Im	Ex	Im	Ex	Im	Ex	Im	Ex	Im	Ex	Im
Fish	37		32		18		16		16		6	
Cereals		29		18		9		8		4		1
Textiles		14		14		13		12		8		
Timber	42		36		27		24					
Paper			6		18				22		7	
Minerals		7	9	13	11	16		20		10	13	8
Metals		7		9		10	18	10	20	13	17	12
Ships		5		8		19						
Vehicles								14		22	21	20
Machinery								8		10		11
Fertilizer									6			
Four most important product categories, %	90	64	83	53	75	59	59	56	64	55	51	46

Source: Central Bureau of Statistics, *Historisk statistikk*, Oslo.

chemical, metal mining, and textiles, experienced dramatic falls in employment during the 1920s and early 1930s and did not reach the 1910 level of employment until about 1940.

Among the natural resource-based industries, mining of pyrites, copper, and titanium ore were the three most important branches until after World War II. Iron ore became predominant following the construction of state-owned ironworks in the northern part of Norway. As far as production of metals was concerned, copper was the single most important branch until aluminum took over after World War I. Primary aluminum has remained the most important metal product since then, followed by crude steel, ferro-alloys, and ferro-silicon. Whereas the latter are largely based on domestic raw materials, the aluminum industry is totally dependent on imports of alumina. It is, in other words, the entrepôt branch. Together with other energy-intensive branches, it forms what has been referred to as the hydro-electric industrial complex. At the end of the 1970s, the aluminum industry accounted for 10 percent of manufacturing employment, 12 percent of GNP and 40 percent of commodity exports. It continues to represent a formidable source of power over industrial policy.

The primary sector's contribution to national income was radically reduced during the 1930s, but its share of employment was not equally reduced. The sector, in other words, was particularly hard hit during the Great Depression, a factor that significantly contributed to the national political compromise between farmers and labor at the time.

In a sense, economic development in the 1930s broke with the pattern that had been followed since the middle of the nineteenth century. The response to the crisis of 1875-1895 was to open up for an export-led industrialization strategy. It followed the principles of industrial capitalism: economies of scale, specialization, and exchange according to comparative advantage. In the 1930s, the response was to turn to producing for a domestic market, to small-scale production and even to bartering.[13] It was in a sense a "step back in history," a return to the practices of previous periods, most particularly the period right before 1875.

The German occupation of 1940-1945 was highly contested by most Norwegians. In economic terms, it meant stagnation. Industrial and infrastructural projects launched by the Germans were largely opposed and some, like the heavy-water project, were even sabotaged by Norwegian resistance. Norway survived the German occupation economically, but did not develop during it. Shipping experienced another profit surge at great loss of lives and ships. The war ended with a strong, latent demand for economic change and, above all, for material growth.

The first part of the postwar growth period, 1946-1959, was characterized by rapid expansion, not by transformation. There was rapid and widespread introduction of new products and techniques in the chemical, electrical, and other branches. These new technologies were mostly imported; Norway had become part of the general U.S.-led international wave of modernization. The export sector and the domestic based industries were not yet integrated. Moreover, the former was competing in an international market, the latter not. Even in this sense it was a truly mixed economy.

For the first time, Norway had an industrial policy. It emerged as an important element of the newborn state interventionism and would repeat the experience of the first industrialization period at the beginning of the century. Industrial policy after the war was to exploit what was still believed to be comparative advantages in an open economy: cheap and abundant hydroelectric power, access to markets abroad provided by a strong merchant shipping sector, and a reservoir of labor still to be found in agriculture.

In terms of restructuring between the sectors, the transformation of Norway after World War II followed the pattern of other Western European countries. In 1950, the primary sector accounted for 30 percent of total employment, but 14 percent of GNP. During the next 25 years, its share of employment fell to 8 percent. But its share of GNP did not equally diminish. The primary sector, improved its average productivity radically during the period through mechanization and restructuring of production.

For manufacturing industry and the service sector, the picture is different. Until the beginning of the 1970s, manufacturing industry grew at about the pace of the economy as a whole, whereas the service sector had the fastest growth rate, absorbing the labor reserve from the primary sector. During the 1970s, however, these trends changed. Manufacturing industry stagnated or

---

[13]The Colbjørnsen-Sømme Three Year Plan suggested that barter would be one solution to a nonfunctioning market.

receded. At the same time, employment grew faster than during previous periods, to a large extent due to increased female labor force participation.

The investment rate in Norway was comparatively high throughout the postwar period. In terms of investments as a percentage of GNP, Norway looked more like Japan than the EEC and the United States during 1960-1975.[14] Investments were financed partly through foreign loans and partly through a combination of domestic state and private capital. Efficiency of investments was, however, rather small compared to international levels.

The bulk of these industrial investments, before the petroleum era, were in the hydroelectricity-based industries. Looking back at the pattern of investments from the point of view of the 1980s, Norwegian companies and the state, to a large extent, invested in overcapacity. The raw material-based economy remained. During the 1960s, in particular, there were heavy investments in expanding hydroelectrical power production and mineral and metal processing, more than doubling power production during that decade.

At the end of the period under survey, the petroleum industry was in a dominant position. In 1973 the government published a white paper calling for a modest growth in oil production and in the use of income from the new source.[15] Oil production started on a large scale in 1974 under a wide range of state control mechanisms. During the next few years, the intentions of the white paper were basically set aside. Oil production increased rapidly and oil incomes made it possible to employ job-seekers through the state sector and to grant substantial salary increases to waged labor. As a result, inflation got a boost and productivity growth was reduced.

Technological Transformation, Entrepreneurs, and Industrial Policy

Risk-taking entrepreneurs in manufacturing led the way into the second period of transformation, which has previously been referred to as the breakthrough period. It started in the 1880s and represents the (first) "Schumpeterian transformation." It lasted, interrupted by market fluctuations and highs and lows in innovative activity, until the Second World War. With some exceptions, it was a technological transformation of the production structure rather than economic restructuring. It was supported by Civil servants recruited from the new profession which brought an entrepreneurial spirit to the emerging state bureacracy

The real breakthrough occurred with hydroelectricity—the combination of waterfalls and electricity. It coincided with the rise of new social actors (a growing middle class and labor), and with national liberation (in 1905, Norway seceded from the union with Sweden).

---

[14]According to OECD statistics, the Norwegian investment rate varied between 28 and 37 percent, the high figure being due to petroleum sector investments in 1973-1974.

[15]Parliamentary White Paper no. 25, (1973-1974).

Industrial projects during "the Schumpeterian crisis" were practically all financed by domestic capital. The coming of hydropower changed this completely. Foreign companies already owned a number of waterfalls producing power to factories at the turn of the century, and they were actively buying up more waterways. The new resource attracted financial and industrial capital in several of the Western countries. While the Union broke up, the Swedish banker Wallenberg entered as a main partner in Elektrokemisk, the first big industrial venture in Norway. It was founded in 1904 partly in order to sell turbines from Swedish ASEA, which Wallenberg controlled (Stonehill 1965; Seierstad et al. 1970). In the course of a few years, Norway opened up to foreign capital on a large scale.

There were two main reasons for this rather sudden change. First, Norway's commercial banking sector was comparatively undeveloped. Shipping had been mostly self-financing its investments, industry was mostly small-scale and not very capital intensive, and primary sector needs were taken care of by a combination of private and state banking. Second, the new industrial projects needed comparatively large inputs of capital. Economies of scale arguments had entered Norwegian economic politics, and there was simply no financing available to meet the new demands. Hence, Norwegian industry became a net importer of capital for practically all of the period after the 1890s, except for the 1930s, when there was no foreign capital available.

The development of Norway's electrochemical and electrometallurgical industries was not primarily a response to international demand. It was partly a coincidence and partly due to entrepreneurial initiative. The entrepreneurs were a mixture of engineers and financiers, mostly the former. They had received their education abroad and looked for ways of implementing their new know-how. Entrepreneurial engineers met researchers working in relatively new chemical and physical research laboratories at the university.[16]

It was as a result of such meetings between entrepreneurial engineers and researchers that the Birkeland-Eyde process, whereby nitric acid was produced by means of the electric arc, was born.[17] The process required cheap

---

[16]The University of Oslo was founded in 1811 but was for most of the nineteenth century a learning place for law, religious studies and humanities only. Natural sciences became increasingly important towards the end of the century, however, and especially in chemistry, research was taking off before the end of the century. An agricultural college was created in 1897, whereas the Institute of Technology was established thirteen years later, modelled after the German polytechnical universities.

[17]Kristian Birkeland was professor in physics at the University of Oslo from 1898, and Sam Eyde was an engineer educated in Germany who worked there as an engineer for several years until he returned to Norway in 1899. He had become aware of prognostics about the dramatic future demands for nitrites to be used as fertilizer during his stay abroad, that production of natural nitrate in Chile had peaked, that nitrite was an important element in the atmosphere and that it might be commercially exploited given the right technology and huge quantities of electric power. The two met in 1903 and in 1904 Birkeland's experiments were already promising enough for Eyde to start organizing commercial exploitation.

electricity to produce a marketable synthetic fertilizer. In the course of a few years, the foundation was laid for what is still the backbone of the mainland industry in Norway: fertilizer, electrochemical, and electrometallurgical industries. During this period the single largest Norwegian company, Norsk Hydro, was established. At present, the company, after having carried out a series of international take-overs, is the largest producer of fertilizer in the world.[18]

Installed hydroelectrical power-generating capacity increased from 34 KW in 1900 to 400,000 KW in 1912, and 1.25 million KW in 1920. Not only did new industries grow up, old ones like pulp and paper, textile, and copper were reinvigorated.

Almost all of the equipment and skills needed for rapid development of infrastructure and industry had to be imported. The domestic contribution was above all some important innovations in process technology.

National innovation efforts continued to be dependent on research training abroad, even after a number of national universities and colleges had been established. Thus, the percentage of Norwegian holders of a doctorate from abroad rose from 11 percent in the 1920s to 24 percent in the 1960s (Skoie 1970, 402).

With a rapidly expanding scientific environment, which was more complex and required more resources than a small nation could master, borrowing from abroad became vital. In the case of Norway, interacting with scientific communities abroad also resulted in a "brain drain," particularly among engineers.

Between the two world wars, the networking between science and business that had been initiated in the latter part of the nineteenth century again proved important. It probably explains why innovation became a major factor behind the solution to the post-1929 crisis. The upswing started in 1933 with a radical fall in unemployment. The explanation for the upswing was to be found in domestic structural transformation. There were even elements of technological transformation in the process. A host of inventions introduced during the 1920s, mainly in the United States, facilitated labor-intensive production. The once so successful Birkeland-Eyde process was surpassed by the new Haber-Borsch process in the fertilizer industry. Adjustment meant rationalization and more unemployed. Strikes exploded and were at one stage met by military force.

Firms were either left to their own fate and went out of business, or they formed cartels and managed better. A large number of new firms, mostly small and medium-sized, were formed, many in the peripheral areas where unemployment was high and wages low. The shipyard industry had an

---

[18]It was founded in 1905 on the basis of the Birkeland-Eyde process assisted by Wallenberg and with French and German capital. The German share was bought out by the French a few years later.

upswing as Norwegian shipowners—this time among the first in the world—shifted from steam to diesel engines. Thus, industrial employment rose considerably, absorbing a rapidly increasing number of new job-seekers, a result of the baby boom of the 1905-1920 period.

During the 1945-1975 period, research and development (R&D) became politicized. The state established a series of sectoral research councils during the first postwar years. In 1967, a bourgeois government created a government research board consisting of five cabinet ministers headed by the prime minister and assisted by an advisory council. Innovation became a public institution. The state provided not only money, but guidance. Research policy targeted R&D to specific goals with detailed control systems. Norwegian educational performance expressed by public schooling and higher education, also mostly the responsibility of the state, was comparatively high in the 1960s and 1970s. But innovation activities were comparatively modest by most OECD standard measures, although slightly higher than those of Finland and Denmark (Ergas 1984). R&D expenditures, however, increased as a share of GNP from 1.2 percent of GNP in 1965 to 1.8 percent in 1987. Public funds accounted for two-thirds of national R&D in 1975 (Skoie 1967; Norwegian Council for Scientific and Industrial Research 1986).

In comparison, private Swedish companies spent substantially more on R&D than did Norwegian companies during the 1960s and 1970s. Thus the private capitalist in Norway appears to have lost the entrepreneurial spirit that was characteristic of the earlier 1900s—or has left it to the state.

Economic Policy and the Role of the State

Formally, the modern Norwegian nation-state was a fait accompli in 1905. In reality, however, the state was still weak. It had to respond to strong cultural and political manifestations of national identity. It had practically no control over the industrialization process. But one of its very first tasks was to respond to popular demand for control over natural resources.

Combining Nationalism with Capital Imports

In 1909, foreigners controlled 80 percent of Norway's mining, 85 percent of its chemical, 44 percent of its paper and textile, and 33 percent of its metal industries (Stonehill 1965). Most important politically was that foreigners were buying up the waterfalls. In 1909, they controlled three-quarters of all falls—two times as many as were actually used in power production in 1905.

As soon as the dissolution of the Union was settled by a referendum, the Storting (Parliament) took up the flag of resource nationalism. In the course of a couple of weeks during 1906, temporary "panic legislation" was written and passed. It prohibited the construction of more than small-sized hydroelectrical plants without the permission of public authorities; it regulated (or limited) the role of foreign ownership of waterfalls; and it decided that Swedish citizens were to be treated as foreigners. The laws were later strengthened and made permanent (1909) under the name "Concession Laws." Such laws were designed to secure public control over not only waterfalls, but also railroads. Foreign ownership rights were to revert to the state after 60-80 years without compensation to owners.

Linking resource nationalism to the socialization of infrastructure was not aimed at nor did it keep foreign capital from continuing to invest in Norwegian industry. The Norwegian government introduced joint ventures as an option to foreign capital. The latter accepted it to a large extent. Thus, in 1909, 44 percent of all hydroelectricity production was foreign owned. In fact, industrial production grew more rapidly after 1909 than before. One reason may have been that the concession laws were liberally practiced, another that the Norwegian state used the laws to enforce decisions whereby Norwegian firms, wherever possible, were selected for subcontracting deliveries to new ventures (Bergh et al. 1980, 105). Some part of the indus–trialization was, moreover, financed by loans from abroad. Thus, between 1900 and 1913, accumulated foreign debt rose from representing one-sixth to one-half of GNP.

The emergence of the state as an economic actor now entered its formation stage. The most important reasons for the growth of the state were first, the mobilization and organization of new social and political actors through social liberalism and later socialism, and a rapidly growing labor movement; and second, the demands of a more complex economy. Emphasis will be placed on the latter, returning to the former later in the chapter.

State intervention in productive sectors was somewhat apparent in agriculture, but was practically nonexistent in the manufacturing industry. The period 1875-1905 was characterized by a profound restructuring of agriculture. The "gospel of communication" bore fruit in the countryside. The production of cereals had been drastically reduced due to strong competition from continental and American grain after the opening up of foreign trade from the 1860s on. Norwegian peasants turned to livestock production, especially along the railroad lines, and they turned from self-sufficiency to production for the market. In the process, the state stepped in to ease the costs of restructuring that migration could not alleviate. It played a prominent role both as a transmitter of knowledge and as a creditor (Bergh et al. 1980). The farming group in the Parliament was a strong force all along since 1814, an expression of the comparatively free-holding Norwegian agriculture.

For a long time fisheries was a very important sector, the contribution of which to GNP increased throughout the nineteenth century until about 1880. Fisheries, in particular those based on herring and cod, accounted for 5 percent of GDP and 43 percent of total commodity exports (Bergh et al. 1980, 46). When industrialization took off, the share of fisheries fell. But fisheries, as did agriculture, maintained a high political profile throughout and long into the twentieth century, in fact until this day.

In the nineteenth century, the fishery resources were rather unstable. In particular, when herring reappeared along Norwegian coasts in the 1830s, fisheries were able to substitute for some of the opportunities lost in agriculture due to the Napoleonic wars and their impact on trade regimes. Fisheries provided employment to between 5 and 8 percent of the active working population, and for many small farmers it was a necessary supplementary source of income.

Even fisheries experienced technological transformation in times of crisis. When the herring temporarily disappeared from Norwegian waters in the 1870s, it forced fishermen out from the coast to off-the-coast and open sea fishing grounds. Bigger boats and new catching equipment were introduced rapidly. Even though the herring returned to the coasts, technological transformation meant increased conflict among fishermen between the owners of big and small boats, and between new and traditional technology.

The Monetarist Disaster

The interwar period offers an "instructive confrontation between economic theory and economic reality" (Sejersted 1985, 89). It was a confrontation between two radically opposite economic policies. One stressed anti-in-flationary goals and a passive state. The other grew out of class conflict and looked at the state as an instrument (labor) or partner (social liberals and farmers).

The period 1920-1938 was above all a period of strong economic cycles and far-reaching restructuring of Norwegian political and economic life through a process of ups and downs. The crisis signal was turned on in 1920, but the recession took on a more lasting character in 1922 .

After 1922, international markets picked up and many economists and politicians argued that the crisis was only a short and temporary one that would soon be behind them. Therefore, they stuck to an orthodox monetarist policy. The krone was revalued by 70 percent over less than two years. As a consequence, unemployment soared from 10 to 20 percent, first in the manufacturing sector.

With practically no industrial policy and a social welfare policy that was still to be implemented, the main area of policy intervention was monetary policy. Gold standard orthodoxy was contested by both business and economists, but it prevailed.

The Great Depression struck Norway with full effect in 1930-1931. Unemployment rose to 33 percent. Since the United States several years earlier had closed free immigration, this outlet, formerly used to a great extent by Norwegian job-seekers, was no longer an option. During the 1920s, readjustment of the krone against foreign currencies and accompanying wage increases resulted in increased demand. This demand centered on consumer goods which were hardly produced in Norway; demand, therefore, was channeled abroad and led to increased imports. Exports were seriously hit by the overvalued krone.

The bourgeois government finally left the old parity in 1931. But it had no real alternative to put in its place. When the Labor party introduced its new economic policy (NEP), the Three Year Plan and an expansionist policy, there was still strong resistance based on another "monetarist" assumption: that investment had to be financed by domestic savings. Since there was at the time a low savings ratio, the NEP was felt to be hazardous. But Labor, led by the practitioner, Colbjørnsen,[19] and the theoretician, Ragnar Frisch, represented the radically new economic thinking along the lines set out by Keynes, and it finally won support.

It won due to three factors, all of them political and institutional. First, the Labor party turned to social democracy. In the 1920s, it adopted a socialist policy with a social democratic flavor, rather than that of Bolshevism, which had the support of a minority in the party. A brief experience with government in 1928 legitimized state institutions to the party cadres and legitimized the party to the nation. With important electoral progress in 1933, Labor was set for a leading role.

Second, the farming community, which was represented to a large extent by the Farmers' Party, was in a deep economic crisis due to low food prices. In order to solve the crisis, it was willing to break out of the bourgeois group and compromise with Labor. This compromising was formalized in the so-called "Crisis Settlement" in 1933.

Third, and as part of the process of moderating Labor, the trade union movement was prepared to enter into compromises with capital organized in the Federation of Employers and the Federation of Industries. A settlement that formalized the common goal—to reach agreement on wages, working conditions, etc.—was reached in 1935. This agreement, "The General Agreement" (Hovedavtalen), has since then formed the basis for wage settlements in Norway.

The foundation also was laid for the institutionalization of a mixed economy in Norway in which the state controls some part of production (and infrastructure) and income, and establishes legal and economic frameworks for private markets. It is further characterized by a clear separation between the market and the state. Thus, in some sectors or branches the market is allowed to operate freely, whereas in others the state is the undisputed decision maker on economic parameters.

---

[19]Ole Colbjørnsen had worked with the Soviet Five Year Plan in the 1920s and was in many ways the father of the new policy in Norway. His thoughts were first presented in Colbjørnsen, Ole and Axel Strømme (1933), En norsk 3-årsplan (A Norwegian Three Year Plan).

The Finalization of the State

With the enormous expectations accumulated during World War II, all was set for a policy of the highest possible economic growth and material living standard. After a brief interlude of a broad coalition government in 1945, Labor won a majority in the Storting for the first time in the fall of that year, a majority it kept until 1963. During the months that followed the 1945 victory, a new price law and other regulating measures were introduced. Public expenditure as a percentage of GDP rose from 17 in 1938 to 25 in 1946; after World War I it had been 7 percent. By 1975 it doubled to reach 50 percent.

This growth was organized through a rapid and broad development of public administration. During 1945-1955, the number of ministries increased from ten to fifteen; the number of public offices was doubled; and the number of public servants tripled. The number of public laws and regulations was increased. At the end of the period (1971-1974), Parliament produced annually an average of 88 laws and 288 public decrees or instructions (Aubert 1976).

The postwar economic policy was based on four premises. First, it emphasized the need for a strong state. But there was a general consensus that Adam Smith ought to be firmly placed alongside state intervention. The ideology of the mixed economy was, thus, penetrating both politics and business. Second, the policy was to be a "no experiments" policy. It was a return to what were known as Norwegian specialities—electrochemical and electrometallurgical industries. Third, the policy reconfirmed the principle of the open economy. However, the newborn social and political coalition was reluctant to give up the extent of protection that development in the 1930s and before had provided for agriculture, domestic market-based industry and services.

The fourth premise of the postwar economic policy was consolidation of the system of socio-political coalitions. It was most visible in the coming of the welfare society. Provision of social services and public health care, better and more education at all levels above primary schools that had been compulsory for several decades, and other aspects of what is now known as the "developed society" were introduced. The establishment of a liberal international economic order was the other main stimulus for a compromise between the liberalizing and the protectionist factions. Bretton Woods represented in itself a compromise, one of "embedded liberalism" (Ruggie 1982). It offered national governments a wide range of intervention if national interests were seriously threatened.

If the industrial policy and the welfare state were to be implemented at the same time—which was the aim of government supported by the national coalitions—huge inflows of capital would again be needed. Government policy from 1946 on was to stimulate savings; the savings rate in Norway in the 1950s and later was one of the highest in the OECD. But it was still far from sufficient to provide for the amount of investments that were planned. Therefore, the Storting accepted the Marshall Plan offer after a debate, whereas Communists and nationalist factions opposed it. The amount of aid did not exceed 20 percent of gross capital formation in any of the four years it was given (1949-1952) (Hoff and Isachsen 1979), but it greatly contributed to the increase in investments after 1948.

In exchange for Marshall Aid, some of the regulatory devices that were ready to be implemented were softened. Escape clauses and other loopholes in the GATT and IMF rules nevertheless made it possible to maintain a system of redistribution and of direct and indirect subsidies to agriculture and some parts of industry. Among other things, the state decided to establish state-owned iron and steel works against the will of important business factions, the Farmers' and the Conservative Parties (Grønlie 1973). The result was that the state operated on a constant deficit which was a source of friction between Labor and the Right.

A similar but less dramatic conflict along a socialist-private capitalist division was seen in other branches of industry. The state had taken over the aluminum industry works expanded by the Germans during the war. Labor opted for a strong state role, but backed off as the expansion of the industry met not only local opposition, but also a need for foreign markets and capital. Alternatives that opted for a national strategy with state control and nationally based marketing and distribution systems abroad were overruled. One explanation may have been that leadership did not dare to behave as did the risk-taking entrepreneurs at the beginning of the century (Tresselt 1968). This explanation may underestimate the market power of the international aluminum cartel. Vertical integration and a dominant position at all levels in the product line were probably a strong barrier to the entry of newcomers. It was only in the late 1970s that the Norwegian aluminum industry started to internationalize in order to take control over sources of supply.

Growth and Redistribution in the 1960s and 1970s

Thus, the immediate postwar period brought the organization of a compromise on industrial and foreign economic policy. In iron and steel works, and aluminum in particular, there was a mixture of state and private ownership, with two of the three aluminum companies owned jointly by the state and foreign multinationals, and the third being a joint venture between a Norwegian and a foreign company.[20] Electricity production had been taken over by the

---

[20]About half of the shares in Norsk Hydro are controlled by the state—in the 1970s and 1980s it has been 51.4 percent. Aardal and Sunndal Verk A/S, long the biggest producer, was first a fully state-owned company, but in 1957 became a joint venture between the state and Alcan. On two occasions, the relationship between Alcan and state interests in the company became the source of political conflict. In 1966, this almost led to the fall of the government.

state as had roads and railroads years before. State control over hydroelectricity production was to become a backbone in the "hydroelectrical industrial complex" that would dominate industrial policy in the 1950s and 1960s (Midttun 1989). For the rest, the private ownership principle was to be the basis of industry and services. State banks were important as financiers of housing, and there were quasi-governmental credit institutions for industry and agriculture. Shipping was the one sector which, due to the fact that more than 90 percent of the business was freight between third countries, was most in favor of a liberal economic order—nationally as well as internationally.

When petroleum was found in the North Sea, Norway was quick to follow up or even lead in the international wave of expansion of exclusive economic zones (EEZ). Moreover, the state was to take control over the new resource. Even though Labor at the time was running a minority government, it gained support for the principle of national public control. At the same time, the Norwegian state continued the "double-track" policy restricting foreign control over natural resources that it innovated in hydroelectricity. Foreign companies were subject to a fairly rigorous tax and planning system. The state has informally made foreign corporate access to North Sea petroleum contingent upon foreign supplies of funds for R&D in Norwegian firms. At the same time, a mixture of organizational solutions in the operation of petroleum production on the continental shelf has substantiated the compromise between national and foreign interests. Similarly, the state (through its wholly-owned Statoil company) shares control over Norway's part of the shelf with one semipublic and one private company.

Trade Policy and Foreign Economic Organization

Commodity trade and shipping together accounted for between 30 and 50 percent of GNP in Norway between 1845 and 1975. In terms of commodity concentration, the share of the four most important commodity categories in Norwegian exports (value) fell from 90 percent in 1866-1970 to slightly above 50 percent in 1975. With the coming of the oil from the mid-1970s on, the share has increased to about 65 percent (varying with oil prices). Imports

---

After the second big debate in 1974, a gradual take-over by the state was agreed to and implemented. As the company experienced serious economic problems during the 1980s, it was finally merged with and taken over by Norsk Hydro in 1985 to become consolidated as Hydro Aluminum. The third company in the industry is Elkem, which controls Karmøy Aluminum jointly with Alcoa. The Norwegian aluminum industry has throughout its history been dependent on imports of bauxite after it decided that the Søderberg process was not commercial compared to the leading foreign processes. It is only recently that the companies have started to invest in their own raw material (bauxite and oxide works) abroad, mostly in Central and Latin America.

show a corresponding decline from about 65 to 45 percent over the 110 years (Central Bureau of Statistics, Historisk Statistikk).

Fish and timber exports against cereal and textile imports characterized the foreign trade structure of the nineteenth century. They were overtaken by metals and minerals towards the middle of the twentieth century. In these commodities, however, Norway's trade was intraindustry trade; the entrepôt character of the aluminum and partly ferro-alloy branches was part of the explanation. With the modern economy came imports of machinery and cars.

Norway's foreign trade and finance policy was highly dependent on England for more than 100 years. In general, it has been heavily influenced by the type of regimes imposed by other countries. Besides England's free trade and gold parity policy, Norway was influenced by Sweden'customs union. For Liebermann (1970), these two foreign regimes were decisive influences on Norway's economy throughout the nineteenth century.

The Swedish-Norwegian Customs Union (1815-1905) reduced duties on goods between the two countries, but at the same time limited the access of the Norwegian merchant fleet to transportation between the two countries and between Sweden and third countries. The latter measure was adopted in order to enable the Swedish fleet to develop. Liberalization of trade between the two resulted in Swedish metal exports gradually outcompeting Norwegian production.

Although foreign trade was liberalized during the 1845-1975 period, differential tariffs were maintained. Infant industry protection continued and in fact increased during the period, whereas there were minimal or no duties on raw material and food imports. A law passed in 1875 introduced a duty-free common market for commodities, but the advantages of the innovation were limited because of disputes over rules of origin matters. A new law in 1887 attempted to clarify these matters, but was not really put into effect because Sweden adopted a more protectionist policy in 1888. Whereas Sweden followed Germany on the protectionist road, Norway, following England, was one of the last European countries to enter it. The customs union, in other words, was rather ineffective in the end.

Tariffs were at the time an important source of state income. Customs duties accounted for almost 75 percent of all tax income to the state in 1840, and at least 40 percent in 1875 (Liebermann 1970). The protectionist lobby in the 1880s was a coalition of industrialists, trade unionists, and municipality council leaders. This coalition has been an almost irresistible force in Norwegian trade politics ever since. In fact, it was decisive in forcing the government to take Norway out of the Multifibre Agreement between 1978 and 1984 (Hveem 1989).

The protectionist lobby did not succeed until late in the 1890s, and it had to make a compromise with the free traders in 1897. In 1905, however, protectionism finally won support, another illustration of the nationalist mood at the time. From then on and until the early 1920s, there were steadily increasing import duties on agricultural and industrial manufactured products.

During the next long international recession—the crisis of 1922-1933—trade policy in Norway was not very different from that of other European countries. During this period, as discussed above, it was the exchange rate policy that was most important.

The high degree of specialization in the Norwegian case might have developed an enclave economy of the Latin American type. The pattern of geographic location resulted in a new and modern smelting industry existing alongside small-scale farming in poor mountainous areas. Coastal and riparian areas were developed, whereas large parts of the inland lagged behind. There was a steady trend towards urbanization during the whole period covered; between 1905 and 1920 it was more rapid than during other sub-periods, except in the 1960s.

The First World War was a mixed blessing to the neutral country. Foreign currency reserves were abundant and the Norwegian krone grew strong. But domestically, social (class) differences became greater and inflation rose. In addition, the obvious imbalances in international supply-demand conditions and the relationship between war winners and losers represented a potential threat to Norway. Its export- oriented economy made it less prepared to handle vulnerability than many other countries. As Bull puts it: "There was no production sector which was only domestic—the foreign economic sector penetrated everywhere. And this foreign economy was in chaos after the war" (Bull 1979, 25).

After the Second World War, Norway was among the countries that signed the original agreements to set up the IMF, GATT, and the OEEC (later OECD). There were, however, important transition rules. Norway had obtained temporary exemption from obligations to liberalize agricultural imports. This exemption was made a lasting element of Norwegian trade policy during the entire postwar period and is now under review by a GATT panel at the request of apple exporters in the United States.[21]

As trade regulation has shifted from tariff to non-tariff barriers (NTB), Norway has followed suit. Comparative statistics are not well developed in this area, but those that exist appear to indicate that Norway, among OECD countries, is using NTBs. According to one source, 14 percent of public expenditure in Norway at the end of the 1970s was in the form of subsidies or transfers of income to particular groups or sectors, whereas the corresponding figure for Sweden was 7 and for Denmark 5 percent (Steen 1989, 147). According to official Norwegian estimates, the level of subsidies was reduced in the 1980s, and for the manufacturing sector was lower than that of Sweden for that period.

---

[21]The issue was settled in the first instance by the panel during the Summer of 1989, giving support to the U.S. interests.

Figure 6.1
Unit value index (excl. ships) and terms of trade. 1920 - 1975. 1961 = 100

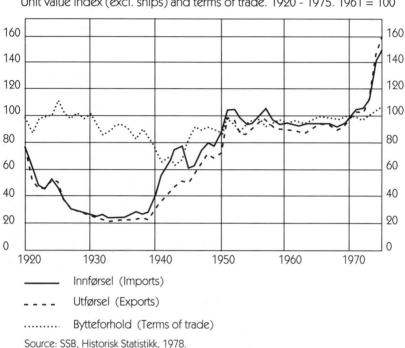

—————— Innførsel (Imports)

- - - - Utførsel (Exports)

.... Bytteforhold (Terms of trade)

Source: SSB, Historisk Statistikk, 1978.

Trade with the other Nordic countries increased after World War II. Some of this increase may have been indirectly due to the establishment of The Nordic Council, a common market for some goods, a common labor market, and institutionalized cooperation in several areas. A proposal to establish a customs union was, however, rejected on two occasions. Instead, Norway joined the European Free Trade Association (EFTA) when it was formed. In a referendum held in 1972, the Norwegian population by a small majority voted against membership in the EEC, whereas Denmark and Britain joined. Norway instead negotiated an association treaty that provides for free flow of manufactures, but regulates fish and some other products and keeps agricultural products outside free trade. Still, exports to the EEC increased and accounted for close to 70 percent of total Norwegian exports at the end of the 1970s. The greater part of Norway's foreign direct investment was also directed towards the EEC.

Throughout the period of industrialization, Norway's terms of trade were relatively stable, with the exception of an adverse trend in the 1930s (see Figure 6.1). Throughout the formation period in the nineteenth century, terms of trade were similarly stable with a predominantly positive trend. The fact that Norway could sell raw materials to England in exchange for cheap textiles and capital goods under favorable terms of trade played an important role in its development process.

Norway's exchange rate policy has turned from relative liberalism to moderate regulation. It has not used the exchange rate as an instrument in the foreign economic sector to the extent that some other Western European nations have. Norway largely followed the British and later the American exchange rate policies up until the 1930s and early 1970s, respectively. But most small Western European countries did so, and their way of handling the international fixed exchange rate regime was to cope with inflationary tendencies by adapting domestic prices through wage control or unemployment, not by revaluing or devaluing their currency. As Maddison puts it with reference to Aukrust (1977), Norway was part of the general trend whereby "smaller countries, and particularly Scandinavia, tended to drift with world price trends" (Maddison 1982, 134).

In 1973, the Norwegian government decided to join the "snake," the moderately-fixed exchange rate system organized to counter the destabilizing effects of the unilateral U.S. decision to free the dollar from the Bretton Woods obligations. In 1978, the Norwegian government reversed its decision and stayed out of the European Monetary System. The fact that the British government did the same thing may have played a role in Norway's decision, but there was also a growing belief in the krone due to the start up of oil production and exports.

Since 1978, the Norwegian exchange rate system has been to allow the krone rate to be decided by a basket of fourteen (later twelve) currencies. The internal composition of the basket and the relative weight of the respective currencies are decided by the Norwegian Central Bank (Norges Bank), assisted by the Currency Council (see below).

The Transition to the Bargaining Economy

The compromise between labor and farmers, and the national agreement in the labor market in 1935, laid the foundation for the bargaining economy of the post-World War II period. The compromise reflected the type of democratic corporatism (Katzenstein 1984), or nationwide formation of coalitions (Olson 1982), that has come to be seen as typical of the Scandinavian countries since the mid-1930s.

The bargaining economy is a society in which a major share of resource allocation is decided upon through institutionalized negotiations between a number of independent decision-making centers in the state, in organizations, and in firms. Through a routine of interactive processes these centers develop a common understanding of problems and become integrated into bargaining processes.

The bargaining economy not only transforms, but in fact transcends the mixed economy. It provides opportunities for social actors to manifest their respective opinions in confrontation, but at the same time to develop mutual understanding of each others' goals. The ultimate purpose is to reach agreement whenever conflicts of interest exist. As a result, state-private conflicts are reduced. So are capital-labor conflicts. Strikes are still allowed and used, but not to a large extent. Instead, the system offers incentives for the actors in the labor market to reach agreement: first, because the state delegates to other social actors the decision-making authority on several matters and second, because the state sometimes finances part of a settlement (Hernes 1975; Olsen 1978; Nielsen and Pedersen 1989).

A strong network of independent nationwide organizations is as much a prerequisite for the functioning of the bargaining economy as an effective state. It is, therefore, not a mere coincidence that the growth of nationwide organizations in Norway occurred along with the growth of state administration during the first post-World War II years. One hundred and seventy national organizations were formed during 1945-1950 (Moren et al. 1976). Before that period, agricultural and fishery organizations were dominant in the economic-productive sector. Therefore, primary sector organizations have developed particularly strong organizational representation of group interests.

This may explain why the primary sector is still able to extract subsidies and other concessions from the state well out of proportion to its contribution to GDP. The manner and extent to which these two sectors integrate with ministries and politicians have led scholars to see the cross-institutional integration as a segment, encapsulating its members from the rest of the economy (Dahl-Jacobsen 1960; Olsen 1978). Their relative strength in the institutional network may also be due to the fact that the two primary subsectors largely represent the peripheral regions of Norway. Their representatives compensate for their reduced economic clout by being relatively better organized than other group interests. So far they have been largely able to solve internal conflicts between large and small producers, but such conflicts occasionally make compromising difficult.

Manufacturing and services organizations grew only after World War II. The evolution of the organizational system, in other words, follows rather closely the pattern of the state. In some instances, the state has even demanded that organizations be established. An organized counterpart is better than anarchic relationships.

It took most of the 1950s to organize consensus and vital compromises, and to prepare the foundation for the new political-economic system. Its finalization coincided with the beginning of the "economic growth miracle" internationally. One of its main purposes was to provide shelter and compensation to those groups that were negatively affected or did not automatically obtain Pareto-optimal outcomes by the functioning of the economy. Therefore, part of the system also organized a consensus between export and import competing interests. The success of this system is, among other things, reflected in the level of subsidies (see above).

As trends in education, changes in production structure, and the building of social services all show, the "miracle" began around 1960. In 1950, only 3 percent of the population of the age of twenty-five had passed higher education. The relative number was about the same in 1960, but then surged to 6 percent in 1970 and continued to increase. The big educational explosion, however, was in secondary education, where the share of nineteen-year-olds who passed exams doubled from 1960 to 1970 and increased further to 27 percent in 1975. A major reason for this explosion was the arrival of women to a position of equality with young men.

The coming of the welfare state was a major factor behind the increase in public expenditure. Public expenditures on social security increased from 8.5 percent of GNP in 1955, to 13 percent in 1963. However, the real rise was to come around the mid 1960s, when the Storting passed a law giving all Norwegians over the age of 70 a state pension. In the 1970s and 1980s, the share of the public sector in GDP remained at or above the 50 percent level.

A large number of tripartite committees is an important feature of the system. They consist of representatives from the state, from capital and from labor. The legitimacy of the committees is reinforced by the fact that the state, both government and the Storting, delegates authority to them.

Presently in Norway there are some 900 councils, committees, and boards appointed by the state, 100 of these being appointed ad hoc. They are composed of representatives of concerned interests, that is, organizations or sectors particularly concerned about policy in a given area. This means that both capital and labor are represented in all institutions of some importance, sometimes by general nationwide organizations, other times by specialized organizations (and in many cases by both). It also means that the regional interest—a dimension that came to prominence in Norwegian politics during the 1930s and became a dominant force in the bargaining economy after World War II—is well represented.

Most of the institutions deal with social relations, cultural- scientific and educational affairs, or work in the various sectors of production and trade. Among the latter, there are comparatively more institutions in the primary than in the industrial (manufacturing) sector.

The institutional network is also part of international bargaining relations and is responsible for handling vulnerabilities caused by changes channelled through the foreign economic sector. Sixty-five of the 900 committees handle matters related to the foreign economy. Practically all of these committees have been set up since World War II. Their number and importance appears to have varied with fluctuations in international markets and regimes as well as with domestic demand. This is illustrated by the fact that there have been three waves of committee "production": one associated with the establishment of Bretton Woods (e.g., the Currency Council), one with the surge in exports in the 1950s (the Export Council), and the last one, in the 1970s, having to do with the emergence of Norway as a petroleum producer (British-Norwegian committees) and the declaration of exclusive economic zones in fisheries, both coinciding with international restructuring and a resultant domestic demand for crisis assistance (Textile Council).

Some committees have been as much arenas for bargaining within collective sectors (for example, sector organizations for labor) as between them. This is particularly true for those sectors that are part of the transfer economy: part of their incomes derive from public support (subsidy) systems. A case in point is again the primary sector. The fact that these committees have been delegated the task of allocating public resources obviously makes them important institutions in the political economy of the country.

The gradual transition from the mixed to the bargaining economy that has taken place in the postwar era is illustrated in the purpose and the composition of the committees. At the same time, there is still some division of labor among state and private sector institutions in performing economic policy functions. The Currency Council (established in 1946) has only state representatives, a confirmation that exchange rate policy is an exclusively public domain, i.e., a matter of coordination between the Foreign Affairs, Commerce, Finance and Industry Ministries, and the Central Bank, with the latter gaining more power recently.

Concluding Remarks

Norway appears to face three serious questions at the start of the 1990s. Is her industrial strategy well founded? Does she suffer from a lack of entrepreneurial spirit? And is the bargaining economy turning out to be a stumbling block to necessary transformation?

Petroleum incomes may have come as manna from heaven. But oil production has made the Norwegian industrial structure even more raw material-based than before, and there are symptoms of the "Dutch disease." Oil production has generated new skills, but relatively few job opportunities. Exports of unprocessed or semi-processed minerals and metals now account for close to two-thirds of total exports. Another traditionally important sector, shipping, has turned to internationalization in order to maintain its market shares.[22]

The current radical political-economic critique describes the economic situation as that of a country that turned down a blind alley. Petroleum will

---

[22]A wave of registrations of Norwegian ships abroad forced the state to introduce the Norwegian International Ship (NIS) register, a free ship register where shipowners are granted tax exemptions and allowed to hire seamen internationally, in practice, in countries where labor is cheaper. The NIS register has resulted in a substantial number of Norwegian-owned ships registering in it.

not give the economy the right push ahead, unless it is divested from the petro-economy into transforming the mainland industry. Norway presently generates less value added in research generated industry than does South Korea. There appear to be few entrepreneurs, and those who exist face difficulties in competitive markets.

The authoritative defense would point out that traditional industries like aluminum and magnesium are doing well, and that Norway should stick to what it knows best, but increase value-added and invest abroad to maintain market shares. This position is questionable when reference is made to the comparative advantage claimed for these traditional export industries. The hydroelectrical industrial complex is indirectly subsidized by the state through low electricity prices.

The other question to be asked is whether the bargaining economy is a disadvantage or an advantage to a country in need of rapid restructuring. There is strong pressure to introduce more market-oriented economic policies, and the pressure is already bearing fruit. Does the need for social and spatial mobility normally associated with structural change run counter to the principles and practice of the bargaining economy? Is what was previously an apparent advantage a disadvantage under present conditions of international restructuring and competition? Are vested interests too strong in their hold on the resources at the disposal of the bargaining economy?

The bargaining economy is based on manipulation of goals and preferences, but at the same time on stable institutions. At present there is another type of transformation that is widely demanded in most of Western Europe: that development should be sustainable (World Commission on Environment and Development 1987). Environmental degradation is a serious problem. Norway is no exception. Latin America will inevitably have to put it on top of its agenda as well. Concerns associated with ecopolitics can no longer be written away as marginal; they are moving to the top of the political and the economic agenda. Will they attack vested interests in present industrial structures so violently that these latter will leave the bargaining economy? And will the ecological movement be willing to enter it in the first place and abide by the rule of compromising? The answer to these questions also offers the answer to the transformation problem in the 1990s and beyond.

REFERENCES

Aubert, V. 1976. *Rettens sosiale funksjon.* Oslo: Universitetsforlaget.

Bairoch, P. 1976a. *Commerce exterieur et developpement economique de l'Europe au XIXe siecle.* Paris: Presses Universitaires Francaises.

————. 1976. "Europe's Gross National Product, 1800-1975." *Journal of European Economic History.* Fall.

Bergh, T., et al. 1980. *Growth and Development.* Oslo: Norwegian Institute of International Affairs.

Bjerke, J. 1966. *Langtidslinjer i norsk økonomi.* Oslo: Central Bureau of Statistics.

Brox, O. 1966. *Hva skjer i Nord-Norge?* Oslo: Pax forlag.

Bruland, K. 1988. *British Technology and European Industrialization. The Norwegian Textile Industry in the Mid-Nineteenth Century.* Cambridge: Cambridge University Press.

Bull, E. 1979. "Norge i den rike verden." In *Norges historie*, edited by K. Mykland. Oslo: Cappelen.

Cipolla, C. M. 1962. *The Fontana Economic History of Europe*, Vols. 1-6. Glasgow: Collins/Fontana.

Colbjørnsen, O. and A. Strømme. 1933. *En norsk treårsplan.* Oslo.

Collett, J.P. and H. Andersen. 1989. *Anchor and Balance. Det Norske Veritas, 1864-1989.* Oslo: Cappelen.

Dahl-Jacobsen, K. 1960. "Lojalitet, nøytralitet og faglig u avhengighet i sentraladministrasjonen." *Tidsskrift for samfunnsforskning.* 1960: 1

Ergas, H. 1984. *"Why do some Countries Innovate more than Others?"* Bruxelles: Centre for European Policy Studies: no.5.

Fagerberg J. 1987. "A Technology Gap Approach to why Growth Rates Differ." *Research Policy*, vol. 16, nos. 3-5.

Freeman, C. and L. Soete, eds. 1987. *Technical Change and Full Employment.* Oxford: Blackwell.

Gerschenkron, A. 1962. *Economic Backwardness in Historical Perspective.* Cambridge, Mass.: Harvard University Press.

Gourevitch, P. 1978. "The Second Image Reversed." International Organization.

————. 1987. *Politics in Hard Times.* Ithaca: Cornell University Press.

Grønlie, T. 1973. *Jern og politikk.* Oslo: Universitetsforlaget.

Habermas, J. 1962. *Strukturwandel der Offentlichkeit.*

Hernes, G., ed. 1978. *Forhandlingsøkonomi og blandingsadministrasjon*, Oslo: Universitetsforlaget.

Hodne, F. 1981. *Norges økonomiske historie 1815-1970.* Oslo: Universitetsforlaget.

Hoff, J. and A.J. Isachsen. 1979. "Marshall-hjelp. Kredittverdighet. Betalingsbalanse." Norsk Utenrikspolitisk Årbok Oslo. Norsk utenrikspolitisk institutt.

Hveem, H. 1989. "Norway - the Hesitant Reformer." In *Internationalism under Strain. The North-South Politics of Four Middle Powers*, edited by C. Pratt. Toronto: Toronto University Press.

Katzenstein, P. J. 1985. *Small States in World Markets. Industrial Policy in Europe*. Ithaca: Cornell University Press.

Keohane, R.O. and J.N. Nye. 1977. *Power and Interdependence*. Boston and Toronto: Little Brown.

Liebermann, S. 1970. *The Industrialization of Norway 1800-1920*. Oslo: Universitetsforlaget.

Maddison, A. 1982. *Phases in Capitalist Development*. Oxford: Oxford University Press.

Midttun, A. 1989. "Forhandlingsøkonomi i en tungindustriell sektor. Det norske vannkraft-industrielle komplekset i 1970-og 1980-årene." In *Forhandlingsøkonomi i Norden*, edited by K. Nielsen and O.K. Pedersen. Oslo: Tanum-Norli forlag.

Moren, J., et al. 1976. *Norske organisasjoner*. Oslo: Tanum.

Nielsen, K. and O.K. Pedersen, eds. 1989. *Forhandlingsøkonomi i Norden*. Oslo: Tanum-Norli forlag.

Norman, V. 1982. *En liten åpen Økonomi*. Oslo: Universitetsforlaget.

Norwegian Council for Scientific and Industrial Research, *Norway's Industrial Future*. Oslo, 1986.

Olsen, J.P. 1978. *Politisk organisering*. Oslo: Universitetsforlaget.

Olson, M. Jr. 1982. *The Rise and Decline of Nations*. Cambridge, Mass.: MIT Press.

Parliamentary White Paper no. 25 (1973-74) on Petroleum Policy. Oslo: Ministry of Oil and Energy, 1973.

Ruggie, J. G., ed. 1982. *The Antinomies of Interdependence*. New York: Columbia University Press.

Seierstad, A., et al. 1980. *Norge og den internasjonale storkapitalen*. Oslo: Pax forlag.

Sejersted, F. 1973. "En teori om den økonomiske utvikling i Norge i det 19. århundre." University of Oslo, Mimeo.

————. 1985. *Historisk introduksjon til økonomien*, Oslo: Cappelen.

Senghaas, D. 1982. *Von Europa Lernen*. Frankfurt: Rowolt Verlag.

Skoie, H. 1966. "The Problems of a Small Scientific Community: The Norwegian Case." Minerva. vol. 8, no. 3.

Steen, A. 1989. "Velferdsstat, korporatisme og selvregulering. Landbrukspolitikk i forhandlingsøkonomien i Norge og Sverige." In *Forhandlingsøkonomi i Norden*, edited by K. Nielsen and O.K. Pedersen. Oslo: Tanum-Norli forlag.

Stonehill, A. 1965. *Foreign Ownership in Norwegian Enterprise*. Oslo: Central Bureau of Statistics (Sosialøkonomiske studier no. 14).

Tresselt, D. 1966. "Strategi og kontroll i norsk aluminiumsindustri." Bedriftsøkonomen 1966 og 1968.

Valen-Sendstad, F. 1964. *Norske landbruksredskaper 1800-1850-årene.* Oslo.

Vekst og velstand. *Norsk politisk historie 1945-65.* 1977. Oslo: Universitetsforlaget.

World Commission on Environment and Development, 1987. *Our Common Future.* Oxford: Oxford University Press.

CHAPTER SEVEN

EXPORT BOOMS
AND DEVELOPMENT
IN ECUADOR

Galo Abril-Ojeda*

Introduction

Compared to the other Latin American countries discussed in this book, Ecuador is a latecomer. By the beginning of this century, when the Southern Cone countries had living standards not very different from those in most European countries, Ecuador did not even have the transportation infrastructure to connect its three sharply contrasting regions: the Coast, the Sierra (highlands), and the Amazon.[1] The two dominant areas, the Coast and the Sierra, were connected by rail first in 1908, and the Amazon area remained practically isolated until the late 1950s.

Under these conditions, there was no interregional trade to sustain economic development. The main production of the Sierra consisted of agrarian products for local consumption. To the extent that any industrial activity existed, it was at a small enterprise level, producing textiles, construction materials, leather goods, and handicrafts. Apart from tobacco, sugar, and a few other food products, most goods consumed in the coastal region were imported. Imports were made possible by the foreign exchange generated from cacao exports.

By exporting agrarian products, the coastal region has constituted the center of economic life in Ecuador during different periods. The information available points to the performance of these exports as a decisive factor in changing the overall level of economic activity in the country. However, the higher level of exports registered from time to time, referred to as "boom" periods in the literature, never generated much development in other sectors or regions. Industrial development, in particular, saw no significant improvement. This chapter asks the following questions: Why didn't the export booms preceding the oil boom generate development in Ecuador? Was Ecuador so backward that it could not take advantage of the possibilities created by the early booms? Why did the oil boom generate

* Comments and suggestions from the other participants in this project, particularly from Magnus Blomström, are gratefully acknowledged.
[1] The Galapagos Islands also belong to Ecuador.

such rapid growth? Had the pre-conditions for development changed by the 1970s? An attempt will be made to answer these questions by presenting a chronological review of the evolution of different economic indicators during the periods to which the export booms are attributed. Simultaneously, institutional, political, social, and geographical factors that have influenced the development path in Ecuador will be addressed. To begin, however, a brief overview of early Ecuadorean history will be presented.

Economic and Institutional Characteristics During Colonial Times

During the sixteenth century, mining production allowed Latin America to enter the world market. The supplies of silver and gold from Latin America, which were largely exported to Spain and Portugal, contributed not only to a recovery of foreign trade between Europe and Asia, but also to a restructuring of the world economy (Wallerstein 1974). The export revenues generated by the mining centers of Potosí (Alto Perú in present Bolivia), and the northern regions of New Spain (among others, the mines of Zaruma, in present Ecuador) also led to major changes in the region's structure of production, especially in agriculture and textiles (Marchán 1987a).

The colonial economy of Quito was drawn into the sphere of Potosí through exports of textiles, which were also exported to the markets of Santa Fé and Chile. By the end of the sixteenth century, livestock (mostly sheep) in the area of Quito numbered between 1,200,000 and 2,000,000 head, according to different estimates. The wool produced in the area was directed mainly to the textile factories (obrajes) of Latacunga and Riobamba, cities of the Central Andean region of Ecuador (Ortíz de la Tabla 1977). By the late seventeenth century, around 3,100 Indians were employed in the textile industry in five Andean cities, representing approximately 10 percent of the tributary population of these production centers, and 20 percent of the obraje labor force of the whole Audience of Quito (Tyrer 1976).

The dominant position of the mining industry diminished gradually by the first half of the eighteenth century, inducing an economic crisis throughout the whole of South America (Assadourian 1980) and causing the decline of the obrajes of Quito (Hurtado 1977).[2] The collapse of the mining market of Potosí, registered by the end of the eighteenth century,

---

[2] In many cases, due to a lack of a labor force (Indians), mining production had been reduced substantially by the end of the sixteenth century. The hard working conditions and rudimentary methods utilized in the production of gold led to a massive extermination of the Indians working in the mines (Jaramillo-Alvarado, 1955). By 1575, the Spanish Crown had attributed 95,000 Indians to the mines of Potosí; by 1633, this labor force had been reduced to 25,000, and to 1,700 by the year 1678 (Martínez 1962).

constituted the principal factor leading to an end of the textile activities in the Audience of Quito. However, the smuggling of English textiles and the earthquake of 1698 that destroyed a major part of the obrajes had already played a significant role in this process (Vargas 1987). The economic crisis that followed induced landowners to sell properties to different religious organizations and some private actors, thereby allowing the consolidation of the hacienda and the latifundio that was predominant in the Sierra until the nineteenth century (Marchán 1987a).

As in other regions of South America, the formation of a national identity and the need for independence from the Spanish Crown were growing steadily. In what concerned the Audience of Quito, the first protest occurred on August 10, 1809. However, it was not until May 24, 1822 that the country obtained independence from Spain and integrated into the "Gran Colombia" (together with Nueva Granada and Venezuela). By 1830, the "Southern District" (Quito) separated from this confederation, turning into an autonomous republic (Reyes 1986). The name Ecuador was adopted in 1835, and the monetary unit (sucre) was introduced by the Monetary Law of March 1884, in response to the chaotic situation generated by the money emission of different private banks lacking sufficient metallic reserves (Carbo 1978).

Throughout the eighteenth century, under the maintenance of a feudal system, the process of political consolidation did not induce major changes in favor of a market economy. Even though by the end of this century the coastal region, through rubber production and exports (until 1885), had reintegrated Ecuador into the world market, geographical isolation among regions impeded the improvement of domestic trade (Andrade 1987).[3]

The different opportunities for the Coast and the Sierra, the low income levels, the economic stagnation, and the two opposing political tendencies ("conservatism" of the Sierra and "liberalism" of the Coast) risked provoking a political disintegration of the nation.[4] But by the end of the nineteenth century, the "Liberal Revolution" (1895) changed the state of affairs.

---

[3] According to Jaramillo (1955), it was easier to reach the Capital of Perú (Lima) than Quito from the southern province of Loja. The long journeys to Quito had to be made through the virtually inaccessible Andean mountains.

[4] The predominant position of the Coast ("Oligarchy" of Guayaquil) on economic matters, against the administrative predominance of the Sierra (the "bureaucracy" of Quito) might have added to the contradictory regionalistic feelings that characterize Ecuador. It is affirmed that this regionalism has very often constituted a barrier to the achievement of a strong political and economic system (Ayala 1982).

Agrarian Export Booms, 1900-1971

Ecuador entered the twentieth century under the umbrella of the political and economic reforms enforced by liberalism.[5] These initial reforms seem to have changed the institutional environment in favor of an economic process (of the export-led type) based on agrarian exports whose different expansion periods define the export booms referred to above. But as will be discussed, it was not before the middle of this century that this process would lead to appreciable changes in economic development.

The Cacao Boom, 1900-1920

Accurate estimates of income, sectoral activity, and export levels for the period 1900-1920, when cacao exports expanded, are not available. Nevertheless, we know that production and income levels by the beginning of the century were extremely low across the country, except for the areas around the province of Guayas (Andrade 1987). Beyond some minor production of sugar, coffee, tobacco, and other agrarian products directed mainly to the domestic market, the production of cacao in the coastal region predominated. By 1914, the share of cacao in total exports rose to 77 percent (Heiman 1943). The highest participation in world market, 16 percent, was achieved in 1916 (Carbo 1987). But this export boom, and the imports it permitted, did not have any major impact or spill-over effects on other productive activities, sectors, or regions.[6] The villages of the Sierra continued to produce mainly food and textiles (in artisan forms) for local use.

Several factors might explain this mono-productive structure and, thus, the low capacity of the economy to respond to external shocks. Some of the factors include the persistent geographical isolation among regions; the concentration of income and wealth; the nature of the social structure; and the weak and unorganized state and political system.[7] Despite initial reforms, practically every village had its own laws and regulations, and the

---

[5] Included among the reforms introduced are the enforcement of the "Code of Commerce" (that regulated mercantilistic life until the early 1960s); a partial nationalization of the Church's properties; the expansion of the school system and introduction of secular education; the introduction of a divorce law and the right to vote for literate men and women; some organization of public finances; and the construction of the railway system.

[6] The economic depression following World War I, the emergence of other production centers, and the plagues that drastically affected the plantations, ended the cacao boom, leading to one of the most severe crises in Ecuadorean history (Carbo 1978).

[7] Apart from foreign interest in plantations, not more than sixteen families and the Church (mainly in the highlands) owned most productive land (in a context where over 80 percent of the population was made up of landless peasants). Those families had, and have even today, a predominant position in the productive, financial, and political systems (Ayala 1982).

state's income came mainly from taxes on foreign trade and loans from a private bank (Banco Comercial y Agricola) which was licensed to issue its own money (Andrade 1987; Carbo 1978). Therefore, a laissez-faire condition characterized economic life, not because of an explicitly adopted economic strategy, but because of the lack of efficient public institutions. This, in turn, was a result of an incipient state lacking in management capacity. In any case, it could be argued that the reason Ecuadoran exports did not have any spill-over effects on other sectors had to do more with the lack of basic services (such as efficient transport and communication systems and developed economic entities) than with inappropriate economic policies.

Only during the period 1925-1929, with a new revolution (the Juliana Revolution in July 1925), did Ecuador take some relevant steps towards what would be considered a structured economic entity, organizing the institution of the state.[8] To some extent, the new reforms improved the management capacity of the state, but not the ability of the economy to adapt to changes in external markets to preserve domestic stability. Low levels of education and technical skills,[9] and the lack of commercial and financial facilities, impeded adaptation to new technologies, innovations to sustain sectoral and regional development, and the development of a more dynamic domestic market. Even when some reforms aimed to improve the economic process, in practice, some of the measures taken appear to have had contradictory results. To a large extent, the regulations adopted were directed at increasing the revenues of the public sector (by further taxation on imports and exports), and providing agricultural and industrial activities with preferential access to financial means (Rodríguez 1987). The "Law for the Promotion of Industrial Development" (enforced already in 1921) and the establishment of the Banco Hipotecario in 1927 (Marchán 1987b), which was created to favor sectoral economic policies, introduced the possibility for private sectors to finance investment with money from the central bank. This possibility, even if it led to some product diversification, may have had adverse effects on domestic savings, encouraging financial capital placements abroad with serious consequences for economic growth. Given its permanence, this possibility may be continuing into the economic process of the present day (Abril-Ojeda 1988).

During this period of reforms, agriculture expanded and diversified, and manufacturing in the Sierra also registered some improvement. Among

---

[8] During this period, new institutional changes occurred improving government management. Public finances were organized, laws and regulations unified, and the role of the Banco Comercial y Agrícola was passed to the Caja Central de Emisión y Amortización, on which basis the Central Bank was created in March 1927 (Andrade 1987; Carbo 1978).

[9] By that time illiteracy predominated (until the end of the 1950s, over 50 percent of the adult population remained illiterate according to U.N. reports).

Table 7.1. Annual Average Rate of Growth of Macroeconomic Indicators, 1950–1987
(1975 prices)

	1950s	1960s	1970s	1980–1987
Population	2.9	3.2	3.0	2.9
GDP	5.0	4.0	9.4	1.0
Agriculture	4.0	3.0	3.0	4.0
Manufacturing	5.4	8.0	10.0	1.0
Exports	5.5	4.5	19.0	2.0
Mfg. investment	—	—	12.0	− 6.0*
Ratios				
Exports/GDP	0.178	0.158	0.235	0.221
GFKF/GDP	0.209	0.216	0.212	0.181
Mfg. Investment/GDP	—	—	0.0274	0.0167*

*1980–1986.
Sources: National Accounts, Nos. 7 and 11; Central Bank of Ecuador; Abril and Urriola.

Table 7.2. Structure of GDP and Exports, 1950–1987
(Percent)

	1950		1960		1970		1980	
	X	GDP	X	GDP	X	GDP	X	GDP
Agriculture	83.10	30.10	95.04	28.20	89.02	25.00	19.28	14.40
Oil and Mining	7.11	1.90	0.78	0.60	1.04	0.70	63.08	10.20
Manufacturing (*)	6.76	11.00	4.09	11.70	9.74	17.20	17.59	18.20
Other Industries (**)	—	4.60	—	6.60	—	7.10	—	5.50
Services (***)	—	47.80	—	48.60	—	49.20	—	47.10
Other Items	3.03	4.60	0.9	4.30	0.20	0.80	0.05	4.60
Total	100.0	100.0	100.0	100.0	100.0	100.0	100.0	100.0
XGDP Coefficients	0.18457		0.16726		0.13245		0.20859	

p = Preliminary figures.
  (*) Excludes refined oil.
  (**) Includes construction, electricity, gas and water.
  (***) Includes private and public services.
Sources: National Accounts Nos. 7 and 11; Annual Bulletin Nos. 2, 7 and 11; Historical Economic Statistics (1948–1983) "Memory"
          1955, 1960, 1972. Ecuadorean Central Bank.
Prepared by: Econometrics Department, Technical Division of the Ecuadorean Central Bank; and CEPLAES.

the new export products, coffee and bananas became the most important.[10] But it was not until after World War II, when there was a significant expansion of exports—the banana boom—that economic growth seems to have achieved a more steady path.

The Banana Boom, 1940-1969

The increase of banana production and exports registered during the 1940s accelerated during the 1950s and 1960s to such an extent that Ecuador became the major exporter of this product in the world market. According to Central Bank reports, banana exports more than tripled by the end of the 1940s. During the 1950s and 1960s, total exports (of which bananas stood for the major share, above 60 percent on average) grew at an annual average rate of 5 percent, agricultural output at 3.5 percent, and GDP at 4.5 percent (faster than the 3 percent growth of population) (see Tables 7.1 and 7.2). By the end of the 1960s, the share of bananas in total exports was reduced to around 40 percent as a result of the expansion of other production centers (mainly in Central America) closer to the world market, and the higher levels of productivity of these new producers (Leffeber 1985).

The banana boom induced an expansion of the domestic market and made possible the initiation of an industrialization process (manufacturing grew at a rate above 6 percent in annual average until the end of the 1960s; see Table 7.1). This process was partly supported by foreign direct investment and external credits (Moncada 1988).

Even though multinational firms such as United Fruit and a few families owned most of the production means and commercialization facilities, small farmers and peasants in the coast participated more actively in this boom than previously. Banana production is both land and labor intensive, and practically the entire region along the Pacific Coast of Ecuador was made up of banana plantations (an exception was the Manabí Province, which has higher mountains better suited for coffee). The low degree of sophistication of the techniques used to sow bananas allowed easier participation by the peasants, regardless of educational levels.

---

[10] The major expansion of agriculture was registered on the Coast with the activation of the sugar industry (Fisher 1983) and the production of coffee and bananas. Between 1926 and 1929, coffee and banana exports grew by 250 percent of their initial level (from $43 to $150 million, at 1937 prices). These exports fell drastically however, during 1930-1934, recovered until 1938, and fell again during the crisis following World War II (U.N. Document E-CN-12-295, p. 21; Benalcázar, 1988). In the highlands, some fifteen factories had been established, employing 2,500 people, with a capital investment of about $2 million (Deler 1987). Most of these firms produced textiles for the domestic market and Colombia (Gonzáles 1937). This meant the recovery of a traditional activity which had flourished during the colonial time (see the second section).

Table 7.3. Employment by Sector, 1950–1986
(Percent)

	Agriculture	Industry (*)	Manufacturing (**)	Services
1950	53.2	22.0	19.4	24.8
1962	56.5	17.5	14.1	26.0
1972	56.8	14.6	10.2	28.6
1986	36.0	18.6	10.6	41.1 (***)

(*)Includes mining and oil, construction, and manufacturing.
(**)Excludes handicrafts.
(***)Excludes the item "new workers" that had not been taken into account in the estimates of the active population for 1972.
  The estimates for 1986 were 4.3 percent.
Source: For 1950 and 1962, "Annual report, 1963." For 1972 and 1986, Central Bank of Ecuador, "Industrial Statistics." Volume I
and II, CONADE.
Prepared by: CEPLAES.

The need for efficient and rapid transportation of fruit to export markets forced the state to improve the transportation network of the production areas. During the 1950s, the construction sector grew at an average annual rate of 9 percent, higher than the 5 percent growth of the GDP (CBE, National Accounts, no.7). By the end of the 1950s, all major cities and towns along the coast were connected by new roads. Through the taxation of exports, even major ports were built. However, most important was that all major cities of the Sierra were also connected by new roads to the coast. Commercial activities, within and across regions, could then expand significantly (these activities grew at 6 percent per year).

The new employment opportunities in the banana plantations brought mass migration of unemployed people and landless peasants from the interior of the country to the Coast. The population of the coastal cities like Guayaquil, Machala, Quevedo, and Santo Domingo de los Colorados grew at an average annual rate of higher than 6 percent (twice the average for the whole country). Unlike the situation prevailing in the 1940s, the relatively higher income levels and the regional distribution now supported some integration and development of internal markets, and even some industrial growth. Food, beverages, tobacco, and other manufactures (handicrafts, leather, construction materials, etc.) produced in the interior of the country could now be commercialized across regions.

By 1950, the share of manufacturing in GDP grew to 11 percent, in 1960 to 12 percent, and in 1969 to 17 percent. The major share of this increase corresponded to processed food, beverages, tobacco (60 percent of manufacturing output) and textiles (20 percent) (CBE, National Accounts, no. 7).

Despite these appreciable improvements, seen in an Ecuadorean historical perspective, the export of bananas did not bring about a steady increase of industrial employment. Poverty continued to be widespread. Beyond the higher levels of employment due to the labor absorption in the banana plantations, the boom seems not to have altered the agrarian employment structure in the Sierra. This is reflected by the fact that the 19 percent share of manufacturing employment in the total active population of 1950 dropped to 14 percent by 1962 (see Table 7.3).

Besides the export taxes appropriated by the state, the major share of gains from banana production and exports was controlled by multinational enterprises and the few families that owned the production means and managed the commercialization of the fruit and the financial system (Moncada 1988). These groups made little reinvestment of profits in Ecuador. Thus, when import-substitution efforts began in the late 1950s, over half of the population still remained trapped within the traditional agrarian structure and did not represent potential consumers of industrial goods because of their relatively low incomes.[11] The political impact was to reduce the capitalists' willingness to tolerate reform projects; they looked at economic concessions to the poor more as sources of increased cost to them than as necessary reforms for the expansion of the domestic market (Conaghan 1988).

In 1964, the first land reform law was enforced, changing and modernizing to some degree labor relations in agriculture. However, the partitioning of productive land into the hands of poor peasants, without access to investment resources and techniques or appropriate infrastructure to support production and its commercialization, did not bring about any appreciable economic improvements (Costales 1971). The growth rate of agricultural output (except for bananas) maintained its traditional path, but deteriorated later during the 1970s when priorities turned in favor of industrialization. The 10 percent share of GDP that "other agrarian products" had maintained during the 1960s was reduced by 1979 to 5 percent (CBE, National Accounts, no. 11).

It should be noted that during the banana boom period, the political system tended to encourage the society to modernize. The state created institutions necessary to improve its management capacity, such as the Monetary Board,[12] Superintendence of Banks, Superintendence of Companies, the National Customs Board, Employment Department, etc. Simultaneously, the agrarian frontier expanded its economic relations and became monetarized, and new urban areas developed, facilitating the mobility of the labor force necessary to support the initiation of an enterprise structure. Even if the results obtained were not far reaching, the agrarian reform

---

[11] The import-substitution scheme recommended by the Economic Commission for Latin America (ECLA) was taken into account in Ecuador in 1957 when the Law for the Promotion of Industry was enforced (Abril and Urriola 1988). However, it was not until 1972, in connection with the oil boom, that the state enforced the system of priorities provided by the law.

[12] The Monetary Board (Junta Monetaria), established in March 1948, is the governing body of the Central Bank and includes different cabinet members and representatives of the productive sectors who enact financial and monetary policies.

marked the end of the huasipungo system,[13] breaking traditional relations in favor of capitalistic ones. Therefore, beginning in the 1940s and particularly in the 1950s and 1960s, the ground was laid for a domestic market that opened new prospects for industrialization. In fact, during the 1960s, while the GDP grew at 4.4 percent annually, manufacturing grew at 8 percent (see Table 7.1), faster than the population growth (3.2 percent), showing that modernization as a strategy for economic development had its roots in that decade.

The Oil Boom, 1972-1983

During the 1970s, the sharp increase in oil export revenues, the foreign debt accumulation, the Andean Pact assignments to Ecuadorean manufactures, and the increase in foreign direct investment (FDI) provided new perspectives for economic development.

Economic Performance

The Amazon oil fields discovered at the end of the previous decade were fully developed by 1972. The trans-Andean pipeline was also completed. Oil exports grew from the one percent level traditionally maintained to 55 percent of total exports in 1973, which was the average level maintained until the early 1980s (see Table 7.2).[14] In 1973, the trade surplus originated in the new oil exports, reaching 3 percent of GDP (between 1971-1973, the GDP had grown at 20 percent per year). In 1974, the quadrupling of oil prices led to an even higher trade surplus (5 percent of GDP).

Until 1979, there was a constant improvement of the terms of trade. Even though export volumes between 1975-1979 remained constant, export revenues grew by more than 30 percent of their initial level. During these years, GDP grew continuously at 6.5 percent per year, fueled by the growth of manufacturing (11 percent per year), construction (6 percent), and public services (12 percent).[15] Meanwhile, agriculture stagnated (at one percent annual growth). Table 7.2 indicates that manufacturing exports also grew during the oil boom period from around 10 percent of total exports in 1970 to 17.5 percent in 1980 (a remarkable increase given the significant expansion of oil exports).

---

[13] A system of relationships that permitted peasants to exploit a piece of land within the hacienda in exchange for gratuitous services for its owner (el patrón).

[14] The 7 percent share of "mining and oil" in 1950 total exports corresponds mainly to gold exports. This share, however, fell in 1951 to 3 percent and to 0.5 percent in 1952, which is the level that has been maintained until recently. Since 1987, gold exports appear to have entered a new pace, but at relatively low levels (Internal Reports, 1986-1988; CBE).

[15] For a chronological description of oil boom events see de Janvry 1988, Annex 3.

Despite the improvement of the terms of trade observed between 1979 and 1980 (when oil prices doubled), GDP growth slowed to 5 percent in 1980 due to the decline in oil and manufacturing output. This tendency continued in 1981 when GDP grew by 4 percent, fell in 1982 to 1.2 percent, and declined dramatically in 1983 to -2.8 percent, thereby marking the end of the oil boom period. This contraction can be attributed to the sharp increase in foreign debt payments (1981-1982), the heavy rains and severe floods (1982-1983) which reduced exports of traditional agrarian products, and the contractive fiscal policy and import regulations introduced to counteract internal and external sector imbalances (CBE "Memoria, 1983").

Role of the State

Since the early 1970s, the state has intervened more directly in the process of allocation of resources and distribution of income. While production and export gains of the agrarian booms were in private hands, the gains from the oil activities were kept under the control of the state. The nationalization of the production and commercialization of oil (crude and refined) gave rise to a political allocation of the rents generated above 10 percent of GDP. Since 1972, these rents have been distributed partly to regional governments, ministries, public institutions (educational, social, and financial) in fixed proportions determined by law, and partly to the private sector (mainly industry), in the form of loans provided under concessional terms, through public as well as private financial institutions.

During the 1970s, oil income revenues came to represent about 60 percent of the public sector's budget. Between 1972 and 1974, public sector revenues grew by 25-35 percent per year, and,kept growing at an average annual rate of 15 percent until the early 1980s (CBE, Fiscal Studies Department, and National Accounts no. 11). The new incomes to the state were not only used to expand public sector activities (current expenditures almost tripled between 1972 and 1983), but also to invest in different projects to improve the overall physical infrastructure of the country. The major expansion of the public sector took place between 1974 and 1979 when expenditures grew from 23 to 29 percent of GDP, faster than public revenues. According to the Fiscal Studies Department (internal reports), the initial, relatively small public sector deficit outstanding (less than 3 percent of GDP) was covered by borrowing from abroad. However, the decline in oil prices and the continuation of the expansive fiscal policy gradually increased the public sector deficit to 8 percent of GDP in 1982. The deficit continued to be covered by foreign borrowing.[16] The annual net

---

[16] Beyond financing the public sector deficit, foreign indebtedness on credits from multinational financial institutions such as the World Bank, the Inter-American Development Bank, Corporación Andina de Fomento (CAF), etc., was also used to support manufacturing investments on concessional terms, in line with the scheme of incentives established to promote industry.

increase of foreign debt (in current prices), which prior to 1976 had been growing at an average annual rate of 20 percent, climbed to 66.5 percent during 1977 and 1981. After 1982, in connection with the explosion of the foreign debt crisis, these rates declined drastically to 10 percent per year (CBE, Foreign Debt Department, internal reports).

Public current expenditures grew faster than capital expenditures, showing that bureaucracy expanded more than public investments. Nevertheless, the different projects undertaken permitted infrastructural and social improvements that could be considered historical for Ecuador.[17] The attempts of the state to improve transport and communication systems are reflected by the faster growth of this sector (10.6 percent per year) than GDP (9 percent) and manufacturing (10 percent). Similarly, "communal, social, and individual" services grew at an average annual rate of 7.5 percent, illustrating the efforts made in the educational, health, and housing sectors, and the expansion of the administrative structures (CBE, National Accounts no. 7). Even if this evolution did not always provide beneficial results, it is clear that the extension of the programs transformed the state into a dynamic income distribution agent that did not exist in previous periods. Despite the concentration of income mainly in favor of middle-income groups around the larger cities, public expenditures also helped to expand the domestic market, allowing manufacturing to grow.[18]

Industrial Policy

The ability of manufacturing to respond to the market expansion was assured by the import-substitution industrialization policy of the 1970s, instituted on the basis of the new incomes from oil revenues and the foreign borrowing referred to previously (let us call this the "income effect" of the oil boom). There are at least three channels through which the state enforced the allocation of resources (or the functional distribution of income) in favor of industry: i) credits on preferential terms for new

---

[17] Thanks to the public projects started during the 1970s, electricity consumption, which until the 1960s was a privilege of a few people in urban areas, presently covers some 75 percent of the total population (Reports to the Congress). The share of education in public expenditures grew from 10 to above 20 percent and illiteracy was reduced from the near 40 percent level to around 20 percent at the end of the 1970s (presently, the illiteracy rate is about 18 percent). Expenditures on health services grew, from 2-3 percent to 7 percent of total public expenditures. Even if a more efficient health assistance was concentrated on the big cities, practically all small villages across the country were supplied by health centers.

[18] The major share of housing programs (on the basis of subsidized credits) concentrated on urban areas (mainly Quito and Guayaquil). During 1973-1978, this sector grew at 8 percent per year. However, the major expansion corresponded to building in these two cities (Abril-Ojeda 1984). The lack of sufficient and appropriate housing, in rural as well as urban areas, is still today one of the most serious problems.

investments and working capital; ii) an appreciated foreign exchange rate that favored imports of capital goods and raw materials; and iii) tax exemptions, protective tariffs, and import restrictions to neutralize foreign competition (Abril and Urriola 1988).

Information on the annual distribution of credit shows the industrial sector has absorbed the major share of new financing since 1972. The share of this sector in the total amount of financial resources provided by the entire banking system grew from 18.5 percent in 1972 to 33 percent in 1985. Meanwhile, commerce reduced its participation from 60 to 34 percent and agriculture remained relatively unchanged (between 12-14 percent). "Other activities," which include stabilization credits to private industries having foreign debt payment difficulties, grew from 9 to above 20 percent (Abril and Urriola 1988). In addition, as suggested above, despite the preferences established to improve the regional distribution of investment (lower interest rates according to the geographical localization of the production units), most of the loans provided were concentrated in Quito and Guayaquil (75 to 87 percent of the total credit volume distributed between 1977 and 1983, the years for which elaborated data has been available). Taking into account that almost all industries are located in the provinces to which these two cities belong (Pichincha and Guayas), that in the latter region the major share of exports are produced (agrarian and fishery products), and that also in Guayas the commercial facilities (ports) are installed, the tendency for a skewed sectoral and regional distribution of income is clear (Abril-Ojeda 1985).

"Dutch-Disease" Effect

On the one hand, during 1972 and 1977, the average rate of growth of new investments in manufacturing was around 20 percent per year; i.e, the response of the sector to the financial means obtained and to the expansion of the domestic market was significant. This beneficial result (the "income effect") of the new inflow of foreign resources diminished by 1980 when the rate of growth of new investments in manufacturing became negative and declined even further after 1983 with the explosion of the debt crisis (Abril and Urriola 1988).

On the other hand, during 1972 and 1982, the official nominal exchange rate valid for all commercial transactions was maintained at 25 sucres per U.S. dollar; meanwhile inflation rates increased from 7.6 to 16.4 percent. (CBE, Monthly Statistical Information). Under this system, the new inflows of foreign exchange, from oil exports after 1972 and foreign debt accumulation after 1976, sharply appreciated the real exchange rate, giving room to the so-called "Dutch-disease" effect. The appreciated domestic currency, together with the loans provided on concessional terms, the tariffs and tax exemptions, and the regulations against foreign competition, favored imports of physical capital and raw materials for industry, worsened the situation of non-protected tradables, such as agrarian products (see Table 7.2), and fostered the expansion of non-tradables such as services and construction (of the type referred to above).

This, however, did not affect all types of tradable goods. Simultaneously, as pointed out previously, some increase in manufacturing exports was registered, although mainly due to a variety of specific incentives, such as commercial loans, tax exemptions and export subsidies, and the preferences obtained in connection with regional trade arrangements (the Andean Pact). It has been estimated that the total amount of tax exemptions and export subsidies (Certificados de Abono Tributario)[19] provided by the state in 1982 corresponded to 45 percent of the total value invested by manufacturing that year or 24 percent of its exports, refined oil products excluded (Abril-Ojeda 1985).

Factor Intensity and Productivity Changes

Major changes in the capital/labor relations and productivity ratios took place during 1972-1982. As seen below, the manufacturing of final consumption goods was developed based on the use of modern capital-intensive technologies accessible in international markets. That is, the import-substitution industrialization policy incentives and the foreign exchange system contributed to introducing labor-saving technologies, increasing factor productivity (even in traditional sectors). Nevertheless, even if labor productivity increased (in terms of output per worker), the income distribution and employment generating goals (behind the Industry Promotion Law) were not entirely fulfilled. During 1974-1982, total employment grew at only 2 percent per year, below the rate of growth of the population, and the agrarian sector reduced the amount of people employed by about 100,000 (or 5 percent of the active population), i.e., at a rate of decline of about 1.7 percent per year. Meanwhile, labor utilization in manufacturing increased 3 percent, and in construction 8 percent per year (CONADE, 1972 and 1986). However, in terms of participation, the share of manufacturing in total employment remained relatively unchanged, at 10 percent (see Table 7.3).

By reducing the level of aggregation and considering also the employment induced indirectly (on activities other than their own), it is shown that some manufactures generated substantially more employment. Agro-industrial activities, such as processed food, beverages, and tobacco have maintained an important share of employment of the manufacturing sector:

---

[19] A reimbursement, corresponding to above 10 percent on average of the export value received by the exporters (most often, other than the producers themselves).

33 percent in 1970 and 30 percent in 1982 (CONADE, op. cit.). Estimates of backward-linkages indicate that for a given increment of one million sucres (of 1975) in the production of each of these activities, on average, they employ only two more persons directly, but indirectly bring about 38 to 39 new jobs in the rest of the economy (Abril and Urriola 1988). As is referred to below, these are activities which, in the context of linkage properties of exports, show an appreciable degree of integration into the rest of the economy.

Regarding labor productivity changes, evidence points to remarkable improvements in the case of Ecuador during the reference period. Between 1950 and 1980, the annual average growth of labor productivity was above 4 percent, i.e, more than the average for Latin American countries (Rosales 1989). Moreover, this productivity improvement was above 6 percent per year during 1970 and 1980, when most Latin American countries showed a setback. Obviously, looking at these changes by sectors, it is found that the major improvements are to be attributed to the industrial sector—the capital intensity that increased due to the import-substitution policy referred to previously. If the effects of the oil boom are not taken into account, by considering the previous period alone (1950-1970), the average annual growth of labor productivity was nearly 4 percent, also higher than most other Latin American countries. These improvements in labor productivity reflect the acceleration, relative to other countries in the region, of the economic development preconditions that took place in Ecuador when the import-substitution industrialization strategy was in force.

Characteristics of the Manufacturing Sector

It can be argued that the incentives provided to promote industrialization and the income distribution effects on effective demand as a result of the expansion of the public sector have been important sources of industrial growth. This expansion, with its positive impact on income, particularly in middle income groups, seems to have amplified the domestic market, allowing the manufacturing of consumer goods to grow.

A closer review shows that the manufacture of these consumer goods, which represents the major share of the sector's total output, has been developed on traditional comparative advantages linked to exports of primary goods. That is, even if supported by a higher level of domestic demand, the new manufactures seem to have developed an "export orientation" using the market infrastructure provided by traditional exports. In addition, the new processed goods, differing from primary export goods, appear to have induced linkage properties to the rest of the economy that are not present in the traditional export basket.

Evolution within the Sector

Looking at the evolution by subperiods (CBE, National Accounts, nos. 7 and 11), manufacturing grew fastest during the decade of the 1970s: 10 percent per year, against 9 percent for GDP.[20] But reviewing the evolution within the sector, it can be seen that capital goods (chemicals, machinery, and equipment) grew above the average for all manufacturing activities, coming to represent 4 percent of sector value added during the 1970s or less than one percent of GDP, on average.[21] This small participation makes it difficult to talk about any significant degree of import substitution. In addition, these are activities strongly dependent on imported physical capital and raw materials, to such an extent that only one activity, "machinery and equipment" accounts for more than 60 percent of the annual trade deficit of the manufacturing sector (Abril and Urriola 1988). This provides an indication of the persistent low level of technical progress and integration of capital goods activities with the rest of the economy. In terms of self-sufficiency (generation of foreign exchange), which constituted an explicit goal behind the industrial promotion scheme adopted in Ecuador, the contribution of the capital goods sector may thus far be considered unsuccessful.

During the 1970s, the processing of primary goods or of renewable natural resources (food, beverages, tobacco, textiles, wood, leather, paper and paper products) accounted for more than 60 percent of manufacturing output. Within this group, the major share corresponds to processed coffee, cacao, fish and tobacco, i.e., traditional goods produced on the Coast that dominate the Ecuadorean export basket. This means that manufacturing developed on the basis of traditional comparative advantages of agrarian products.[22]

It is important to point out that manufacturing exports of processed agrarian products grew during the oil boom period, representing 90 percent of the sector's total exports (CBE, National Accounts, nos. 7 and 11). This

---

[20] The rapid average growth of the oil sector after 1972 (63.5 percent per year) explains the relatively low participation of manufacturing in GDP, which rose from the 16 percent share it maintained until 1969, to 17 percent in the 1970s, and to 18 percent in the 1980s (CBE, National Accounts, no. 11).

[21] This lies below the 6 percent of average participation in GDP valid for LDCs (UNCTAD 1986).

[22] It should be observed that there has been a tendency for processed food, beverage, and tobacco activities to reduce their participation in sector value-added, and for textiles to increase it during the reference period. In the first case, it is mainly due to the fall in the participation of the exports of sugar; a product which has constantly lost in productivity with respect to foreign competitors. In the second case, the increase seems to be related to the expansion of the cloth industry (directed to domestic and external markets). But this is an activity completely dependent on imported synthetic fibers that are more competitive than the traditional domestic natural fibers.

confirms the theory about an expansion of manufacturing related to traditional export lines and, to a greater extent, of an export-led performance. Two factors appear to indicate that these activities are not a reliable source of growth[23]: the variability of prices of this export basket in the international market (leading to sharp oscillations of export revenues with adverse effects on GDP growth), and the strong subsidies that have been provided these types of exports. However, different observations contradict this perception.

Some estimates of the linkages of export activities to the rest of the economy reflect good integration properties (backward linkages) of agro-industrial exports (Abril and Urriola 1989).[24] Taking the export sector as a whole, the estimated effects support the "enclave" hypothesis concerning an export sector with a relatively low degree of integration into the rest of the economy. However, by reducing the level of aggregation and looking at the effects by export groups, it is found that processed food, textiles, leather, and wood products, despite their 18 percent share in the gross output of the export sector, represent the major share of the backward linkages induced. The backward linkages in this case are greater than those for oil and mining that have the lowest integration coefficient of all groups, despite representing the major share of gross output of the whole group (72 percent). In other words, for the case of manufacturing exports related to renewable natural resources (mainly agro-industrial goods), the "enclave" hypothesis is not entirely valid. That is, even if industrialization during the oil boom period has been pushed by subsidies and preferences (inducing as time passed different kinds of inefficiencies), the properties observed in connection with agro-industrial exports reveal that Ecuadoran industrialization perspectives might have been improving substantially.

Foreign Direct Investment and Regional Trade Arrangements

Undoubtedly, foreign direct investment (FDI) and regional trade arrangements during the oil boom period have played an important role in contributing to the improvements described. Even if in relation to Latin

---

[23] At various times, the economic efficiency of Ecuadorean manufacturers has been seriously questioned. Some estimates indicate that a one percent shift in credit towards industry decreases the GDP growth by about one-fifth of a percent (Anderson, 1989). This may have to do with the fact that a large portion of this credit is allocated to large firms that have good collateral, are highly protected from foreign competition and have excess production capacity, so that new loans are either not contributing or only marginally contributing to growth.

[24] Of the total volume exported in 1985, 13.5 percent or 24 percent of GDP corresponded to bananas, coffee, cacao, shrimps, and miscellaneous, 58 percent to crude oil and refined oil products, 19.5 percent to processed food, textiles, leather, and wood products, 0.2 percent to machinery, equipment, and other manufactures, and 8.8 percent to other exports (where transport services stood for the major share).

America FDI has been insignificant in amount, foreign enterprises were present in practically all industrial activities. During the market expansion after 1970, FDI almost doubled from what it was at the end of the 1960s. Excluding investments in the oil sector, in 1974 FDI in industry grew by 56 percent (Schamis 1981).

Despite the restrictions imposed by Decision 24 of the Cartagena Agreement, FDI participated in all lines of production reserved for local enterprises. Nowadays, foreign firms participate in practically all agro-industrial activities, including food processing for export markets (Urriola and Cuvi 1986). For the most part, the technological level embodied in such production is high and adjusted to the condition of enterprises abroad. Investment in intermediate sectors, where local technology is scarce, have seldom been covered by multinationals. To the extent they have invested, it has been made in the final phases of production, such as in the assembly of car parts or in the packing processes of imported goods, such as pharmaceutical products (Belisle 1988). In any case, it cannot be denied that many of the improvements observed in present-day Ecuador, such as the increase in labor productivity ratios and the higher levels of entrepreneurial activities, are the result of the multinational presence.

An undesirable effect, meanwhile, has to do with the rigidity characterizing the system of incentives and with the mechanisms utilized for the regional allocation of investment. To some extent, FDI through partnership in mixed enterprises has taken advantage of regional trade arrangements established by the Andean Pact to avoid barriers against outside imports within the Pact region (often complemented by subsidized local credits or foreign loans). Foreign indebtedness for private investment increased substantially during the FDI period being discussed, and accounts for about 30 percent of the private foreign debt, presently refinanced by the Ecuadorean state (CBE, "Memoria", 1983).

The arrangements of the Andean Pact determined some arbitrary allocations of industrial investment among member countries without major consideration of technological constraints, comparative advantages and future market conditions. When the foreign debt crisis arose, protective measures were generally introduced to the region so that most export industries (particularly in the wood and electrical branches) reduced their production levels to a minimum. During 1983 and 1985, some estimates indicated a nonutilized installed capacity of 40 percent on the average for those branches. (It should be mentioned that because of the negative real costs of financial capital for imports of capital goods, most investment had, from the start, been excessive).

Summary and Conclusions

Except for the oil boom period, any strong evidence for the expansion of the export sector (the agrarian booms) leading to higher levels of activity overall in the economy has been difficult to find. The lack of access to necessary data has impeded a more accurate determination of facts. However, it seems clear that during the agrarian export booms, the higher level of economic activity surrounding the coastal production centers did not contribute significantly to the development of other sectors (such as industry) and regions (the Sierra and Amazon areas).

The overall picture throughout this chapter points to different factors underlying the retardation of economic development. Among these factors, until early in this century, were the geographical isolation of the regions forming the Ecuadorean continental territory; the resulting market fragmentation and limited domestic market; and a weak and unorganized political system. By the end of the 1930s, the country could still be characterized by the existence of isolated villages, with low levels of trade among one another, and production mainly for self-consumption under more feudalistic forms of participation.

The absence of a strong political system and national identity persisted for a long time. The opposing interests of the oligarchy of the Coast (Guayaquil) and of the state bureaucracy of the Sierra (Quito) might have perpetuated this situation. Thus, in line with the "domestic institutions and policy school," it could be argued that the absence of a domestic socioeconomic and political organization played a central role in the retardation of economic development during earlier periods.

The institutional reforms enforced after the "Liberal Revolution" improved the managerial capability of the state. But it was not until the 1940s, in connection with the expansion of banana production and exports, that there was some improvement of development preconditions. The land and labor-intensive character of the production of bananas led to a major integration of different areas within and across regions, forced the improvement of the transportation infrastructure, and favored factor mobility. The need for labor on banana plantations increased migration currents from the interior of the country, giving room to a greater spread of income distribution. All these factors permitted some expansion of the domestic market, providing new perspectives for sectoral and regional development. In that way, the ground was laid for the initiation of the industrial process that has its roots in the decade of the 1950s.

The land reform introduced in 1964 brought an end to the minifundio system. Despite its initially unsuccessful economic results, this reform changed and modernized agrarian labor relations, enhancing the possibilities for a market economy to develop. During this decade, the productivity of labor showed clear signs of improvement; this phenomenon accelerated during the 1970s at rates of growth superior to the average for Latin American countries.

The acceleration of productivity growth coincides with the significant increase of foreign exchange inflows from petroleum exports, foreign indebtedness and foreign direct investment, as well as with the regional trade arrangements that established preferential treatment for Ecuadorean industrial exports. The import of technology, made easier by the import-substitution industrial policy, might have facilitated productivity improvements. In some sense, all of these factors, plus the retardation of economic development relative to other countries that characterized Ecuador until the 1960s, give credence to the "convergence hypothesis." This hypothesis argues that the more backward a country, the higher the rate of productivity growth achievable by borrowing technology from the more advanced nations. Since 1972, an important role has been played by the comprehensive state programs in sustaining this process, by reducing illiteracy, expanding the educational system, providing health services, and improving the energy distribution systems.

Even if the expansion of the public sector may presently be a deterrent to economic growth, the fact that its direct control over oil production gains and distribution permitted an easier transfer of resources among sectors and regions was a contributing factor to economic development (not present in previous boom periods).

During the oil boom, manufacturing exports increased substantially, diversifying the traditional export basket. To a greater extent, the new export products followed the traditional comparative advantages provided by agrarian products. However, integration of the new manufacturing exports into the rest of the economy shows that the efforts made were historical in the sense that the monoproductive structure of the economy was altered with beneficial results. For this type of export-led development perspective to lead to real benefits, there is an urgent need for a revision of the rigid import-substitution policy incentives in coordination with the appropriate macroeconomic policy measures. The limited room in the production process achieved by the capital goods sector also speaks in favor of implementation of policies to improve the level of domestic technology and its process of innovation and integration into the rest of the economy.

Ecuador has a long haul ahead despite the prevailing conditions and the increase in factor productivity registered as an important source of growth. The experience thus far of external shocks (i.e., variations in the terms of trade) leading to drastic alterations of GDP growth indicates that long-term policies directed at a major diversification of the productive structure are needed beyond the short-term measures aimed at changing relative prices against the world market.

A more diversified economy may permit an easier dissemination of external shocks among sectors, reducing their impact on the rate of growth of the GDP. From the point of view of a temporal allocation of resources, the irrationality embodied in the radical annual changes of GDP growth surely constitutes one of the main factors behind the retardation of Ecuadorean economic development.

REFERENCES

Abril-Ojeda, G. 1984. *El desarrollo y la importancia de la industria de la construcción en el Ecuador*. Quito: Cámara de la Construcción.

_____. 1985. *Política monetaria y desarrollo industrial en el Ecuador; 1970-1983*. Quito: Banco Central del Ecuador.

_____. 1988. *Reactivación con equidad; una respuesta a la crisis ecuatoriana*. Quito: CEPLAES.

_____, and R. Urriola 1988. "Eficiencia de los incentivos de fomento industrial en el Ecuador, 1972-1986." Quito: CEPLAES. Mimeo.

_____. 1989. "Alternative Policy Combinations for the Promotion of Industry and Economic Development." Quito: CEPLAES, Mimeo.

Almeida, P. and M. Naranjo. 1987. "Pensamiento dominante y economía nacional en la década de los años veinte." In *Crisis y cambios de la economia Ecuatoriana en los años veinte*, edited by C. Marchán. Quito: Banco Central del Ecuador.

Almeida, P. and R. Almeida. 1989. *Estadísticas económicas históricas, 1948-1983*. Quito: Banco Central del Ecuador.

Anderson, J. 1989. "Impact of Monetary and Fiscal Policies on Ecuador's Real Growth and Inflation." University of San Diego, School of Business Administration. Mimeo.

Andrade, B. 1989. "Reseña de una década que forjaría historia." In C. Marchán, ed., *Crisis y cambios de la economía Ecuatoriana en los años veinte*. Quito: Banco Central del Ecuador.

Assadourian, C. S. 1980. "La minería andina colonial." In C.N. Assadourian, et al., *Minería y espacio económico en los Andes*. Lima: Instituto de Estudios Peruanos, siglos XVI-XX.

Ayala, E. 1982. *Lucha política y origen de los partidos en el Ecuador*. Quito: Corporación Editora Nacional.

Belisle, J. F. 1988. *La industria farmacéutica ecuatoriana*. Quito: CEDIME.

Benalcázar, R. 1988. "La función desempeñada por el comercio exterior en el desarrollo de la economía durante 1950-1985." Quito: Banco Central del Ecuador. Mimeo.

Carbo, L. A. 1978. *Historia monetaria y cambiaria del Ecuador, desde la epoca colonial*. Quito: Banco Central del Ecuador.

CEBCA. 1989. *Lineamientos para impulsar la producción de bienes de capital en el Ecuador* (con énfasis en la política financiera). Quito: Comisión Ecuatoriana de Bienes de Capital.

Central Bank of Ecuador, 1985 and 1988. National Accounts, nos. 7 and 11. Quito: Banco Central del Ecuador.

Central Bank of Ecuador, Memoria: 1955, 1960, 1963, 1972, and 1983. Quito: División Técnica, Banco Central del Ecuador.

Conaghan, C. 1988. *Restructuring Domination, Industrialists and the State in Ecuador*. Pittsburgh: University of Pittsburgh Press.

CONADE. 1972 and 1986. *Industrial Statistics*. Quito: Consejo Nacional de Desarrollo.

Costales, A. and P. Costales 1971. *Historia social del Ecuador. Reforma agraria*. Quito: Casa de la Cultura Ecuatoriana.

Deler, J. P. 1987. *Ecuador del espacio al estado nacional*. Quito: Banco Central del Ecuador, Biblioteca de Geografía Económica, vol. II.

de Janvry, A., A. Fargeix and E. Sadoulet 1988. "Adjustment and Equitable Growth. The Case of Ecuador." Paris: OECD Development Centre. Mimeo.

Fisher, S. 1983. *Estado, clases e industria*. Quito: Editorial El Conejo.

González, J. L. 1937. "Breves notas sobre la industria textil en el Ecuador". Boletín. Quito: Ministerio de Previsión Social, Trabajo, Agricultura e Industrias, Año I, no. 4, 37-50.

Hurtado, O. 1977. *El poder político en el Ecuador*. Quito: Ediciones PUCE.

Heiman, H. 1943. *Estadísticas de las exportaciones del Ecuador 1940-1942* (con series históricas anteriores). Quito: Ministerio de Economía.

Jaramillo, A. P. 1955. *Historia de loja y su provincia*. Quito: Edit. Casa de la Cultura Ecuatoriana.

Leffeber, L. 1985. *Economía política del Ecuador, campo, región, acción*. Quito: York University and FLACSO.

Marchán, C. 1987a. "La economía política del Ecuador durante la colonia". In Vargas, 13-14 and 52-53.

_____. 1987a. "Crisis nacional, aprovechamiento regional y discriminación social de sus efectos económicos (1920-1927)." In C. Marchán, ed., *Crisis y cambios de la economía ecuatoriana en los años veinte*. Quito: Banco Central del Ecuador.

Martínez, E. E. 1962. *Diferencias y semejanzas entre los países de América Latina*. México: Universidad Autónoma.

Moncada, J. 1988. "Marco histórico del proceso de industrialización en el Ecuador. Bases para la definición de opciones de desarrollo industrial." Quito: CEPLAES. Mimeo.

Ortíz de la Tabla, J. 1977. "El obraje colonial Ecuatoriano. Aproximación a su estudio." *Revista de Indias*, no. 148-150.

Reyes, O. E. 1986. *Breve historia general del Ecuador*. Quito: Imprenta Colegio Técnico Don Bosco, volumes II and III.

Rodríguez, F. 1987. "Inestabilidad monetaria internacional y nacional. Cambios en la orientación de la economía y de la política en el Ecuador (1914-1927)." In *Crisis y cambios de la economía Ecuatoriana en los años veinte*, edited by C. Marchán. Quito: Banco Central del Ecuador.

Rosales, O. 1989. "Competitividad, productividad y posibilidades de reinserción comercial en América Latina". Santiago de Chile: CEPAL, ILPES, Documento EIN-55.

Schamis, G. 1981. "Notas para la discusión del papel de la inversión extranjera directa." Quito: CEPLAES. Mimeo.

Superintendencia de Compañías. 1988. *El desarrollo empresarial en el Ecuador, en las dos últimas décadas*. Quito.

Tyrer, R. 1976. "The Demographic and Economic History of the Audience of Quito: Indian Population and the Textile Industry, 1600-1800." PhD dissertation, University of California, Berkeley.

United Nations. 1988. "El desarrollo económico del Ecuador." Document E-CN-12-295, in Benalcázar.

UNCTAD. 1986. *El sector de bienes de capital en los países en desarrollo*. United Nations, II D.4, 1986.

Urriola, R. and M. Cuvi. 1986. "La agroindustria alimentaria en el Ecuador de los años 80." Quito: CEPLAES. Mimeo.

Vos, R. *Industrialización, empleo y necesidades básicas en el Ecuador*. Quito: Corporación Editora Nacional.

Vargas, J. M. 1987. *La economía política del Ecuador durante la colonia*. Quito: Corporación Editora Nacional.

Wallerstein, E. 1974. *The Modern World-System*. New York: Academic Press.

CHAPTER EIGHT

POLITICS AS A DETERMINANT
OF ECONOMIC PERFORMANCE:
THE CASE OF FINLAND

Tarmo Haavisto and Ari Kokko

Introduction

The development of the Finnish economy over the past 100 to 150 years has in many respects been similar to that of the other Scandinavian economies. As the previous chapters have shown, four key factors—domestic natural resources, innovative private entrepreneurs, a well-educated and technically skilled labor force, and opportunities to participate in international trade— have been essential for long-run development and growth in all of the Scandinavian countries, including Finland. Together, these factors have made it possible to build a competitive productive base and have helped the countries to develop from positions as peripheral raw material producers to advanced industrial nations, with per capita incomes at the top of the international scale.

However, Finnish history differs from that of the other Scandinavian countries in one important respect. Economic development and growth was relatively late and uneven in Finland, and there was for a long time a clear gap in income and productivity between Finland and the other Scandinavian countries. The difference with respect to Sweden (which is most similar to Finland in terms of natural endowments and other characteristics) is estimated to have been around 25 percent of average GDP per capita before the First World War, and remained unchanged or even increased somewhat during the period up to 1950.[1] Compared with the distance between high income and middle income countries today, this difference may appear modest. Never-

---

* The authors wish to thank the members of the project group and Ricardo Ffrench-Davis for valuable comments to earlier drafts.

[1] Estimates differ depending on source. According to Maddison and Alestalo, the income gap increased to nearly 40 percent by 1950 (Maddison 1977, 126; Alestalo 1986, Table 1); Maddison and Hjerppe assert that it remained largely unchanged (Maddison 1982; Hjerppe 1988, 50).

theless, it represented a distinct gap in the level of development, which was quite apparent in, for example, the differences in economic structure. Before World War I, 80 percent of the economically active population in Finland was employed in agriculture, compared to less than 50 percent in Sweden. In 1950, Finland was still a primarily agricultural economy, with almost half of the population in that sector; by that time, the employment share of Swedish agriculture had fallen to about 20 percent. (Alestalo, Andorka, and Harcsa 1987, 13; Jörberg and Krantz 1976, 384).

At the same time, social and institutional development in Finland was correspondingly less advanced, and some of the distinctive features of the Scandinavian welfare state were lacking until well into the 1960s or 1970s. Most notably, the move towards corporatism in the structure and conduct of the labor market occurred much later in Finland than in the other Nordic countries. Less than 30 percent of the Finnish labor force was organized in unions in 1950, when the corresponding figure for the rest of Scandinavia was more than twice as high; at that time, the rate for Sweden was already 76 percent (Kosonen 1987, 165). Collective bargaining in Finland did not appear until after the wars, whereas it had been introduced in the neighboring countries already in the interwar period. Full employment was not a major policy goal until the recent decades, while in the other countries, most notably Sweden, deliberate deficit financing of government budgets in order to keep demand and employment high began during the Great Depression in the 1930s.[2]

On the other hand, extremely rapid structural changes have taken place in Finland after the 1950s. Growth rates have generally been higher than in the rest of the region, and many of the differences with respect to the neighboring countries have disappeared. For example, the income gap with respect to Sweden converged to less than 5 percent of per capita incomes by the late 1980s, and Finland has now evolved to a welfare state of the Scandinavian type. These particular features of Finnish development pose some questions that may also have important implications for today's developing nations: Why didn't Finland begin to catch up to the Swedish lead before the 1950s? What factors explain the fast development thereafter? What can the Finnish story tell about the development of welfare states?

The emergence of the welfare state—including the evolution of economic and social institutions and rules for the market—is difficult to trace. But a brief look at the convergence theory, which explicitly tries to explain relative growth rates, is useful in determining why Finland lagged behind, and helps isolate some of the factors that have characterized Finnish development. From this, it will later be possible to return to discuss the welfare state. The

---

[2] The characteristics of the Scandinavian welfare state will not be discussed in much further detail. For a good overview, see Eriksson, Hansen, Ringen, and Uusitalo 1987.

convergence hypothesis, in its crudest form, simply asserts that the growth rates of productivity (and thereby income) are inversely related to the initial levels of productivity. [3] The more backward a country, the higher the rate of productivity growth achievable by borrowing technology from the more advanced nations.

Recent evidence seems to verify the existence of simple convergence of this sort, at least among the industrialized nations. For example, growth rates of GDP per capita for OECD countries over the period 1870-1970 have a significant negative correlation with initial income levels (Baumol, Blackman, and Wolff 1989, Chapter 5). However, it is not surprising to find strong convergence in an *ex post* sample of successful countries. On the contrary, any sample group which is relatively homogeneous today probably exhibited larger variations in its characteristics a century ago. Therefore, some important additions have been made to the convergence hypothesis. The role of education is emphasized by Baumol, Blackman, and Wolff (1989), who use a considerably larger sample, and find that the introduction of educational variables helps explain most cases where convergence has not occurred. Abramowitz (1986) stresses the point that backwardness only carries a *potential* for rapid growth. To fulfill this potential, it is necessary for the social capabilities of the less developed country—in terms of level of education and technical competence, and commercial, financial and political institutions—to be relatively advanced. Hence, convergence of a notable scale can only be expected when the laggards have the capacity to successfully exploit technologies already employed by the leaders. Another variable that affects the possibilities for convergence is the degree of homogeneity in the resource endowments and demographic characteristics of leaders and followers, which increases the likelihood that the leading technologies are appropriate for the less developed country. Geographic proximity probably also enhances the convergence process by increasing the depth and frequency of the social, political, and economic contacts that underlie the diffusion of technology. Productivity and income differences between neighboring countries are more likely to disappear than differences between nations that are far apart.

For the relationship between Finland and Sweden, the standard criteria for convergence seemed to be fulfilled already during the first part of the century. The countries were—and are—not only bound together by a common border, a common history, and close social, political and economic contacts, but also largely homogeneous with respect to geographical and demographic characteristics and social capabilities. The Finnish political institutions were developed early, and universal and equal suffrage was

---

[3] For more details, see Abramowitz 1986, Baumol 1986, Baumol, Blackman, and Wolff 1989, Chapter 5.

introduced already in 1907 during Russian rule. In Sweden, this did not occur until 1921. The educational levels were more or less comparable from the first decades of this century: the development of secondary education had advanced somewhat further in Sweden, but the share of third level students was higher in Finland, even in a general European comparison. The Finnish rates of savings and investment were also comparable to or somewhat higher than those in Sweden.

Thus, the standard explanations do not fully answer the question why Finland did not catch up to the Swedish lead before the 1950s, nor do they give good answers for why growth rates accelerated and fast convergence began thereafter. In the following, it is suggested that political factors have been important determinants of economic performance, and that a shift in the general policy orientation around the 1950s explains much of the difference in growth rates. In summary, this chapter argues that policies during the interwar period favored small-scale agriculture, and allowed an inefficient economic structure based on the small family farm to survive longer than what would otherwise have been the case. A major reason for this "rural bias" was the need to improve living conditions for the rural population and neutralize the social unrest that led to the Civil War in 1918. Policies after World War II, in contrast, were marked by a shift in emphasis from agriculture to manufacturing, and a growing concern for the international competitiveness of industry. Here, the relation to the Soviet Union played an important role, both because the war reparations forced Finland to concentrate resources on the industrial sector and because the Soviet market was opened to Finnish exporters. In addition, the domestic political structure grew to resemble that in the rest of Scandinavia, which made it possible to begin to develop the Finnish welfare state.

The remainder of this chapter is organized as follows. The first section briefly describes the development of the Finnish economy before independence and the emergence of the class conflicts leading up to the Civil War. Thereafter, the interwar period and the rural bias are discussed. The third section concentrates on the postwar period and the reasons for the accelerating growth rates. The final section comments on the development of welfare states of the Scandinavian model.

Finland Before Independence: Economic Development with Class Conflicts

In the middle of the nineteenth century, Finland was undoubtedly one of the poorest and least developed nations in Europe. The earliest available cross-country comparisons of income levels show that Finnish GDP per capita around 1870 was still lower than anywhere else in Western Europe (Maddison 1982, 8). Agriculture was the overwhelmingly dominant economic sector, but suffered from low productivity because of inefficient production technologies, poor soil quality, and unfavorable climate. All of these weaknesses had been brutally revealed in 1867-1868, when Finland was struck by the last serious peacetime famine in Western Europe, which cost the lives of nearly 10 percent of its population—for some regions, the death rate was closer to 20 percent (Lefgren 1973).

Important advances had already been made, however, during the first half of the century, and it seemed likely that Finnish economic development would follow the same pattern as in the other Scandinavian countries. For centuries, Finland had been a peripheral part of Sweden and subordinated to decisions made in Stockholm (which might partly have explained the low level of development). The Swedish defeat in the war against Russia in 1809, which led to Russian supremacy over the Finns, changed this and led to important institutional reforms. A separate Finnish state was created within the Russian empire as a markedly autonomous Grand Duchy under the tsar's direct rule. Government and law in the new state were managed largely without Russian interference: in principle, only the governor general was appointed by the tsar. The Finnish language gained official status on the same terms as Swedish and came to dominate also in literature and culture. These changes reinforced the national identity, and laid a base for overall development.[4]

Economic development was also directly influenced by the union, particularly after the middle of the century. A national currency, wholly independent from the ruble and fixed to the gold standard, was established in 1860, and helped to accelerate the growth of the market economy. After the 1850s, the early stages of the industrialization process were nourished by the removal of the tariffs on Finnish exports to the Russian market. The first Finnish textile factories, sawmills, paper factories, and ironworks date back to this time, and emerged partly as a response to the opening of these export opportunities.

The fast growth of the forest industry was particularly notable. There, exports of raw wood and sawn products to England and Germany added to the demand from Russia and boosted production. Domestic demand for both consumer goods and machinery was stimulated by the exports, so that the effects spread to most other parts of the economy. As in the rest of Scandinavia, private entrepreneurs and innovators, including some foreigners, played an important role in this growth process. In all, the pattern of export-led industrial development had many similarities to that of Sweden.

The structural transformation of the agricultural sector made necessary by the falling relative prices of grains during the second half of the century was another parallel to the Swedish case. The emergence of cheap American

---

[4] See Pihkala 1985.

grain and tariff-free imports from Russia made grain production unprofit-able, and forced Finnish farmers to turn to animal husbandry and dairy production. Undoubtedly, the shift was warranted, considering the com-parative advantages of the country: earlier, grain farming had been a necessity rather than a choice, but now incomes from timber sales facilitated an improvement in the use of resources. As a result, total production expanded, the degree of commercialization increased and, as in Sweden, butter became an important export product, accounting for some 20 percent of total exports at the turn of the century.

In spite of these obvious similarities, there were also important differ-ences between the developments in Finland and the rest of Scandinavia during the nineteenth century. First, the exports of manufactured goods had from the beginning been almost exclusively directed to the protected Russian market. Finland's advantaged position there deteriorated towards the end of the century, as tariffs were introduced and gradually increased to protect Russian infant industry. The domestic market was still too small to support the industries that had been most export oriented, and only a few producers were able to compete in other foreign markets. At the same time, there were attempts to limit Finnish independence on other fronts, e.g., culture and education, which culminated with the February manifesto in 1899. This manifesto marked a "russification" program that included, among other measures, the abolition of the Finnish military, an edict on the use of Russian in education and administration, and an integration of the two countries' postal systems. Both the industrialization process and the general rate of development therefore slowed down, and the secondary and tertiary sectors remained much smaller than in Sweden.

In agriculture, the differences were more serious. Living conditions for large parts of the rural population improved only slightly or not at all during the latter part of the nineteenth century, in spite of better farming methods and increases in agricultural production. One reason was that only the larger landowners, who could raise money for the necessary capital inputs by selling timber to the expanding wood industry, benefitted much from the change to dairy production and the improvements in farming technologies. Another reason was that rural population increases led to shortages of land and a large oversupply of labor in the countryside. Industry was less advanced than in Sweden, where it had absorbed much of the excess rural labor. Overseas emigration was also smaller than in Sweden and Norway, probably because fewer people could afford to pay the price for the journey to America. Instead, tenant farming became common and the number of rural laborers grew; yet, widespread unemployment and underemployment could not be avoided. In short, a large rural proletariat was formed.

These matters constituted perhaps the most important difference between Finland and the other Scandinavian countries during the nineteenth century: whereas the transition from primary to secondary sectors was managed

Table 8.1. Landholding Structure in Finland, 1910

Farm size, hectares of arable land	Distribution of farms by size group		
	Total %	Freehold %	Tenant %
0.5–5	54	35	78
5–10	23	29	15
10–25	17	25	6
25–100	6	10	1
100–	0	1	0
Number of farms	221,239	125,172	96,167

Source: Peltonen, 1988, 32.

relatively smoothly in Sweden, Norway, and Denmark, serious social and political problems were encountered in Finland. They would, as will be seen, come to have profound effects on the country's development over the following century, not only as major causes for the Civil War in 1918, but also as important determinants of the policies in the following three decades.

Worsening Income Distribution and Class Conflicts Before the Civil War

The rapid population growth and the inability of the urban sectors to absorb labor, as noted above, led to a deterioration in the income distribution, the emergence of different forms of leaseholding, and the growth of a large class of landless rural laborers. According to data from 1901, only 23 percent of all rural households owned land, while 34 percent farmed rented land and 43 percent were landless (Rasila 1982, 142). Statistics on agricultural structure according to size and type of landholding supplement the picture. Over two-fifths of the farms with more than 0.5 hectares of arable land (and nearly three-fifths including also smaller holdings) were tenant farms in 1910, as Table 8.1 shows.

The development toward increased tenant farming led to poverty and low living standards for the majority of the rural population. By tradition, the tenancy contracts for both the crofters (who made their main livelihood from farming) and the cottagers (who had smaller landholdings and were more dependent on other employment) stipulated that land rents were to be paid in labor.[5] This meant, in practice, that the conditions for the tenants were becoming worse over time as the value of the direct land rents increased with the rising wage levels. Lease conditions also became tougher. For instance, increasing timber prices led to restrictions on the tenants' rights to sell timber

---

[5] According to Peltonen 1988, 41, 72 percent of the total land rent was paid in labor in 1912.

from their leaseholdings: earlier, this had constituted an important source of cash income. It is estimated that the income for tenant farmers only reached some 40-70 percent of that for comparable freehold farms (Peltonen 1988, 42). The working conditions for the rural laborers were equally tough or worse. The ones who found employment worked long hours for low wages, but increasing unemployment and underemployment were the most serious problems.

The worsening living conditions led to social unrest and serious discontent among the rural people. From the beginning of the twentieth century, there were increasingly frequent demands for improvements. The Conservatives, including the free farmers and landlords who gained from the leaseholding system, were unwilling to accommodate such reforms. The newly established Social Democrats, on the other hand, adopted the tenants' and landless agricultural workers' requirements into their programs. By themselves, the labor parties were weak, since the industrial sector was still small and the waged laborers were few and unorganized. By taking up the demands of the rural groups, they gained an important ally to the "Red" side. The Social Democrats managed to become an important political force already in 1907, when universal suffrage was introduced, and won the majority of the seats in the Parliament in the 1916 elections. Thus, largely as a result of their close ties with the countryside, the Social Democrats made their parliamentary breakthrough in Finland earlier than in the other more industrialized Scandinavian countries.

The Finnish Socialists' rapid advances and their close contacts with the Russian Bolsheviks, however, led to a serious polarization of the political spectrum. The opposition, the more nationalistic Conservative and Agrarian Parties, feared both the domestic Socialists' radical demands for reforms and the threat of Russian nationalism (which had been evident ever since the February manifesto in 1899) and Bolshevism, and turned to Germany and Sweden for support. The political situation was, therefore, very unstable, in spite of the Social Democrats' clear parliamentary majority, and equilibrium could be maintained only as long as the tsar's administration and army stayed in power and upheld law and order.

The Civil War

The Russian revolution in 1917 broke the peace and triggered a series of dramatic events. Fearing a spreading Bolshevik revolution, Finnish conservatives and nationalists declared the country's independence in December 1917, with strong support from Germany. However, the country was in a more or less chaotic state, since the Bolshevik victory had suddenly eliminated the ruling Russian administration and army. A direct confrontation between the opposing political forces was almost unavoidable. In January 1918, the Reds set up their own administration in Helsinki, and forced the

"White" government to flee north to Vasa in Ostrobothnia. The Civil War had started.[6]

In May 1918, the war was won by the Whites with the help of German troops. The son-in-law of the German Kaiser, Prince Fredrik Karl of Hessen, was elected the king of Finland, but he was never installed as a monarch. The German front in the First World War collapsed during the autumn of 1918, and Fredrik Karl was forced to decline the crown. Instead, the commander of the White army, General Mannerheim, signed a new constitution in July 1919, and the country's first president was elected shortly thereafter.

Between the World Wars: Land Reforms, Rural Bias, and Inward-Looking Policies

The Civil War had established the political right wing in a superior position, but it was evident that the political and social problems underlying the war had not been solved. As long as the ownership structure and the living conditions in the countryside remained unchanged, there also remained a threat against the new Finnish nation. The fear of a new peasant revolution, made worse by the proximity of the communist Soviet Union, forced even the political right to realize that radical improvements for the majority of the rural people were necessary. The first measures were taken in the form of two land reforms which were, in fact, set up and administered almost entirely by the conservative National Coalition and the Agrarian Union—the other parties did not actively take part in most of this work (Ahvenainen and Vartiainen 1982, 187). The reforms were not unique for Finland: in the same way, "green revolutions" took place in virtually all the countries "on the western fringe of the red revolution in Russia" (Heaton 1966, 472). As in Finland, the reasons were not based on economic or social arguments, but rather on what was perceived as a political necessity. As noted by Derek Urwin:

> "There is sufficient evidence to suggest that the driving motive was fear and anticipation of future peasant revolutions. The national elites were not disposed toward land reform because of western influence and the penetration of western culture, but rather because of traditional peasant commitments and the size of the rural population" (Urwin 1980, 68-69).

Therefore, the aim of the land reforms was to eliminate the political threat from the left by transforming the rural proletariat into independent farmers. As a first step, the crofter system was abolished in 1918. All tenants leasing private lands were given the right to redeem their leaseholdings at

---

[6] See Rasila 1969 and Jutikkala 1962 for a more detailed analysis of the events surrounding the Civil War.

prices estimated according to the 1914 price level, with an amortization period of thirty-seven years (Rasila 1982, 144). This meant that the real cost to the former tenants was kept very low: land prices were not adjusted to inflation, although the cost of living index had increased by a factor of ten between 1914 and 1918. The accumulated inflation during and after the Second World War also exceeded 1,000 percent, and wiped out most of the remaining debt.

The radical 1922 Land Laws made up the next step, providing that all landless citizens with some minimum agricultural skills were entitled to land for farming purposes. The title that could be claimed according to the laws was maximized to 20 hectares of arable land and an additional 20 hectares of forest (in northern Finland, 75 hectares of forest), although most of the newly established farms were considerably smaller. Land was to be taken mainly from state and company properties, but rules for partition and redemption of private lands were also formulated. (In the end, only a few thousand hectares of private lands were ever redeemed, as the number of voluntary transactions turned out to be higher than expected). The prices of land were set by the state, and credit was provided on favorable terms. Loans and grants for the clearing of new farmland were also introduced (Jutikkala 1982, 208-211).

The land reforms led to great changes in the countryside. During the first decades after independence, the tenant farmers disappeared almost entirely and the number of landless rural laborers decreased significantly. Instead, and exactly according to the objectives of the land reforms, the share of independent farmers in the rural population increased rapidly. By 1940, the share of owner-occupied farms was among the highest in Europe (Alestalo, Andorka and Harcsa 1987, 20). They made up over 70 percent of all rural households, to be compared with the estimated 23 percent in the beginning of the century.

The impact on economic policies and political structure was even larger. The release from the burden of land rents and the access to land had undoubtedly improved the economic position of the laborers and former tenants, but most farms were still too small to provide an acceptable standard of living. In fact, the land reforms had actually led to a fall in the average size of farms. The political stability that was sought could not be achieved with a majority of rural households on or below the poverty line, regardless of whether or not they formally owned their farms. Further measures were necessary. Economic policies had to have a rural bias so that even the small farms could survive.

Economic Policies and Agricultural Expansion after the Civil War

Finnish agriculture moved away from grain farming and became increasingly specialized in animal husbandry around the turn of the century, both because of the rising world market prices of butter, and because Russian grain could be imported without tariffs. One of the first measures after independence was to set up protection for grain farming. Earlier, there had been tariffs on imports from outside the Finnish-Russian market—these tariffs were reestablished at approximately the old rates, but now they provided effective protection since the inflow of duty-free Russian grain had been cut off. The rates were increased in several steps during the 1920s, and corresponded to roughly a fifth of the domestic prices until the Great Depression in the early 1930s, when world market prices fell dramatically. In the 1931-1935 period, grain tariffs were well over 100 percent of CIF prices (Jutikkala 1982, 213).

Protection was also extended to animal products, but remained insignificant in comparison with export premiums and subsidies. Costs in animal husbandry had increased with the increasing domestic grain prices. As a compensation, export premiums, which allowed exporters of pork and eggs duty-free imports of fodder grains and fats, were introduced in 1928. Some years later, the premiums were converted to outright export subsidies. Concerning dairy products, butter had traditionally been the most important export good next to forest products. Before the Great Depression, special support was not considered necessary, but falling prices on the export markets led to subsidies also for butter and cheese exports after 1933. As intended, exports increased, but not to very high levels. Instead, the main benefit to the farmers was that domestic prices increased by the whole amount of the subsidy. In addition, subsidies on inputs like fertilizers and new varieties of seeds kept costs low.

With the stimulus of these policies (and an unusually warm climate during the whole interwar period) agricultural output expanded quickly, and the self-sufficiency targets were approached rapidly.[7] Even though the population was growing, it was possible to limit imports to only 10 percent of total consumption by the end of the 1930s; before the First World War, the import share had been 61 percent (Jutikkala 1982, 219). Production of bread grains more than doubled during the interwar period, and production of butter, cheese, eggs, and pork came to exceed domestic consumption.

The emphasis on agriculture in economic policies meant that the real income development of the rural population was more advantageous than that of any other population group, even though productivity growth was slower than in both industry and services.[8] In other words, real resources were transferred to agriculture from the other sectors, in striking contrast to

---

[7] Jutikkala notes that the warm weather acted as if it "shifted the whole country 300 or 400 kilometers to the south" (Jutikkala 1982, 207).

[8] Average labor productivity growth in industry in the 1920-1938 period was 4.3 percent per year compared to 1.9 percent in agriculture (Hjerppe 1988, Table 15, 95).

policies in today's developing countries where an "urban bias" is the rule. The improvements in the rural living conditions were sufficient to lead to a notable expansion in the number of farmers, so that total labor input did not fall in spite of the beginning of mechanization of production and the fall in the number of rural laborers. The number of farms with more than 2 hectares of arable land increased from 185,000 to 235,000 between 1920 and 1940. The amount of arable land increased by about one-third during the same period, from 2.015 million hectares to 2.631 million hectares (Alestalo, Andorka and Harcsa 1987, 21; Jutikkala 1982, 211).

Of course, these policies were not inexpensive. Average incomes stayed low because people were not encouraged to move from agriculture to industry, where average labor productivity was twice as high (Hjerppe 1988, 95). Also, the degree of commercialization of agriculture fell because of the increasing share of the small, self-sufficient family farms that retained most of their production for their own consumption. This held down domestic demand for manufactured goods.

Agricultural Support and Political Structure between the Wars

The first stages of the comprehensive support to agriculture had not been difficult to realize. The ideologically based arguments for the land reforms were extended to embrace agricultural support in general. The food shortages that had plagued the country during and after the war were still fresh in everyone's memory, contributing to the general acceptance of rural devel-opment and food self-sufficiency as important goals. However, the urgency of these arguments decreased with time. Instead, changes in the political structure made agricultural support more or less self-generating. The votes of the new, small independent farmers, many of whom had probably belonged to the leftist block before the Civil War, made the Agrarian Union the most important actor in the ruling political block. Excluding two short-lived minority governments in the late 1920s, the Agrarians were strongly represented in all governments before World War II, and could argue forcefully for continued agricultural support. In addition, there was a strong consensus within the Agrarian Union for these policies, whereas there had been some resistance to the original land reforms. An important cornerstone of the party was formed by the largest landowners, who had lost both the labor of the crofters and considerable land areas almost without any real com-pensation. The crofter liberalization might have been an unpleasant neces-sity, but there were no reservations concerning the tariff protection and the subsidies, although they were nominally designed to benefit the majority of smaller landowners. Since the large farmers were more commercialized and most of the agricultural support was based on the quantities produced for the market, they had even more to gain than small farmers.

The Social Democrats, who had moved back toward their "natural" voter base, the urban proletariat, represented the only real opposition to the protection of agriculture, since it increased food prices and lowered urban real wages. From their weaker position, they were unable to change the direction of the policies, and the brief Social Democratic minority government in 1928 actually fell on a proposition to abolish the tariffs on barley and rye.

Continuing Emphasis on Agriculture: Effects of World War II

In the late 1930s, signs of changing agricultural policies appeared. In domestic politics, the agricultural support seemed to have neutralized the immediate threat from the left, but the political climate was still much tougher than in the rest of Scandinavia, and there was a real threat of a takeover by the extreme right wing in the early 1930s (Alestalo and Kuhnle 1987, 29 ff.; Kalela 1987). In response, the parties in the center joined forces, and the first red-green coalition government between Agrarians and Social Democrats was installed in 1936. The self-sufficiency targets were also approached, as noted, and overproduction of grains (particularly rye) began to be noticed. Since the most urgent causes for the rural bias were eroding, some cautious steps were taken toward a more efficient agricultural structure. A revision of tariffs and land policies in 1938 indicated a change away from unrestricted support. Tariffs were lowered, and support to new settlements was cancelled. Instead, mechanization and expansion of the size of existing holdings were to become priorities.

The Second World War broke out before any significant redirections of agricultural policy had been made. The war ended in the loss of about 12 percent of the total territory to the Soviet Union. Karelia, the southeastern part of the country, which had been a major agricultural region, was one of the lost areas, and nearly half a million people were evacuated to be resettled elsewhere in Finland.

The reconstruction of productive capacity, the large war reparations to the Soviet Union, and the Finnish declination of the Marshall Aid program limited the investment possibilities, so that relatively few of the evacuees from Karelia could be resettled in urban centers or directed to industrial employment. Instead, a new land reform was instituted. Most of the Karelian families were given small plots of land and were expected to continue as farmers, although generally on smaller and less productive farms than before. Some 70,000 demobilized front soldiers were also included in the resettlement program. Almost all farms with more than 20 hectares of arable land were forced to give up parts of their holdings to the refugees, and a total of 123,000 hectares of new farmland were cleared. In all, including forest land, almost 2.8 million hectares were redistributed in the resettlement program, i.e., almost twice as much as during the crofter liberalization. As a result, average farm size fell from around 10 hectares in 1941 to less than

9 hectares in 1950, with even larger reductions in average field area (Pihkala 1982, 342-345 and 395).

Again, this committed future economic policies to strongly support agriculture for many years, since even the weaker newcomers had to survive on their land. The redirection of agricultural policies that had been announced in 1938 was forgotten and not taken up again until the end of the 1950s. The number of farms continued increasing to a maximum of about 331,000 in 1959, which must have been quite exceptional in the Western European context (Hjerppe 1988, 70). Not until that time did agricultural policies change distinctly to favor larger holdings and higher productivity. By then, economic policies in general had already been directed in favor of industry for several years.

The interests vested in agriculture have had enough political weight to conserve the strong support also after the 1950s. Taking both direct subsidies and price controls into account, total support is presently estimated to be in the vicinity of 90 percent of average agricultural net incomes, in spite of the change in production structure toward larger units and seemingly more productive methods (Pihkala 1982, 395; Alestalo, Andorka and Harcsa 1987, 50). Another sign of this is that in the 1980s, the agrarian parties still have stronger parliamentary representation in Finland than anywhere else in Western Europe, with over a quarter of the votes (Pesonen and Rantala 1985, 221).

Industrial Policies and Trade Policies in the Interwar Period

In comparison with agricultural policy, the lack of any direct industrial policy in the interwar period appears obvious. Outside the agricultural sector, economic policies throughout the whole period were characterized by a conservative liberalism with heavy reliance on market forces, and the aim was to minimize the role of the public sector. An example of this conservatism was the continuing ambition to balance the government budget: deficits were not accepted even during the Great Depression of 1929-1933, which led to the breakthrough of Keynesian ideas in Sweden.[9]

Formal industrial policy was limited to development of infrastructure, including education, and support to investment through beneficial tax rules.[10] During and immediately after the First World War, several foreign companies in the country had also been bought up by the state. These companies— including Kemira, Enso-Gutzeit, and Outokumpu—formed the base of a relatively large state-owned industry, using Scandinavian standards: to the

---

[9] See Kalela 1987, 65 ff. for more details.
[10] Ahvenainen and Vartiainen 1982 present a more detailed survey.

present, its GDP share has fluctuated around 5 percent. The firms have, however, generally been administered strictly on the basis of economic profitability and have complemented the existing production structure by entering into fields with high risks or particularly high capital require-ments—mining, power production, and chemical fertilizers. Direct compe-tition with private domestic entrepreneurs has been rare, but competing imports have usually put pressure on the state-owned companies and assured efficiency (Ahvenainen and Vartiainen 1982, 183-184).

Trade and exchange rate policies had a more important impact on the industrial sector. The Civil War and the Russian Revolution froze most contacts with Russia, where many industries had enjoyed large markets thanks to the customs union. The most important of these was the paper and pulp industry, but metal products, textiles, and many other consumer goods had also been exported to the East. It turned out that only the forest industries were competitive enough to be able to redirect exports to the West; the other producers had to rely on the home market demand. The redirection of production was greatly eased by the exchange rate policies immediately after the war. Unlike most other countries, Finland did not attempt to (and was not able to) return to the prewar gold standard. Instead, the Finnish mark devalued by almost 80 percent with respect to the dollar and the pound, which improved the competitiveness both for wood and paper exports and for the domestic import substituting producers. The currency did not stabilize until the export industry found its markets after 1922.

At that time, the growth of international protectionism had already begun to be noticed, and escalated to an outright tariff war in the early 1930s; bilaterally balanced trade accounts also became common. Finnish develop-ment followed the international trends, and the average tariffs in the interwar period rose to around 20 percent.[11] Outside the already established forest industry, exports were, at best, seen as a way to complement domestic demand and fill up capacity, although a new devaluation in the early 1930s improved the international competitiveness of many Finnish products.

Wood and paper exports were the important exception, and their continuing success also benefitted other industries that had lost their Russian export markets. The export revenues financed some of the investment that was needed for the shift to import substitution, and demand for inputs and capital goods for wood and paper production itself stimulated domestic producers in several industries. Not least importantly, the larger farmers' incomes from sales of timber increased domestic demand for a multitude of consumer goods. The growth rate of industrial output was, therefore,

---

[11] Before 1913, tariffs had averaged around 10 percent (Hjerppe 1988, 133).

remarkably high even during this period, although from a very low base.[12]

However, looking at the entire economy, the share of agriculture remained high, agricultural productivity was low, and the income gap with respect to more industrialized countries remained large. At the same time, it must be noted that the polarization of the political spectrum was halted and the threatening class conflicts were largely neutralized: in the long run, this might have been the most important consequence of the interwar policies, as will be discussed later.

The Post-War Period: Policies for Growth and Competitiveness

The likelihood that Finland would catch up with the other Scandinavian countries seemed, in many ways, even smaller after World War II than before. The Finnish economy had been seriously hurt by the war—over 88,000 lives had been lost, large parts of the capital stock had been destroyed, and 12 percent of the territory had been annexed by the Soviet Union— whereas its Scandinavian neighbors had been left relatively unharmed. A heavy burden was added by the war reparations to the Soviet Union, which at worst, between 1945 and 1948, corresponded to 5-6 percent of GDP. [13] Since the Soviet Union claimed the bulk of these payments in machinery and metal products, much of the capacity of the metal industry was also locked up until the early 1950s. On the international scene, Finland chose to stay outside the Marshall Aid program that was a decisive stimulus to recovery and growth in most other Western European countries. In domestic policies, the support to agriculture continued at a high level, sustained by the 1945 land reforms and the resettlement of the Karelian evacuees.

Nevertheless, the years after the war marked the beginning of fast growth and convergence. As seen in Table 8.2, the average yearly growth rates of GDP during the period 1950-1979 were higher in Finland than in the other Scandinavian countries (with the exception of the late 1970s, when the Norwegian economy began to profit from the North Sea oil). As a result, the gap in per capita incomes compared to Denmark and Sweden diminished to less than 5 percent by the late 1980s; meanwhile, oil revenues have brought

---

[12] The average growth rate of industrial output in the 1920-1938 period is estimated at 7.9 percent per year (Hjerppe 1988, 65). However, the impact of the Civil War on industry was very severe, and the volume of output in 1918 had fallen below the level of 1897. This low base might bias the growth figures upwards. Yet, industrial growth was rapid even taking this into account. The average annual growth rate between 1913 and 1938 was about 5 percent: this figure, in turn, is biased downwards, since it includes the war years, when output fell significantly.

[13] Pihkala 1982, 342, and 354. Contemporary estimates were considerably higher, at between 10 and 15 percent of GDP (Jörberg and Krantz 1976, 430).

Table 8.2. Average Yearly Growth Rates of GDP for Finland, Denmark, Norway and Sweden, 1950–1979, Five-Year Periods
(Percent)

	1950–54	1955–59	1960–64	1965–69	1970–74	1975–79
Finland	5.5	3.6	5.8	4.3	5.4	2.3
Denmark	2.6	3.1	5.6	4.3	2.7	2.6
Norway	4.3	2.8	4.5	4.4	4.2	4.8
Sweden	3.5	3.3	5.2	3.6	3.4	1.5

Source: Kosonen 1987, Table 6.2, 154.

Norway to the top of the Scandinavian income league. The structural changes over the same period occurred even faster. The share of the primary sector in total employment fell from almost 50 percent in 1950 to about 10 percent in 1985, while both industry and services expanded their shares correspondingly.

Finland has also caught up with the neighboring countries in the field of social and institutional development, and has become a welfare state of the Scandinavian model. In the 1980s, the Finnish social security system, the role of the state in health care and education, and the corporatist development of the labor market with collective bargaining and close contacts between labor, capital, and the state, are all comparable to conditions in the rest of Scandinavia.

Against the background of the rural bias of the interwar years and the wartime losses, it seems clear that the fast development after the 1950s could not have been generated without important changes in policies. The overall direction of policies has indeed shifted significantly to support industrial growth and competitiveness and a higher outward orientation. Like the rural policy bias during the 1920s and 1930s, postwar policies have also emerged in response to political events and political motives. Before the policy changes are discussed in detail, however, it is necessary to look once more at the development in the agricultural sector. Because of the interwar policies and the resettlement program, agriculture still accounted for almost half of total employment around 1950, much of which was in small inefficient family farms. This implied not only that the economy was weak and unproductive, but also that a tremendous potential for growth existed—all opportunities for growth had simply not been exploited because of the earlier policies. With the gradual erosion of the policy bias favoring small-scale agriculture (combined with increases in agricultural productivity and rural population) followed a change towards a more sound economic structure. This effect, which came from the removal of obstacles to structural change, would have stimulated fast growth even if nothing else had happened with policies and ideology. The stagnant character of the interwar years, hence, made up an important precondition for the magnitude and speed of the subsequent changes.

Weakening Rural Bias and Structural Change

In the aftermath of World War II, the resettlement of the Karelian refugees again committed economic policies to agricultural support, as seen earlier. The first years after the war were marked by strict state control of agricultural prices and distribution, with recurrent revisions of product prices to keep the farmers' incomes at an acceptable level. However, the high inflation rate and wage increases in industry meant that agricultural incomes kept lagging behind, which created a heated political debate about income distribution: the farmers' demands for higher prices were countered by the growing urban population's demands for real wage increases. The political compromise in 1947 (which paralleled the Swedish agricultural policies of the early 1930s) prescribing direct state subsidies to the farmers in return for constraints on the increases of consumer prices for food products moderated this conflict and was an important turning point for the agricultural policies.[14]

From 1951 until the end of the 1960s, agricultural prices and incomes were indexed to the overall income development in the economy; thereafter, they have been included in the general income policy agreements together with other wages, taxes, and social policies.[15] For some time, these policies continued the emphasis on small-scale agriculture, and the number of farms continued growing during the 1950s, as we have seen above. However, the change in the structure of agricultural support—from direct financing through high consumer prices toward producer prices and subsidies via the government budget—changed the rules of the game. Labor productivity in industry grew by almost 5 percent per year in the period 1946-1960, whereas agricultural productivity growth remained under 3 percent, so that the amount of subsidies needed to secure acceptable living standards for the rural majority increased just as steadily (Hjerppe 1982, 95). This put heavy pressure on the government budget, and contributed to the state's bias in favor of larger production units and more efficient methods of production during the late 1950s. At that time, overproduction was also beginning to be a serious problem.

The main measure to increase farm sizes was the establishment of credit facilities to allow the farmers to purchase and clear new land, and to avoid the partition of estates when the younger generation took over. Consequently, the field area expanded and did not peak until 1968 (Pihkala 1982, 387). Mechanization was encouraged by tax policies, and the number of tractors and other agricultural machines grew rapidly during the late 1950s. The

---

[14] The Swedish "cow trade" in 1932-1933 between Agrarians and Social Democrats secured political support for active stabilization and unemployment policies in exchange for agricultural protection (Hedlund and Lundahl 1985, 52 ff).

[15] See Valtioneuvoston kanslian julkaisusarja 1985(3), 37-46 for a detailed account of the agreements.

absolute number of farmers did not begin to fall until after this time. Since the early 1970s, these measures have brought the agricultural productivity increases to almost the same level as in industry.

Several other factors were also eroding the relative strength of the rural bias already during the late 1940s, before the changes in agricultural policies took place. The increasing mechanization depressed the demand for rural labor, and the laborers who did not manage to buy their own land were among the first to leave the countryside. Most importantly, however, the rate of urbanization and structural change was speeded up by demographic changes. The population growth in the interwar period had been relatively high, around one percent per year in the 1920s, with over nine-tenths of the growth concentrated in the rural areas, where most people lived and where families were much larger than in the cities. After the Second World War, the large age groups of the 1920s were moving into the labor force, but could not find employment in their home districts. The average farm was so small that it was impossible to provide full-time employment for the second generation. Clearing of new land was still supported in the policies, but after the loss of Karelia and the resettlement program, the unused land was increasingly unsuitable for agriculture. The employment problems remained when the parents retired: the farms were usually too small to provide an acceptable living for more than one of the children.

The sons and daughters of farmers were, therefore, forced to seek employment in the urban areas, which led to a fall in the population and employment shares of agriculture from the first postwar years. Meanwhile, the birth rate in the rural areas accelerated again with very large age groups in the 1946-1950 period. In the 1960s, this fed the rate of rural-urban migration in a similar way as in the early 1950s, independently of the orientation of economic policies. By that time, migration from Finland to Sweden had also become important: over 200,000 people, mostly younger people from the rural areas, moved to Sweden between 1960 and 1970. This undoubtedly made the structural transformation easier, since it moderated the need to create new employment in the domestic industry and service sectors. Thus, the fast urbanization has largely been an intergenerational phenomenon. Most farms, even the smaller ones, survived as long as the older generation was still able to work, and so the real fall in the number of farms did not occur until the 1960s and 1970s, when these generations retired (Kosonen 1987, 162).

Summing up the discussion about the role of agriculture, it can be noted that the agricultural sector has decisively influenced Finnish political and economic development in three different manners in three different periods. In the late nineteenth century, the oversupply of rural labor could not be absorbed by any other sector, and created serious social and political problems. In the interwar period, a "rural bias" emerged as the result of the wish (which coincided with the larger landowners own interest in subsidies and protection) to neutralize these social problems. Thus, structural change and economic growth were constrained. After the war, a gradual adjustment process has been possible as industry and services (and migration to Sweden) have absorbed the rural labor surpluses. With this transformation of the economy, rapid growth and convergence have followed.

Postwar Recovery and Industrial Growth

Although changes in the agricultural sector were necessary for the transformation of the Finnish economy, there were other changes in policies that paved the way for the extremely rapid industrialization and development in the postwar period. The support to agriculture remained, as noted, but it was evident early on that a strong emphasis on industrial growth and competitiveness was replacing agricultural development and food self-sufficiency as the leading economic-political goals. The decisive shift in policies took place at the end of the war with the program for economic recovery.

The economic responsibilities of the state had grown during the war as a large part of industry had become directly involved in the wartime production, and as rationing, wage and price controls, and other rules were applied on most transactions. The central role of the state remained also after the war, when economic recovery became the primary objective. The reconstruction of infrastructure and productive capacity, the war reparations to the Soviet Union, and the resettlement of the front soldiers and the Karelian refugees required enormous amounts of capital that the private sector could not supply on its own. The state, on the other hand, could direct the available resources to the best uses and promote investment and growth.

The list of priorities was relatively easy to set up. On the domestic scene, the most important objective was considered to be the resettlement of the Karelian refugees and the demobilized front soldiers, in all over 120,000 families. Overall, however, top priority was given to the recovery of the industrial capacity, largely because of the war reparations the Soviet Union claimed in the form of complete factories, ships, machines, and other intermediate products. The development of the metal industry and the restoration of the needed power production capacity was therefore emphasized heavily. Reconstruction of the home market industry, urgent repair and maintenance work, and investments in agriculture followed further down on the list. Investment resources for housing, education, and administration were given lower priority and received few resources (Pihkala 1982, 350).

During the war, private consumption had been depressed to only about two-thirds of its prewar level and the demand for consumer goods was therefore high. However, making up for the foregone consumption was not an immediate priority. In order to keep the growth of consumption down and allocate the available goods for investments, wartime rationing was retained for several years; all commodities had not been freed from formal rationing until 1954. The structure of imports was also controlled through a strict licensing system that favored the import of raw materials and investment goods at the expense of consumption goods. In addition, wage and price controls remained, but it appears as though their role for these purposes was limited: high wage increases, with equal nominal rises for all employees, were granted immediately after the war, and wages were later indexed to the cost of living. The level of private consumption was, nevertheless, kept relatively low, particularly during the first few years after the war.

Most of the reconstruction was financed via the government budget, both by heavier taxation and considerable borrowing, but also, and maybe most importantly, through inflation. Government expenditure had accounted for only 13 percent of GDP in 1938, but increased to about a third after the war. Government incomes also increased, but not quite as rapidly, which led to large deficits. Thus, public debt increased from 5 percent to over 60 percent of GDP after the war, and continued growing in nominal terms during the following years (Pihkala 1982, 354-355). At the same time, the large wage increases in 1945, when the wages for industrial labor almost doubled, added to the high investment demand, and caused very rapid inflation. The ratio of public debt to GDP was thereby halved by 1948, in spite of continuing deficits. A new surge of inflation in the beginning of the 1950s eroded the real value of the debt further. In that way, the recovery program was largely inflation-financed, which emphasizes the "comparative advantage" of the state: it is unlikely that the massive resource accumulation and redistribution could have been managed any other way.

With the help of this administrative allocation of resources, economic recovery was relatively fast, particularly in comparison with the slower development after the Civil War. The prewar level of GDP was reached in 1947, and momentum was shifted to industry, where output in general grew by over 13 percent per year between 1945 and 1948. By 1950, private consumption per capita had also grown some 20 percent above the 1938 level (Laurila 1987, Table 10; Pihkala 1982, 347). However, agriculture lagged behind in the growth process. The production volumes from the late 1930s were not reached until some twenty years later, in spite of the continuing increase in the number of farms and the resources spent to expand the field area. The reason was partly that the land used for the new settlements was of lower quality than the lost Karelian land, but also that the shortage of foreign currencies prohibited the import of seeds, fertilizers and other inputs until the 1950s. Thus, the GDP share of industry exceeded the share of the primary sector for the first time in 1949, and economic structure was moving away from its rural bias. Industrial structure also changed, primarily because of the war reparations to the USSR.

The War Reparations

The payments of the war debt were considered so urgent that a special war reparations agency (*Soteva*), with exceptionally far-reaching authority, was set up for its administration. The agency contracted the needed production capacity, allocated investment goods and other resources, but was also empowered to expropriate raw materials, machines or whole establishments for the use of the state or private entrepreneurs (Pihkala 1982, 341-342). During the first years after the war, it directed large resources for investments in the metal industry, which was to produce most of the goods for the debt payments. The initial concentration on investment was possible since the first payments were made in the form of used ships from the Finnish merchant fleet and prefabricated wooden houses, which the wood industry could produce simply by increasing the utilization of existing capacity.[16] By 1946, the metal industry had grown enough to account for most of the debt deliveries, partly because the state-owned armaments and munitions factories had rapidly been converted to production of goods for the war reparations. Even more important was that the heavy investment and machinery imports had renewed the capital stock, so that a modern metallurgical and engineering industry was created. The metal industry's output reached above the prewar level already in 1945, and almost doubled by 1949. Its share of total industrial output increased from about 15 percent during the 1920s and 1930s to 24 percent in 1950 (Hjerppe 1982, 412; Ahvenainen and Kuusterä 1982, 224).

The final payments on the war reparations were made in 1952. By that time, the metal industry had gained a strong foothold on the Soviet market, and the political détente made it possible to continue the shipments to the East in the form of bilateral commercial trade. This proved to be of great importance for the diversification of Finnish exports and, thereby, the overall development of Finnish industry.

Soviet Trade

Finnish trade with the Soviet Union had reemerged already in 1944, soon after the truce treaty was signed between the countries. To begin with, the relation was based on pure barter trade and was of a temporary character, but a clearing agreement was signed in 1947, and the trade relation was deepened further when the Treaty of Friendship, Cooperation, and Mutual Assistance was signed in 1948. The treaty explicitly extended the political relation between the countries to include also commercial and trade relations.

---

[16] The capacity of the merchant fleet in 1945 had fallen to only 38 percent of the prewar level as a result of the deliveries to the USSR and the war destruction (Pihkala 1982, 352).

In 1951, the bilateral one-year trade agreements were replaced by the first five-year trade and payments agreements, which have been renewed regularly. The five-year agreements include rough plans for the values and quantities of goods to be exchanged during the plan periods, including payments and pricing principles. Bilateral clearing has been retained until the present, with the ruble as accounting currency. More detailed yearly plans are then added, listing the groups of commodities to be exchanged during the year.[17]

The opening up of Soviet trade after almost three decades of frozen relations had a large impact on the diversification of exports. After World War II, the forest industry's products comprised over 90 percent of total exports, whereas the metal industry made up less than 5 percent of the total. When the war reparations were completed, the metal industry turned to exporting and increased its share rapidly, to over one-third of total exports by the mid-1970s (Saralehto and Vajanne 1981, Appendix 2). Initially, the Soviet share was about four-fifths of the metal exports, but fell to only one-fifth in the early 1970s as other countries became increasingly important markets. A similar trend has been seen also for other industries, such as textiles and clothing, chemicals, and food products (Alho *et al.* 1986, Chapter 2). For individual products, the development is even more obvious. Over 80 percent of the export of ships went to the USSR in the 1950s, which fell to 70 percent in the 1960s, and 50 percent in the 1970s. Exports of equipment for the pulp and paper industry and electronics and computer technology have been built up in a similar way (Yudanov 1983, 207-208). In all, trade with the Soviet Union has come to cover almost a fifth of Finland's total trade.

Hence, looking at the pattern of geographical diversification for most nontraditional exports, it appears as though Soviet trade has served as an important stepping-stone for export to other countries. Undoubtedly, the Soviet export market has been large enough to support specialization and scale economies, which the domestic market could never have offered. This may have contributed to making Finnish products competitive also on the world markets. These effects are, however, not comprehensively researched, and constitute an interesting field for further study.[18]

The long time horizon in Soviet trade has provided another benefit for the Finnish exporters. The realized trade has followed the five-year agree-

---

[17] For a more detailed description of the trade agreements, see Alho *et al.* 1986 and Möttölä, Bykov, and Korolev 1983. However, considerable changes will take place after 1990.

[18] Kivikari 1985 and Tolonen 1985 present some analyses of this, but without conclusive results since exports to the Soviet Union and other markets have expanded concurrently. Therefore, it would be interesting to follow the sectors where the volume of East trade is presently falling. What happens to competitiveness in other markets?

ments relatively well, and it has always been possible to sell the planned quantities of goods. The deviations have instead shown up as larger trade, or, in some instances, occurred because of failure to fulfill the export plans (Hemmilä 1983). It has, therefore, been possible to plan research and development (R&D) expenditures and investments with the reassurance that costs will be recovered.

The direct employment generated by exports to the Soviet Union has increased from around 50,000 in the late 1960s, to 130,000 in the beginning of the 1980s (Alho et al. 1986, 90). This corresponds to the whole increase in total employment over the same period, and focuses attention on yet another important point, namely that the development of Soviet trade has been inversely related to the rest of Finnish trade. This countercyclical nature was particularly evident after the oil crisis in the early 1970s. The major Finnish export sectors—paper, wood products, and metal products—were all sensitive to business trends, and Western exports fell dramatically in the depression following the oil crisis. Concurrently, the value of imports from the USSR was inflated by the increasing price of oil, which was the major import commodity at that time. In that situation, it was convenient to balance the bilateral account by redirecting exports to the Soviet Union, and thereby keep capacity utilization in industry relatively high. Similarly, the negative impact of the second oil crisis in the early 1980s was reduced by the bilateral trade. It is estimated that economic performance in the period 1973-1985 would have been significantly weaker without this alternative (Alho et al. 1986, Chapter 5).

Thus, the heavy investment made for the war reparations paid off in the sense that they established Finnish industry, with the metal industry in the forefront, in the important Soviet market. From there, producers seem to have been able to diversify to third markets, thanks in part to the specialization and scale economies gained from exports to the Soviet Union, but also because of the R&D effects of the five-year agreements. Moreover, the exports to the East varied inversely with other exports, which stabilized the economic fluctuations and kept employment and capacity utilization at a high level after the oil crises.

Increasing Trade Orientation and Effects on Economic Policies

As in most other European countries, Finnish trade in the immediate postwar years was based on different bilateral clearing and barter agreements. However, unlike the rest of Western Europe, Finland retained the restrictive trade practices for more than a decade. The reconstruction after the war translated into high demand for imports, whereas export potential was still limited, particularly outside the forest industries. Strict licensing was, therefore, considered necessary, and tariffs remained at the same high level as during the interwar period, at around 20 percent. Heavy devaluations were, nevertheless, required in 1945 and 1949 to keep the balance of payments controllable.

After the improvement in export prices and the surge of demand because of the Korean War, pressure on the balance of payments decreased, and import quotas could be relaxed somewhat. Yet, the liberalization of trade did not begin until after 1955, when quotas on most raw materials and investment goods were lifted altogether. In 1957, after another devaluation of some 40 percent, most of the remaining quantitative trade restrictions were abolished, and the trade liberalization continued during the following decade with membership in EFTA (in 1961) and the removal of all tariffs on imports of industrial products from other member countries (in 1967). By 1972, average tariffs had thereby fallen to about 3 percent (Pihkala 1982, 374). During the mid-1970s, similar agreements with the EEC and the COMECON removed most remaining tariffs on industrial products. Thus, since the 1960s, trade policies have not differed significantly from those in the rest of Europe.

With the gradual relaxation of trade barriers and the effects of the exports to the Soviet Union, the volume of trade has increased at an average rate of about 7 percent per year over the postwar period (Saralehto and Vajanne 1981, Chapter 2). This development has also led to a markedly higher export orientation in the whole industrial sector. Yet, the increasing importance of trade has not been immediately apparent from aggregate statistics. The combined share of exports and imports in GDP remained constant, at around 40 percent, from the beginning of the century until the end of the 1960s, with large declines during the wars. However, the rapid growth of the tertiary sector, which comprises mainly nontradables, renders the aggregate figures misleading: the export share of the value added in primary and secondary sectors increased quickly to around 60 percent in the late 1960s and nearly 80 percent by the early 1980s (Hjerppe 1988, 134-135). Hence, the role of exports has become increasingly important, and this structural change has brought with it very specific demands on economic policies: it has become necessary to take the competitiveness of the export sector into account in the formulation of policies.

The strongest link between economic policies and concern for exports has probably been the management of the balance of payments. The largest Finnish export industries—forest products and metals—have proved to be highly sensitive to business trends, as noted earlier. During depressions in the international business cycles, the balance of payments has, therefore, immediately turned to deficits; in the worst troughs, the deficits have been large. The policy response has taken the form of recurrent devaluations. The Finnish ten-year devaluation cycle (1949, 1957, 1967, 1977-1978) is highly correlated with the major depressions in the European economy that occurred during the same period (Pihkala 1982, 385-386). To keep the entire economy strong, it has been necessary to uphold or restore the strength of the export firms, sometimes at the expense of other objectives.

For industry, this has naturally been an advantageous environment, since the state has not interfered in the workings of the economy if such actions have threatened to disturb growth, investment, and competitiveness. Most clearly, this was stated during the depressions in 1957-1958 and 1966-1968 when devaluations and restrictive monetary and fiscal policies ensured competitiveness and continued growth possibilities, but at the cost of high unemployment and falling real wages in the short run (Kosonen 1987, 185).

Thus, the key policy objectives, at least until the late 1960s, were growth, investment, and the international competitiveness of exports. These priorities were partly different than those in the other Scandinavian countries. In those countries, full employment and income distribution were main issues; in Finland they were clearly subordinated to the growth targets (Kosonen 1987, 183). The growing dependence on exports and the instability of export earnings are important explanations for this order of priorities. Stabilization policies could simply not be pursued in response to each depression in the business cycle without adverse effects on growth and competitiveness. In that situation, devaluations were the only remaining instrument. Concurrently, the political structure has contributed to push policies in the same direction, in favor of export competitiveness.

Political Structure after World War II

Unlike their Swedish and Norwegian party brothers, who dominated their political arenas, Finnish Social Democrats were relatively weak after the war, and could not pursue their own objectives—traditional social democratic policies with heavy emphasis on distributive justice and full employment—without serious resistance from the other parties. The working class was also weakly organized. In 1950, only 29 percent of the labor force was unionized, to be compared with around 70 percent for the rest of Scandinavia (Kosonen 1987, 165). Meanwhile, the Agrarians remained in the leading political role by virtue of their position between left and right, in spite of the growth in the urban working class and the gradual consolidation of the Social Democrats as the largest individual party. The political debate during the first years after the war was, therefore, focused on disputes regarding food prices and real income development for rural versus urban groups as central themes.

The 1947 compromise regarding food prices, discussed above, was the first step toward a concentration of the diverse political goals. The compromise placed the responsibility for the development of rural incomes with the state. Together with the indexation of producer prices, this meant that the level of urban incomes would more or less directly determine rural incomes as well. It also meant that the zero-sum contest for a fixed amount of resources was cancelled and replaced by a common growth objective. Instead of improving the relative position of one population group at the expense of another, it was recognized that growth would benefit everybody. With this agreement about the common general policy objectives, the red-green coalition was strengthened. Attempts to pursue the motives of both workers and farmers at the same time have, however, resulted in complicated compromises, often with many different variables involved—wages, food prices, taxes, social security benefits, and so forth. In many cases, agreements to support export competitiveness have been the easiest compromises, since exports have stood for a major contribution to growth (Hjerppe 1988, 157). The policy bias from the economic structure has thus been enhanced by the political structure.[19]

This changing focus in policies is clearly stated in the reports of the Industrialization Committee in 1951, where it is noted that industry, rather than agriculture or forestry, will be the future base of the economy (Komiteanmietintö 1951:12). Even the wide program declarations in the early 1950s by the Agrarian leader Urho Kekkonen (who became president some years later), favored industrial development, investment, and exports (Kekkonen 1952).

In summary, Finnish postwar economic development has been rapid, and has caught up with much of the lead of the more advanced industrialized countries. The convergence has been characterized by a fast structural transformation from the primary sector to industry and services. The secular weakening of the rural bias from the interwar period is a strong explanation for the structural change, but new developments have also been critical.

The reopening and consolidation of trade with the Soviet Union, under the auspices of the Treaty of Friendship, Cooperation and Mutual Assistance, is one such factor, illustrating the heavy weight of political decisions. The change in the policy orientation, from agricultural to industrial and from inward-looking to outward-oriented, is another. Thus, both economic and political factors have contributed to the emphasis on growth and international competitiveness.

Democratic Corporatism and the Finnish Welfare State

The role of political factors in the conduct and performance of the economy is perhaps most obvious in the emergence of democratic corporatism and the growth of the Finnish welfare state after the late 1960s. This has brought Finland closer to the other Scandinavian countries, but in a wider perspective, it can also be said to mark the long-run development of the small European states in contrast with economic and political developments on

---

[19] The Swedish (and Norwegian) EFO-model for wage-setting, in which the wage increases in the protected sectors are formally related to the productivity growth in the exporting industries, is a parallel to the Finnish case.

other continents. As a conclusion, the last paragraphs will, therefore, briefly sketch this development.

The political development in Sweden, Denmark, and Norway has exhibited certain features that have been characterized as democratic corporatism. In the words of Peter Katzenstein:

"Democratic corporatism is distinguished by three traits: an ideology of social partnership expressed at the national level; a relatively centralized and concentrated system of interest groups; and voluntary and informal coordination of conflicting objectives through continuous political bargaining between interest groups, state bureaucracies, and political parties. These traits make for a low-voltage politics" (Katzenstein 1985, 32).

The mobilization of the working class into strong labor unions, the growth of the Social Democrats and the emergence of the common welfare state (in Sweden termed *folkhem*, meaning "peoples home"), the centralized wage agreements, and the coalitions between rural and urban groups in all of the three countries manifested the traits of democratic corporatism already by the 1930s. Therefore, political and economic development has been marked by peaceful and almost predictable advances ever since. In more economic terms, the lack of widespread rent seeking has been characteristic; in political terms, it has been the absence of a winner-take-all mentality (Katzenstein 1985, 157).

In the Finnish case, a similar development did not occur until after the Second World War. The coalition governments with Agrarians and Social Democrats after the war laid the groundwork for comprehensive political cooperation. (The first coalition between Agrarians and Social Democrats in the 1930s was, in contrast, more an emergency response to a threatening political situation. The risk of an extreme rightist takeover was considered to be quite real). The increasing organization of the Finnish labor force, which reached the average Scandinavian level in the late 1960s, was another important precondition, evening out the power relationship between labor and capital. The general income policy solution in 1968, after several years of disturbing inflation and increasing balance of payments deficits, might be considered as the final acknowledgement of Finnish corporatism. The income policy deal was a wide compromise solution with broad political backing, ranging from social policies and tax policies to the abolishment of indexation in wage contracts.[20] It opened the way for several similar policy packages, and contributed to the fast growth of the public sector during the 1970s, several decades after the other Scandinavian countries.

---

[20] See Kosonen 1987, 225, and Valtioneuvoston kanslian julkaisusarja 1985/3.

What delayed the development of democratic corporatism (and a welfare state) in Finland? Two of the most important preconditions for the emergence of corporatism were fulfilled in Finland early. First, Finland, like the other countries, was a small state, which made it dependent on the international environment. Small states, according to Katzenstein, cannot afford deep internal conflicts in a turbulent world. Second, Finland, like the others, was an open trading economy. Such economies are largely dependent on international economic developments outside their own control, and must be united to be able to adapt to changes.

However, a third important prerequisite was not fulfilled. In the other Scandinavian countries, political compromise was possible because of a weaker (or less oppressive) political right and a strong and independent peasantry. This led to the emergence of a more moderate left because it "evolved in a domestic structure that was not divided by deep status divisions" (Katzenstein 1985, 161). The moderation of the left was, in turn, necessary for the possibility of compromise and coalition. As seen earlier, the majority of the Finnish peasantry was instead in an almost feudal position. The political structure before the Civil War was marked by a deep polarization, and the left was radical and revolutionary.

The economic policies of the interwar period changed this. The comprehensive agricultural support created a generation of independent peasants, and placed the Agrarian Party in the political lead. During the period 1920-1950, this also contributed to the formation of a more moderate urban left, which is not surprising since, until the present, the majority of the urban working class has had its roots in rural areas. Finnish political development has thereby come to more closely resemble that of the rest of the region, while at the same time diverging somewhat from development in other parts of the world. In this respect, the roots of the Finnish welfare state may be found in the growth of a large independent class of small farmers during the interwar period. The Finnish story—the comparatively slow growth during three decades—may also give an indication of the costs involved in this development.

REFERENCES

Abramowitz, M. 1986. "Catching Up, Forging Ahead, and Falling Behind." *Journal of Economic History,* vol. XLVI, no. 2, 386-406.

Ahvenainen, J. and A. Kuusterä. 1982. "Teollisuus ja rakennustoiminta." In *Suomen taloushistoria 2,* 222-261.

Ahvenainen, J. and H.J. Vartiainen. 1982. "Itsenäisen Suomen talouspolitiikka." In *Suomen taloushistoria 2,* 175-191.

Alapuro, R., M. Alestalo, E. Haavila-Mannila and R. Väyrynen. 1985. *Small States in Comparative Perspective. Essays for Erik Allardt.* Oslo: Norwegian University Press.

Alestalo, M. 1986. *Structural Change, Classes and the State. Finland in a Historical and Comparative Perspective.* Helsinki: Yliopistopaino.

Alestalo, M., R. Andorka and I. Harcsa. 1987. *Agricultural Population and Structural Change: A Comparison of Finland and Hungary.* Helsinki: Yliopistopaino.

Alestalo, M. and S. Kuhnle. 1987. "The Scandinavian Route: Economic, Social, and Political Developments in Denmark, Finland, Norway and Sweden." In *The Scandinavian Model Welfare States and Welfare Research,* edited by Erikson et al., 3-38.

Alho, K., O. Forsell, J. Huttunen, M. Kotilainen, I. Luukkonen, O.-T. Mattila, J. Moilanen and P. Vartia. 1986. *Neuvostoliiton-kauppa Suomen kansantaloudessa.* Helsinki: ETLA.

Baumol, W.J. 1986. "Productivity Growth, Convergence, and Welfare: What the Long-Run Data Show." *American Economic Review,* vol. 76. 1986: 1072-1085.

Baumol, W.J., S.A.B. Blackman and E.N. Wolff. 1989. *Productivity and American Leadership. The Long View.* Cambridge, Mass.: MIT Press.

Cipolla, C.M., ed. 1976. *The Fontana Economic History of Europe,* vols. 1-6. Glasgow: Collins/Fontana Books.

Eriksson, R., E.J. Hansen, S. Ringen and H. Uusitalo, eds. 1987. *The Scandinavian Model. Welfare States and Welfare Research.* New York: M.E. Sharpe.

Heaton, H. 1966. *Economic History of Europe.* Tokyo: Harper & Row.

Hedlund, S. and M. Lundahl. 1985. *Beredskap eller protektionism? En studie av beredskapsmålet i svensk jordbrukspolitik.* Malmö: Liber.

Hemmilä, P. 1983. "Realization of Finnish-Soviet Five-Year Trade Agreements and Variations in Trade." In *Finnish-Soviet Economic Relations,* edited by Möttölä et al., 65-78.

Hjerppe, R. 1982. "Teollisuus." In *Suomen taloushistoria 2:* 408-431.

Hjerppe, R. 1988. *Suomen talous 1860-1985. Kasvu ja rakennemuutos.* Helsinki: Suomen Pankki.

Jutikkala, E. 1962. "Origin and Rise of the Crofter Problem in Finland." *Scandinavian Economic History Review*, vol. X, 78-83.

Jutikkala, E. 1982. "Omavaraiseen maatalouteen." In *Suomen taloushistoria 2*, 204-221.

Jörberg, L. and O. Krantz. 1976. "Scandinavia 1914-1917." In *The Fontana Economic History of Europe*, edited by C.M. Cipolla. vol. 6 (2), 377-459.

Kalela, J. 1987. *Pulapolitiikkaa. Valtion talous- ja sosiaalipolitiikka Suomessa lamavuosina 1929-1933*. Helsinki: Työväen taloudellinen tutkimuslaitos.

Katzenstein, P. J. 1985. *Small States in World Markets. Industrial Policy in Europe*. Ithaca and London: Cornell University Press.

Kekkonen, U. 1952. *Onko maallamme malttia vaurastua?* Helsinki.

Kivikari, U. 1985. "Finnish Soviet Trade in the Light Industries." *Forschungsberichte*. The Vienna Institute for Comparative Studies, no. 109, 25-100.

Komiteanmietintö. 1951:12. "*Teollistamiskomiteanmietintö* 1951." Helsinki.

Kosonen, P. 1987. *Hyvinvointivaltion haastet ja pohjoismaiset mallit*. Tampere: Vastapaino.

Laurila, E.H. 1987. *Yksityinen kulutus Suomessa ajanjaksona 1880-1980*. Helsinki: ETLA.

Lefgren, J. 1973. "Famine in Finland: 1867-1868." *Intermountain Economic Review*, vol. IV, no. 2.

Maddison, A. 1977. "Phases of Capitalist Development." *Banca Nazionale del Lavoro Quarterly Review*, no. 121, 103-137.

Maddison, A. 1982. *Phases of Capitalist Development*. Oxford: Oxford University Press.

Möttölä, K., O.N. Bykov and I.S. Korolev, eds. 1983. *Finnish-Soviet Economic Relations*. London: Macmillan Press.

Peltonen, M. 1988. "Agrarian World Market and Finnish Farm Economy." *Scandinavian Economic History Review*, vol. XXXVI, no. 1, 26-45.

Pesonen, P. and O. Rantala. 1985. "Outlines of the Finnish Party System." In *Small States in Comparative Perspective. Essays for Erik Allardt*, edited by Alapuro et al., 211-228.

Pihkala, E. 1982. "Teollisuus-Suomi 1945-1980." In *Suomen taloushistoria 2*. 1982: 335-407, 432-480.

Pihkala, E. 1985. "Relations with Russia, Foreign Trade and the Development of the Finnish Economy 1860-1939." In T. Mauranen, ed., "Economic Development in Hungary and Finland." *Communications*. Institute of Economic and Social History: University of Helsinki.

Rasila, V. 1969. "The Finnish Civil War and Land Lease Problems." *Scandinavian Economic History Review*, vol. XVII, 115-135.

Rasila, V. 1982. "Väestönkehitys ja sosiaaliset ongelmat." In *Suomen taloushistoria 2*, 132-153.

Saralehto, S. and L. Vajanne 1981. *Suomen ulkomaankaupan indeksit vuosina* 1949-1980. Helsinki: ETLA.

Suomen taloushistoria. 1982. vols. 1-3. Helsinki: Tammi.

Tolonen, Y. 1985. "Effects of Soviet Trade on the Structure of Finnish Export Industries." *Forschungsberichte.* The Vienna Institute for Comparative Economic Studies, no. 109, 101-117.

Valtioneuvoston kanslian julkaisusarja 1985/3. "Tulopoliittiset ratkaisut vuosina 1950-1984." Helsinki.

Urwin, D.W. 1980. *From Ploughshare to Ballotbox. The Politics of Agrarian Defence in Europe.* Oslo: Universitetsforlaget.

Yudanov, Y.U. 1983. "Soviet-Finnish Economic Cooperation: Significance for the National Economy of Both Countries." In *Finnish-Soviet Economic Relations*, edited by Möttölä et al., 198-212.

CHAPTER NINE

THE TRANSITION FROM PRIMARY EXPORTS TO INDUSTRIAL DEVELOPMENT IN COLOMBIA

*José Antonio Ocampo**

Introduction

Among the large and medium-sized countries of Latin America, Colombia stands out as a case of late export-led growth and an equally late transition from primary exports to manufacturing development. In the nineteenth century it unsuccessfully struggled to develop a stable export base. This process mirrored the political instability of the country as it underwent a myriad of national and regional civil wars in the long and difficult process of building a nation after independence from Spain in 1819. Although as a by-product of export expansion the country experienced some modernization of important economic sectors after 1850, on the eve of the twentieth century it was one of the most underdeveloped nations of the continent. Moreover, by then, Colombia had done very little to overcome the regional fragmentation generated by a complex geography. Finally, but not least important, the century closed in the midst of the devastation and monetary disorganization generated by the bloodiest declared civil conflict, the War of the Thousand Days (1899-1902).

Against this background, the economic record of the twentieth century is remarkable. Starting with the Rafael Reyes administration (1905-1909), the country entered into a process of sustained economic development which, although not spectacular in terms of growth rates, has been very stable. In political terms, although persistent violence became one of its well-known features, the country was also able to build one of the strongest democratic traditions of Latin America and the Third World. The initial basis for economic expansion was the production of coffee on small and

* I am grateful to Magnus Blomström, Rosario Córdoba, Ari Kokko, Patricio Meller, Martin Paldam, and Miguel Urrutia for comments to prior drafts of this paper, and to María Stella Hidalgo for research assistance.

medium-sized farms in the western part of the country, combined with a subsidiary development of a few enclave sectors. Although rather late in the process, a rapid structural transformation took place from the 1930s to the mid-1970s that was supported by the demand generated by preexisting export expansion, the integration of the domestic market, and active state intervention in foreign trade transactions. This process was followed by slower growth and a slowing down of the rate of structural transformation since the mid-1970s.

This chapter analyzes the characteristics of export expansion in Colombia since the nineteenth century and its relation to manufacturing development. Regardless of the fascinating and complex interplay between economic development, democracy and violence in the history of Colombia, this chapter concentrates on issues specific to economic history. It is divided into four sections, the first of which is this introduction. The second briefly reviews developments in the nineteenth century. The third considers export growth in the twentieth century. The fourth analyzes structural transformation and manufacturing growth in the twentieth century and the role of economic policy in that process.

Several themes will recur throughout the chapter. The first is the central role played by geography in the modern transformation of the country. Following a traditional hypothesis of the development literature—recently revived by Romer (1986), Lucas (1988), Shleifer (1989), and others—it is argued that the presence or absence of external economies played a crucial role in the structural transformation of Colombia. In a country in which geographical fragmentation posed a basic constraint to economic growth, external economies associated with the construction of a modern transport infrastructure played the leading role. However, due to certain features of the development process, it followed an "unbalanced" pattern (Hirschman 1958). On the other hand, aside from its purely cyclical effects, exogenous terms of trade shocks played a crucial role in the transition between different phases of development. Finally, it is argued that economic policy played a rather subsidiary role in the process and, indeed, that policy shifts were largely a lagged effect of changes in the underlying economic conditions.

The Nineteenth Century Legacy

Since the mid-sixteenth century, the present territory of Colombia was the major gold producer of the Spanish Empire. After a period of decline, which covered most of the seventeenth century, gold production experienced significant growth in the eighteenth century. Despite the continuing expansion of freehold production in Antioquia in the northwest, the slavery crisis during the last decades of the colonial period and its gradual dismantling in the first decades of the Republican period were reflected in a new decline of production in the first half of the nineteenth century.

The attempts to diversify exports, which had started with the Bourbon reforms in the last decades of the colonial period, were continued by the first Republican administrations. However, the results were not immediate. Throughout the first half of the nineteenth century, three-fourths of all gold mined was exported to the rest of the world. However, the privatization of the tobacco monopoly as a part of the Liberal Party's reforms of the mid-century, and the successful introduction of steam navigation on the Magdalena River, generated a new export staple. Tobacco was soon joined by other commodities and some artisan products (Panama hats) to initiate a new period of export growth.

The rate of growth of the export quantum in the second half of the nineteenth century was 3.7 percent, or 2.2 percent per capita. Although fairly rapid by the standards of that time, this expansion barely compensated for the stagnation of the first half of the century. Thus, at the turn of the century, real exports per capita were only some 36 percent above the levels of the late colonial period. Indeed, per capita exports were equivalent to a third of the Latin American average, the lowest level in the region along with Haiti and Honduras. What is more important, export growth was largely based on a myriad of regional booms of individual commodities. These booms were generally unleashed by world scarcities of the individual commodities involved. Their local production was largely improvised and could not stand up to international competition when normal supply conditions were reestablished at a world level. Moreover, in many cases, production did not go beyond the destructive extraction of preexisting forest resources (Ocampo 1984).

Of the rather extensive list of commodities which Colombia sold to the rest of the world during the past century, long-run growth concentrated only on gold and coffee. In the first case, the expansion of Antioquia—increasingly based on large-scale exploitations using modern technology and foreign capital—was finally able to reverse the long-run decline in gold production in the 1870s. The expansion of coffee was fairly slow up to 1870. In the sellers' market that characterized the world coffee economy in the last three decades of the century, domestic production boomed for the first time (Ocampo 1984). Most of the expansion concentrated in the western part of the country on large semi-feudal haciendas using tenant labor (Palacios 1983). Nonetheless, as will be discussed later, both gold production and hacienda coffee underwent a crisis in the early twentieth century.

The greatest hindrance to economic development in the nineteenth century was the inability to develop a stable and sizable export sector. Geography was a great constraint, but so were the backward forms of production—traditional haciendas and subsistence small-scale farming—

which prevailed in variable proportions throughout the country. Although an entrepreneurial class played an important role in the transformation of the economy, and its role was enhanced by the Liberal Party reforms of the mid-century, its efforts were largely wasted in the exploitation of short-term world market scarcities. As a result, the country remained largely isolated from the international flows of capital, labor, and trade. Moreover, the ephemeral character of the export booms was a central obstacle to the development of the external economies necessary to make the growth process self-sustaining.

This was particularly true in relation to the transport infrastructure. In fact, despite the introduction of steam navigation on the Magdalena and other rivers, and the construction of the first railroads, the mule continued to be the major means of transportation until the early twentieth century. By 1898, the railway network was only 498 kilometers long, scattered throughout the country (McGreevey 1971). As late as 1919-1922, when the network had tripled, it was, in per capita terms, still only one-fifth of the Latin American average, the second lowest in the region after Haiti (Ocampo 1984, 53).

Nonetheless, the growth of exports in the second half of the century led to a general economic expansion which was visible in many areas: in the partial modernization of the transport infrastructure, the growth of major cities,[1] the accumulation of capital in these urban centers, the establishment of modern banking, and some technological innovations, particularly in mining. Some domestic factors reinforced the process, particularly the growth of cattle raising, supported by the introduction of artificial pasture and new breeds from abroad. This sector remained, in fact, the most important of rural Colombia throughout the period. On the other hand, the rapid growth of the population (1.5 percent) propelled a significant internal migration. By the end of the century, this process had filled up some of the empty lands that separated major urban centers. Particularly important for their economic repercussions were the southward move of the Antioqueños along the central mountain range of the country and the migration from the highlands in the eastern range towards the Magdalena River. By the end of the century, the triangle formed by the major cities of Colombia (Bogotá, Medellín and Cali) was fairly widely populated.

A weak export base and market fragmentation were the major determinants of the backward stage of manufacturing production. Attempts to

---

[1] The proportion of total population in the five largest municipalities (not necessarily the same in all population censuses) fell from 5.2 percent in 1835 to 3.9 percent in 1851; in 1870 it was only slightly above the mid-century level, 4.2 percent; thereafter, it rose substantially, to 6.2 percent in 1912. For the ten largest municipalities, these proportions were 8 percent in 1835, 6.3 percent in 1851, 6.6 percent in 1870 and 8.8 percent in 1912.

establish some modern industrial firms from the 1830s to the 1870s under the umbrella created by transportation costs and cyclical protectionist trends largely failed. It was only in the last two decades of the century that the first successful pioneering firms were established. However, on the eve of the new century, most of them remained small establishments, not very different from large artisan shops. In fact, the few true factories concentrated on gold mining, particularly in Antioquia. Therefore, it is in these activities rather than in manufacturing activities, where the birth of modern industry must be found in Colombia (Ospina 1955; Safford 1965; Brew 1981; Mayor 1989).

As modern manufacturing experienced a long and painful start, artisan production remained a fairly important activity. The only measure of the relative size of artisan activities in the nineteenth century comes from the 1870 population census data on employment. These data indicate that artisan activities generated 11.6 percent of male and 63.2 percent of female employment. By 1918, these proportions had fallen to 10 and 56.3 percent, excluding the Caribbean coast (comparable data for 1870 are only slightly smaller than the national averages—12.1 and 62.7 percent, respectively). Although these statistics are not comparable to current employment data, they indicate that despite its relative stagnation between 1870 and 1918, the artisan sector was quite large and remained so even in fairly advanced phases of export-led growth (Ocampo 1987).

This sector experienced, however, a substantial structural transformation throughout the century. Some activities grew as a by-product of the demand induced by the growth of exports, either directly (jute bags for coffee exports) or indirectly (sewing, carpentry, printing, etc.). Some even experienced phases of export growth (Panama hats). Simultaneously, the domestic production of cotton textiles collapsed under the weight of import competition.

The collapse of the international prices was the major and probably the only factor behind the desintegration of domestic artisan production. Indeed, except for some brief periods, tariffs on ordinary textiles remained high, but were unable to counteract the trends in international prices. More generally, tariff policy had little impact on the evolution of either artisan or manufacturing activities. In fact, throughout the century, the evolution of tariffs was determined more by fiscal demands than by economic or political principles. Thus, as a result of these demands, the free trade ideology that prevailed from the late 1840s to the 1870s actually increased tariffs. The return to protectionist policies in the 1880s, on the other hand, reduced tariffs, since specific duties were not adjusted rapidly enough to keep up with inflation (Ocampo and Montenegro 1984, Chapter 4).

Figure 9.1
Terms of Trade of Colombia, 1885-1988 (1980=100)

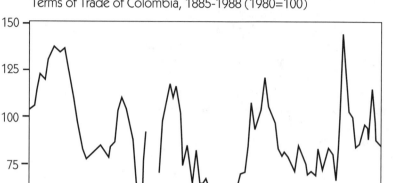

Sources: 1885-1910, OCAMPO (1984); OCAMPO and MONTENEGRO (1984); 1928-88, ECLA.

Table 9.1. Export Growth in Colombia, 1900–1988

	Coffee Exports (Thousand bags)	Quantum Indices (1970–74 = 100)		Purchasing Power of exports (1970–74 = 100)	Exports of Goods and Services as % of GDP (1975 Prices)
		Primary Products	Total		
1900–04	542				
1905–09	604	8.8	7.2	7.4	
1910–14	837	12.8	10.5	13.2	
1915–19	1,244	17.2	14.1	12.8	
1920–24	1,906	27.1	22.2[1]	23.1[1]	
1925–29	2,451	34.3	28.0	38.3	24.0
1930–34	3,149	43.0	35.2	33.1	24.4
1935–39	3,972	53.6	43.8	34.8	24.0
1940–44	4,370	57.5	46.9	31.2	20.4
1945–49	5,429	68.4	55.9	47.1	21.0
1950–54	5,337	72.6	59.3	78.0	18.4
1955–59	5,523	74.1	60.3	70.3	17.2
1960–64	6,139	84.7	70.1	68.1	16.0
1965–69	6,076	92.3	80.9	73.6	15.6
1970–74	6,656	100.0	100.0	100.0	14.9
1975–79	7,990	113.5	123.8	162.7	15.1
1980–84	9,685	139.2	147.8	169.1	14.1
1985–88	10,613	180.8[2]	229.0	268.0	17.3[3]

[1] 1923–24   [2] 1985–86   [3] 1985–87

Sources:

(1) Coffee exports: Ocampo (1984), *Anuario de Comercio Exterior* and *Federación Nacional de Cafeteros*.

(2) Quantum indices and purchasing power of exports: 1905–40, Ocampo and Montenegro (1984); 1940–86, Ocampo (1989c).

(3) Exports of goods and services as a % of GDP: National Accounts of ECLA (1925–50), *Banco de la República* (1950–65) and DANE (1965–87).

Export Growth in the Twentieth Century

The Export Boom

The twentieth century came upon Colombia in the midst of a deep economic crisis. The devastation of some areas of the country during the War of the Thousand Days was compounded by the disorganization generated by the monetary financing of the budget, which generated three-digit inflation during the war years. Moreover, the effects of the civil conflict were combined with the collapse of international prices (see Figure 9.1), which dramatically affected the coffee haciendas (Deas 1976). The other important export sector, gold, experienced a similar recession at the turn of the century because of the exhaustion of the resource base. However, the economic reconstruction was rapid. Monetary stabilization came soon after the war, initiating a strong tradition of monetary and fiscal conservatism. Moreover, starting with the Reyes administration (1905-1909), the country initiated a new phase of development.

As Table 9.1 indicates, the basis for expansion in the first three decades of the century was the rapid growth of exports: 7 percent a year between 1905-1909 and 1925-1929. The terms of trade were erratic throughout this expansion, but overall they showed an upward trend (see Figure 9.1) and, thus, supported the growth of import capacity (see Table 9.1). In the second half of the 1920s, export expansion also facilitated the access to international capital markets for the first time since the War of Independence.[2] This allowed Colombia to end the phase of rapid export expansion in the midst of a spectacular import and investment boom (CEPAL, 1957, and Ocampo and Montenegro 1984, Chapter 2; see also Table 9.5).

The leading export sector was coffee, which grew at a rate slightly above that of total exports during the period, 7.3 percent a year, and increased its share in total sales abroad to 70 percent in the 1920s (see Table 9.2). In the early part of the century the coffee boom was reinforced by the development of a large-scale banana plantation by the United Fruit Company. In the second half of the 1920s, oil extraction also supported the global expansion of exports. Bananas and oil, together with gold, then in

---

[2] Colombia had inherited a war debt which it renegotiated periodically, but never regularly paid in the nineteenth century. The access to new capital flows was, thus, limited to direct investment and a few loans for railroad construction. After the 1906 renegotiation, the export boom finally allowed the country to regularly pay its debt, but significant new flows did not come for some time. By 1923, the external debt of the national government was still $24 million, equivalent to 41 percent of exports (Junguito 1989; Ocampo 1988).

Table 9.2. Composition of Colombian Exports
(Percentage)

	Coffee	Gold	Oil, fuel oil and coal	Other primary	Manufactures[1]
1905–09	39.0	19.7	—	—	41.3
1910–14	47.4	16.3	—	—	36.3
1915–19	55.1	7.9	—	—	37.1
1920–24	75.5	5.6	—	—	18.9
1925–29	67.7	3.2	14.7	—	14.3
1930–34	60.5	7.5	20.2	—	11.7
1935–39	53.6	16.7	19.4	—	10.3
1940–44	60.5	17.4	14.3	—	7.7
1945–49	72.1	5.6	14.6	—	7.7
1950–54	78.7	2.7	13.6	—	5.0
1955–59	76.2	2.5	14.3	—	7.0
1960–64	68.9	2.8	16.1	9.1	3.1
1965–69	61.0	1.7	13.5	15.0	8.7
1970–74	50.5	1.8	6.9	19.8	21.0
1975–79	57.9	2.7	3.9	16.6	18.8
1980–84	48.7	6.4	6.6	19.0	19.3
1985–89	35.6	7.4	23.6	—	33.5

[1] ISTC 5-8.
Sources: Anuario de Comercio Exterior. Banco de la República for gold exports for the whole period and for the composition of exports in 1985–89.

decline, made up the enclave sector of the economy, which concentrated an additional one-fourth of total sales to the rest of the world. Other products were then relatively unimportant.

The coffee sector underwent, in turn, significant structural changes with respect to its nineteenth century pattern. The haciendas, typical of the eastern part of the country, stagnated. As we have seen, the civil war and the collapse of international prices had severely affected these productive units at the turn of the century. However, they were unable to resume growth when peace was reestablished and world coffee prices recovered between 1910 and 1920. As a result, the production in the departments of Cundinamarca, Santander and Norte de Santander, where haciendas were dominant, increased at a very slow pace: from some 500,000 bags in 1900 to 825,000 in 1932—i.e., 1.6 percent a year. The major problem faced by these productive units was the inability to discipline the labor force under the semi-feudal tenant system in what was still a frontier region. In fact, many of the haciendas came under increasing pressure from tenants in the 1920s who demanded improvements in labor conditions, the right to plant coffee on their subsistence plots and, in some cases, the title to the land, As a result of rural turmoil, the coffee haciendas, particularly of Cundinamarca, became one of the focuses of the land reform adopted by the reformist Liberal Party administrations of the 1930s (Bejarano 1979; Palacios 1983).

On the other hand, coffee production boomed in the western part of the country along the steep but rich volcanic soils of the central mountain range that had been populated by the Antioqueños in the nineteenth century.

Indeed, production in the departments of Antioquia, Caldas, Valle, and Tolima increased from 110,000 to 2,423,000 bags in the same period—i.e., 10 percent a year. Production concentrated in those departments on small and medium-sized properties. As a reflection of this concentration, by 1932, 59.5 percent of coffee production in Colombia came from 145,000 small and medium-sized farms—those with coffee plantings of twelve hectares or less (Machado 1977; Ocampo 1989a).

The expansion of coffee plantings in the western part of the country began during the first decade of the century when international prices were still depressed. This reflected the rich resource base on which the boom was built, but also the search by the U.S. for alternative supply sources in response to Brazil's use of its near monopoly power to regulate the international coffee market, and what meant, in fact, a technological revolution. Indeed, coffee made possible the permanent use of land in a region where slash and burn was the dominant agricultural technique. The introduction of stable cultivation of the land was, by itself, a major technical leap forward.

Nonetheless, the consolidation of coffee as the dominant staple of Colombia could not have been possible without the development of a series of subsidiary activities that generated the external economies necessary to make the expansion self-sustaining. The sizable commercialization network and the production of jute bags and pulping machines were some of the activities which grew as a by-product of the expansion of coffee, but also created the externalities necessary to keep the growth process going. However, it was the significant expansion of the modern transport infrastructure which made the crucial difference with respect to the nineteenth century pattern.

By the early 1930s, the railway network (3,262 kilometers) was 6.6 times larger than that which existed at the end of the nineteenth century (McGreevey 1971). Moreover, by this time the joint Pacífico and Caldas Railroads made up the first integrated network, connecting the coffee regions to the Pacific coast. The opening of the Panama Canal in 1914 had made possible the development of a large-scale port on the Pacific. This was a more natural outlet for the new coffee regions in the western part of the country than the northern Caribbean coast. Steam navigation on the Magdalena and Cauca Rivers and the birth of motor vehicle transportation reinforced the process.

The "democratic" character of production was not mirrored in the commercialization of coffee, which since the 1920s was subject to increasing concentration in the hands of a few domestic and foreign firms. The largest foreign firms derived their market power from their vertical integration with the merchant fleet or the roasting/retailing business, mainly in the U.S. The high commercialization margins paid by coffee in the areas where peasant production prevailed may have been partly determined by this process. The interregional differences of such margins were broken up in the early 1930s by the Federation of Coffee Growers. The intervention of the Federation was also crucial in eliminating the advantages of foreign firms and, thus, increasing domestic participation in external commercialization in the postwar period (Arango 1982; Ocampo 1989b).

The Federation, founded in 1927, also played an essential role in the consolidation of coffee production as an administrator of public policy in the sector. Its domestic market intervention was made possible by the building of the first coffee warehouses during the Great Depression. Starting with the short-lived agreement signed with Brazil in 1936 to regulate the international market, the Federation also was in charge of the negotiation and administration of international agreements. The management of the National Coffee Fund, created in 1940 to facilitate Colombia's participation in the Inter-American Agreement, further enhanced the scope of its activities.

This was further encouraged by the earmarking of variable but significant amounts of coffee taxes first to the Federation, and later to the Fund.[3] Tax income, together with profits derived from management of the Fund, facilitated considerable participation in the domestic and international markets, which included the financing of production; marketing, processing and transportation of the crop; management of stocks; direct marketing of coffee abroad; commercialization and subsidization of agrochemicals necessary for its production; and technological innovation and diffusion. This intervention included the participation with share capital in a series of new companies—two commercial banks, several investment banks, the Grancolombian Merchant Fleet, etc.

The private charter of the Federation was no obstacle to its gradual adoption of public duties. Subsequent to the creation of the Federation, an institutional mechanism was adopted to administer the sector: a National Coffee Committee, in which the government was represented, adopted the policy decisions, which the Federation then implemented. With the creation of the National Coffee Fund in 1940, the Committee was given a public charter, but its operation was contracted with the Federation. In its early configuration, the government had only one representative on the Committee. In the mid-1930s, the reformist López administration tried to control

---

[3] The coffee taxes included the small export tax, created in 1927, a fraction of the income generated by the various discriminatory exchange rates created since the early 1930s, the retention quota established in 1958, and the ad-valorem export tax created in 1967. As Table 9.6 indicates, taxation was relatively low up to mid-1950s, except for a brief interlude during the Second World War associated with the Inter-American Coffee Agreement. Taxation became very important afterwards, for reasons which will become clear below.

the Federation. Although it failed in its task, it expanded the government representation on the Committee and gave the government some veto powers. The President was also given the authority to name the General Manager of the Federation. This peculiar management of the coffee sector gave significant stability to a basic area of economic policy during periods of political turmoil. Obviously, its counterpart was the strength of private coffee interests, which became overwhelmingly influential in economic policy.

In contrast to the largely national control of the coffee economy and the "democratic" character of its production, the concentration of production and commercialization in the hands of a few foreign firms was the major feature of banana and oil production. Thus, it is not surprising that together with modern transportation they became the major fields for the struggle of the first modern trade unions in the late teens and throughout the 1920s (Urrutia 1969; Archila 1989). Confrontations between the working class and the export enclaves reached a climax in the famous strike against the United Fruit Company in 1928 (White 1978; LeGrand 1989), which was given literary prominence in García Márquez' One Hundred Years of Solitude. This strike played a crucial role in the domestic political process, particularly in the fall, two years later, of the Conservative hegemony that had dominated the government since the mid-1880s, and the rise to power of the reformist Liberal Party.

The Slowdown of the Coffee Engine and the Long Transition to a More Diversified Export Structure

The export boom did not come to an end abruptly. As a reflection of the lagged production effects of plantings in the 1920s and early 1930s, coffee exports continued to expand at fairly rapid rates in the latter part of the decade. Moreover, its structure, based on small and medium-sized properties, was further strengthened in the 1930s and 1940s (Ocampo 1989b). On the other hand, increasing international prices and the domestic devaluation of the early 1930s generated a new gold boom as other enclave sectors stagnated or declined (see Table 9.2). As a result of the expansion of coffee and gold, the total export quantum continued to grow at a rate similar to that of GDP between 1925-1929 and 1935-1939—4.5 percent a year (see Table 9.1).

Nonetheless, the collapse of commodity prices and Colombia's terms of trade during the Great Depression was the crucial turning point in the history of exports in Colombia. The slowdown of export growth and the gradual reorientation of economic growth inwards deepened in the 1940s and 1950s. Between 1935-1939 and 1955-1959, the export quantum grew at a very slow rate (1.6 percent), significantly below that of GDP. The root of this dramatic slowdown was the lack of dynamism of coffee production.

It was reinforced, however, by the stagnation or decline of the enclave sectors (see Table 9.2).

The slowdown of the coffee sector was initially a lagged effect of the collapse of commodity prices during the Great Depression. Nonetheless, it continued when prices improved rapidly in the first decade of the postwar period (see Figure 9.1). This indicates that, aside from the external events which may have set off the process, the slowdown was also associated with internal events. The most important of these events were the gradual exhaustion of the agrarian frontier in the western regions where coffee had expanded rapidly during the first decades of the century, and the aging of plantations.[4] In fact, the early postwar boom induced a 65 percent increase in the area planted with coffee between 1945-1949 and 1960-1964 (i.e., 3.4 percent a year—still much slower than that typical up to the 1930s), but production increased by only 32 percent (1.9 percent a year). The fall in land productivity (1.5 percent a year) was faster than that which could be expected by aging alone. Thus, the undeclared civil war generally known as La Violencia—which was very much in evidence during this period in the coffee regions of western Colombia—probably contributed to the process (Ocampo 1989b).

Despite the continuing lack of dynamism of coffee and enclave exports, the rate of growth of the global export quantum returned to its long-run trend[5] in the mid-1950s, although it continued to lag with respect to GDP growth (see Table 9.1). Thus, the real expansion that took place between 1955-1959 and 1970-1974 (3.4 percent a year) was largely based on the diversification of the export base. This process was initially based on primary commodities, including some which the country had exported in the nineteenth or early twentieth centuries. Gradually, however, manufacturing exports took over and became the most dynamic component of sales abroad in the early 1970s. By then, the share of "minor" or nontraditional exports had increased to 40.8 percent (see Table 9.2).

This turnaround in the evolution of exports was a by-product of a new collapse of the terms of trade (see Figure 9.1). Indeed, in the postwar period, the performance of nontraditional exports has followed, inversely and with a shifting lag, the evolution of the terms of trade and, thus, international

---

[4] In the traditional coffee technology, which was dominant until the 1960s, the productivity of the coffee trees reaches a peak when they are 10-12 years old, after which it declines at an average rate of some 1 percent a year (CEPAL and FAO 1958). Based on different records of plantings since the 1920s, it can be estimated that the proportion of trees 15 years old or more, which was 40 percent or less until the late 1930s, increased to 70 percent by the mid-1960s.

[5] If estimated with a semi-log regression of the export quantum with respect to a time variable, such a trend is 3.7 percent a year between 1905 and 1988.

coffee prices.[6] As will be seen below, the crucial link has been the exchange rate, which has appreciated (depreciated) during coffee price booms (slumps). Therefore, the diversification of the export base since the mid-1950s may be seen as a "Dutch benefit" resulting from the adverse terms of trade shock experienced by the Colombian economy. To the contrary, the sharp but short coffee boom of the second half of the 1970s (see Figure 9.1) and the capital inflows of the early 1980s had the opposite ("Dutch disease") effects.

At the same time, the international price boom reversed the deterioration of the coffee sector typical of previous decades. The renewed growth of coffee production was based on the new intensive cultivation technologies that became available in the 1960s. With a fairly constant area under cultivation, production and exports increased by some 80 percent with respect to the levels typical in the early 1970s. Although the new technologies were not characterized by significant economies of scale, the technological revolution at the farm level accelerated the moderate tendency to the concentration of coffee production that was perceivable since the 1960s (Junguito and Pizano 1989, Chapter III).

The joint effect of increasing coffee sales, reduced dynamism of nontraditional exports, and a new gold boom was the (unstable) growth of the global export quantum at a rate—4 percent between 1970-1974 and 1980-1984—not unlike the long-term trend and that which had been typical since the mid-1950s. Nonetheless, exports continued to lag with respect to GDP. In the first half of the 1980s, exports (as a proportion of GDP) reached an all-time low since National Account Statistics have been collected. It was only in the second half of the 1980s, when the combined effect of renewed oil, rising coal, and a new boom of "minor" exports induced by the most recent collapse of coffee prices, that the long-run fall in the share of exports in GDP, which had been typical since the 1940s, was finally reversed.

---

[6] The evolution of the nontraditional export quantum shows three kinks in the postwar period: in the late 1950s, the mid-1970s, and the mid-1980s. These breaks took place around or soon after major shifts in the evolution of real international coffee prices. With semi-log regressions against time variables, the trend rate of growth of such exports can be estimated at 5.6 percent in 1945-1957, 18.2 percent in 1958-1973, and 3 percent in 1974-1984. Since the mid-1980s, rates of growth have returned to levels similar to those of 1958-1973.

Table 9.3. GDP Structure in Colombia
(1975 prices, percentages)

	Agriculture	Mining	Manufactures	Construction	Transport	Public utilities and communications	Government services	Commerce and financial services	Other services
1925–29	47.7	3.1	7.8	3.4	2.3	0.2	7.5	9.6	18.3
1930–34	46.2	3.5	7.6	2.1	1.9	0.2	7.6	15.0	15.8
1935–39	43.7	3.6	10.2	2.8	2.8	0.3	7.4	15.1	14.0
1940–44	37.5	3.2	15.7	4.0	4.6	0.6	7.0	13.8	13.7
1945–49	40.0	2.9	14.9	3.9	4.8	0.5	6.5	13.2	13.4
1950–54	33.2	3.4	17.6	3.3	6.4	0.7	7.2	15.9	12.5
1955–59	30.9	3.3	19.5	3.9	6.7	0.9	6.8	15.7	12.3
1960–64	28.4	3.2	20.7	3.4	6.7	1.1	6.9	16.6	12.9
1965–69	26.5	2.9	21.2	3.5	6.8	1.3	6.9	17.8	13.1
1970–74	23.9	2.3	22.5	3.5	7.3	1.6	7.2	19.4	12.2
1975–79	23.4	1.4	22.9	3.3	7.9	1.9	7.2	19.9	12.0
1980–84	22.6	1.4	21.3	3.7	8.1	2.6	8.1	20.2	12.0
1985–87	21.7	3.6	21.3	4.2	7.4	2.7	8.5	18.9	11.7

Source: National Accounts of ECLA (1925–50), *Banco de la República* (1950–65) and DANE (1965–87).

Structural Transformation and Economic Policy

Economic Structure and Economic Policy in the Early Twentieth Century

In the second half of the 1920s Colombia was a traditional, open economy. The primary sector contributed more than half of GDP, mostly in agriculture (see Table 9.3). Moreover, as the 1938 population census indicates, an overwhelming proportion of the population was rural (69 percent) and most employment was generated by the agricultural sector (62 percent). On the other hand, manufacturing and transport, among other sectors, remained fairly small, and the former was still dominated by traditional activities (mainly the production of nontradable foodstuffs—see Table 9.4). Exports made up some 24 percent of GDP (see Table 9.1). As Londoño (1989a, 1989b) has recently shown, both agriculture and exports were relatively large with respect to other countries with a similar population and GDP per capita.

Some changes had taken place with respect to the early twentieth century. The most important change was the opening up of the economy (exports probably accounted for no more than 12-14 percent of GDP in the first decade of the century).[7] Urbanization had also been very rapid. Be-

---

[7] These proportions are those consistent with an expansion in the export quantum of 7 percent and a growth of GDP of 3.5 to 4 percent a year.

Table 9.4. Structure of Manufacturing Value Added in Colombia
(1975 prices)

	Early manufacturing sectors				Intermediate					Late				
	Foodstuffs	Tobacco	Wood and wood products	Subtotal	Beverages	Textiles and apparel	Oil derivatives	Non metallic minerals	Subtotal	Paper and printing	Chemicals and rubber	Basic metals	Metallic products, machinery and equipment	Subtotal
A. As a proportion of value added, excluding wood, paper and products														
1925–29	62.8	14.6		77.4	4.2	5.0	1.7	2.8	13.7		7.4		1.5	8.9
1930–34	66.9	9.4		76.2	4.9	7.9	1.6	2.3	16.7		5.7		1.3	7.1
1935–39	52.1	8.7		60.8	8.4	15.1	2.7	4.4	30.5		6.7		2.0	8.7
1940–44	46.1	7.9		53.9	9.2	20.4	3.0	5.6	38.2		6.2		1.6	7.8
B. As a proportion of total manufacturing value added														
1937–39	43.8	8.1	6.4	58.2	8.0	15.8	2.7	4.4	31.0	2.1	6.6		2.1	10.8
1940–44	42.6	7.3	5.8	55.6	8.5	18.9	2.7	5.2	35.3	1.8	5.8		1.5	9.0
1945–49	39.4	7.0	5.1	51.5	10.9	18.1	3.5	5.4	37.9	2.2	6.4		2.0	10.6
1950–54	37.5	6.5	4.4	48.4	12.3	16.8	3.7	5.6	38.4	3.1	7.7	1.0	1.4	13.2
1955–59	33.6	5.0	4.4	43.0	9.6	16.9	4.7	5.6	36.9	3.5	8.9	5.6	2.2	20.1
1960–64	31.8	4.3	3.8	39.9	9.1	17.2	5.3	5.4	37.0	4.1	9.2	6.6	3.2	23.1
1965–69	33.5	4.1	2.8	40.4	8.6	16.6	5.4	4.9	35.5	4.7	9.1	6.4	3.8	24.1
1970–74	27.8	3.7	2.5	34.1	8.7	17.2	5.4	4.8	36.2	6.2	10.8	6.5	6.2	29.7
1975–79	27.9	2.7	2.2	32.7	9.3	16.2	5.1	5.2	35.7	6.4	11.6	6.5	7.1	31.6
1980–84	29.8	2.4	1.9	34.0	10.0	13.6	5.0	5.5	34.2	6.7	12.0	6.3	6.9	31.8
1985–86	28.7	2.5	1.9	33.2	9.8	13.5	5.5	5.6	34.4	7.0	12.5	6.0	6.9	32.4

Source: National Accounts of ECLA (1925–50), *Banco de la República* (1950–65 and CANE (1965–1986). For intermediate and late industries in 1925–45 (excluding beverages, apparel, paper and printing), Chu (1972). Original index data from ECLA, *Banco de la República* and Chu has been converted at 1975 prices using the value added of the different subsectors according to the DANE Manufacturing survey of that year.

Table 9.5. Imports and Fixed Investment

	Quantum Index, (1970–74 = 100)	Imports of Goods and Services as % of GDP (1975 prices)	Composition of Imports[1]			Fixed Investment as a percentage of GDP (1975 prices)	
			Consumer goods	Intermediates and fuels	Capital goods	Machinery & equipment	Total
1910–14	5.4						
1915–19	4.5						
1920–24	7.7						
1925–29	19.8	24.1	43.5	21.3	32.2	9.9	23.1
1930–34	12.8	13.1	47.9	28.9	19.8	2.8	12.3
1935–39	19.2	15.9	41.6	28.9	23.6	4.6	14.8
1940–44	14.2	11.2	29.1	45.6	19.6	3.9	14.1
1945–49	25.4	14.4	23.6	33.7	35.7	6.6	17.5
1950–54	40.9	18.4	14.6	48.7	36.5	9.1	17.5
1955–59	44.1	15.9	9.4	53.4	36.6	7.2	16.6
1960–64	49.0	14.0	7.3	47.1	44.0	6.4	14.8
1965–69	62.3	14.1	7.9	48.5	41.9	5.9	15.0
1970–74	100.0	16.8	9.9	51.5	38.4	7.4	16.4
1975–79	121.8	16.0	13.2	52.0	34.7	7.5	15.6
1980–84	177.9	19.3	11.9	52.3	35.8	8.6	17.4
1985–87	164.4	15.6	9.0	56.2	33.6	6.9	15.8

[1] Excludes "others."

Sources:

(1) Quantum index: 1905–40, Ocampo and Montenegro (1984); 1940–87, Ocampo (1989c).

(2) Imports and Fixed Investment as a % of GDP: National Accounts of ECLA (1925–50), Banco de la República (1950–65) and DANE (1965–87)

(3) Composition: CEPAL (1957), Banco de la República and DANE.

tween 1912 and 1938, the population of the country as a whole grew at an annual rate of 2.1 percent, whereas that of the twelve major cities expanded much faster—3.9 percent a year. The share of agriculture in GDP probably fell during this period: from some 60-65 percent to less than 50 percent. At the same time, this sector experienced substantial structural change as the production exportables (coffee and bananas) increased while nontradables (foodstuffs, including cattle raising) fell in relative terms.

Transportation and manufacturing also experienced significant changes. As mentioned above, the railroad network expanded considerably while steam navigation was flourishing and the first highways were being built. Nonetheless, many of the investments in infrastructure came rather late in the process, as a result of the investment boom of 1925-1929, the most spectacular since National Account Statistics have been collected (see Table 9.5). As discussed above, it was enhanced by access to external financing in the last phases of the export boom.

On the other hand, the relative decline of artisan activities accelerated as modern manufacturing slowly expanded. As the 1945 Industrial Census indicates, the creation of important manufacturing firms accelerated during the Reyes administration and the First World War, both periods marked by protectionist policies and restricted access to imports. The process intensified once more during the investment boom, which preceded the Great

Depression. Nonetheless, the most important manufacturing firms remained modest even in fairly advanced phases of the export boom. Indeed, manufacturing continued to concentrate in nontradable foodstuffs. Textile production, in particular, remained fairly small prior to the Depression and even experienced a relative regression in the 1920s (Ocampo and Montenegro 1984, Chapter 3). As a result, manufactured consumer goods continued to represent an overwhelming proportion of imports (see Table 9.5).

The relative over-expansion of agriculture and exports and the underexpansion of manufacturing were, undoubtedly, associated with the particular constraints imposed by geography in Colombia. Modern manufacturing could hardly prosper in an economy which, aside from its low income, was characterized by a considerable fragmentation of the domestic market. The growth of modern transportation during the first phases of the export boom actually reinforced this feature of the economy as the infrastructure was initially built up to connect the different regions of the country with the rest of the world (Ospina 1955; McGreevey 1971). However, by connecting its different segments, what was initially a fragmented, outward-oriented, transport infrastructure served as the basis for an integrated domestic network.

However, this came very late in the process. It was only in 1928 that the first highway connecting the Cauca and Magdalena Valleys was provisionally opened up (no railway was ever built for that purpose). This was a crucial element of the domestic transport network since it connected Bogotá with Cali (the third largest city of the country) and the Pacific coast. Moreover, even then, modern transportation was still made up of chaotic fragments of railroads, highways, and steam navigation. By the end of the boom, it was only by a mix of means of transportation that Bogotá was connected with Medellín, Cali, and Barranquilla. Moreover, modern transportation still did not serve to connect major urban centers with their surroundings. It was only with the change in transport policy towards highways in the 1930s that an orderly internal transportation network began to take shape.

Economic policy played a very subsidiary role in the transformation process of Colombia during the first decades of the century. The return to monetary stability soon after the civil war was crucial, as well as the design of a new monetary and fiscal system under the guidance of Kemmerer two decades later. Nonetheless, as was typical of an economy in which state activities remained fairly restricted, its major role in the development process was its contribution to the construction of the transport infrastructure.

On the other hand, the 1905 and 1913 tariff reforms reinforced and, in fact, made explicit the protectionist trend that had been visible since the mid-1880s. These reforms raised average (collected) tariffs to the highest levels of the Republican period (see Table 9.6). They also increased tariff dispersion to protect incipient, manufacturing firms as well as import-substitution agriculture. Nonetheless, as in the nineteenth century, the real effects of protectionism were limited because other preconditions for industrialization and even modern agricultural development were not given.

Few other important changes in tariffs took place prior to the Great Depression except for a controversial "emergency law" that substantially reduced tariffs on agricultural products in 1927 as a mechanism to control the inflationary effects of the export boom. The most important change was, however, the erosion of the protectionist effect of the tariff reforms of 1905 and 1913 as a result of inflation. Following a nineteenth century pattern, these reforms had established a system of specific duties based on the weight of the goods.

The Period of Rapid Structural Transformation, 1929-1974

Major Features of the Process

From the 1930s to the mid-1970s, the Colombian economy experienced a substantial structural transformation. Until the early 1960s, this process was, in fact, faster than that predicted by the cross-country Kuznets-Chenery pattern (Londoño 1989a, 1989b). It was visible in many fields. Between 1925-1929 and 1970-1974, the contribution of agriculture to GDP fell from 48 to 24 percent. At the same time, manufacturing, transportation, public utilities, communications and, to a lesser extent, commerce and financial services sharply increased their share in the generation of aggregate value added (Table 9.3).

Urbanization proceeded rapidly. By 1973, 59 percent of the population was living in urban areas and 25 percent in the four major cities; in 1938, these proportions had been 31 and 8 percent, respectively. This process coincided with an equally spectacular change in the structure of employment: the generation of employment in primary activities fell from 62 percent in 1938 to 35 percent in 1978 as secondary and, particularly, service activities, expanded. Urbanization was accompanied also by a sharp demographic transition. Population growth, which had already been rapid in the nineteenth century, rose to 2.1 percent in the first half of the twentieth century. Later on, it accelerated even further, reaching 3.2 percent in the 1951-1973 period. The rapid fall in fertility reduced the rate to 2.1 percent in the 1973-1985 period and to less than 2 percent in recent years (see population censuses and Misión de Empleo, 1986).

Global structural change was accompanied by an equally significant transformation of the different economic sectors. Following a modified Chenery classification, Table 9.4 shows the share of "early," "intermediate," and "late" sectors in the generation of manufacturing value added. As

Figure 9.2
GDP (% DEVIATION TREND)

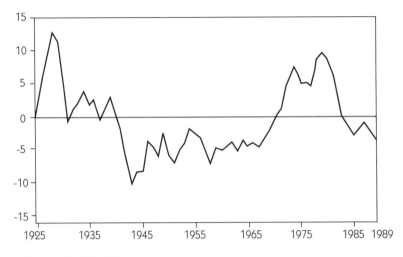

Sources: See Table 9.3.

can be seen, manufacturing development underwent three distinct phases. During the Great Depression and the Second World War, industrial growth was led by beverages (beer), oil derivatives (gasoline), nonmetallic minerals (cement) and textiles (cotton). During a transitional phase, which covers the first decade of the postwar period, these sectors continued to expand and, indeed, peaked as a share of manufacturing value added in the period 1950-1954, but the contribution of late industries to industrial activity started to increase. From the mid-1950s to the mid-1970s, the central feature was the rising share of all late industries—paper and printing, chemicals and rubber, basic metals, and metalmechanic activities—at the expense of both early and intermediate sectors. Throughout this process, artisan activities declined in relative proportion and underwent significant internal transformations. Particularly, textile and tailor's shops lost, as carpentry and metalmechanic repair shops gained relative importance (Berry 1983).

The process was supported by a significant accumulation of physical capital and a fair development of domestic entrepreneurship. Technological innovations also played a crucial role in the process (Echavarría 1989). Domestic private firms led the first stages of industrial growth. Many of them were, in fact, family businesses, which did not always make a successful transition to a corporate structure. Starting in the 1940s, but particularly in the 1950s and 1960s, multinationals and (to a much lesser extent than in other Latin American countries) public enterprises played an increasing role in industrial development.

Despite the rapid structural transformation and the "unbalanced" features of the process (see below), economic growth was remarkably stable. Indeed, as Figure 9.2 shows, GDP growth has remained close to the long-term trend of 4.5 percent a year since 1925. This rate has not been very different from Third World or Latin American averages. Thus, it is the stability rather than a high rate of growth which has been the essential feature of the modern economic growth of Colombia. Moreover, as Figure 9.2 indicates, the strongest slowdowns have been associated with large external shocks: the Great Depression, the Second World War (which interrupted the normal flow of imports), the post-Korean War collapse of commodity prices, and the debt crisis in the 1980s. With respect to the magnitude of such shocks, the loss of GDP has been moderate in most cases.

Foreign trade also experienced substantial changes throughout the process. The fastest and earliest were those experienced by the composition of imports, which by the mid-1950s had the structure typical of a semi-industrialized country (see Table 9.5). As mentioned already, exports also experienced substantial structural changes from the mid-1950s to the mid-1970s. However, the most significant process was probably the long-run decline in the share of exports in GDP. This trend was not quite mirrored by imports, which followed a cyclical pattern similar to the purchasing power of exports and the terms of trade. What is more interesting, given the high (direct and indirect) import content of investment in machinery and equipment, is that this cyclical pattern was transmitted to capital accumulation. This behavior was induced by the effects of the world economy on the domestic business cycle and the real exchange rate (see below).

The Role of Economic Policy in Structural Transformation

As elsewhere in Latin America, the association in Colombia of rapid structural transformation and industrialization with a downward trend of the export coefficient— "inward-oriented development"—has attracted a great deal of attention in the literature. Recent orthodox analysts have questioned, in particular, the role that economic policy played in the process and the distortions it generated. It is my view, however, that while economic policy did play a role in the structural transformation, it was not the determining factor, nor was it always based on the abrogation of price signals.

Major policy decisions affecting economic structure were associated with exchange rate and trade policies and, secondly, with financial arrangements and direct government investment. Overall, these policy decisions reflected a significant shift in the conception of the role of the state in economic affairs which, as in the rest of the capitalist world, started to take shape in the 1930s. It was also accompanied by moderate intervention in labor, agrarian and, more generally, social affairs. In macroeconomics, it was characterized by a great deal of continuity within a general trend of fiscal and monetary conservatism. This meant considerable intervention, particularly in financial affairs, in order to guarantee the moderate growth of monetary aggregates in the phase of sharp fluctuations in international reserves.

The first characteristic of foreign exchange management has been the maintenance of exchange controls since September 1931, when they were adopted as a way to arrest the run on the peso generated by the devaluation of the sterling pound. Although the nature and severity of controls have varied through time, they have been consistent for most current transactions and have only been temporarily abandoned for capital transactions in the period 1948-1967, when a freely fluctuating rate applicable to them was adopted. Exchange controls have been accompanied, however, by a very active exchange rate policy.

Three periods in the evolution of such policy can be differentiated. The first was characterized by a massive devaluation in 1931-1934, followed by fourteen years of a fixed rate.[8] The second period, from 1948 to 1967, was typified by frequent maxi-devaluations and multiple exchange rates. The latter system generally included four rates: a basic rate for most imports and some exports, a freely fluctuating rate for capital transactions and nontraditional exports, and two tax rates for coffee and oil. Finally, in 1967 the country established an active crawling rate system and returned to the principle of a unique rate.[9] It should also be noted that, in contrast to similar systems in other Latin American countries, the crawl of the peso has never been preannounced.

Regardless of variable regimes, exchange rate policy has had two basic features which Figure 9.3 clearly depicts: a long-run upward trend and a cyclical pattern opposite to that of the terms of trade.[10] The first may be interpreted as a precondition for structural change in an economy with comparative advantages in a particular commodity (coffee). The second may be seen as a sign of the dual role which exchange rate policy has played since the 1920s. During price booms, it has served as a mechanism to transfer coffee resources to the rest of the economy—more specifically, to reduce the cost of machinery and equipment and intermediate goods for the rapidly growing capital-intensive sectors (i.e., manufacturing, public utilities, and transportation). During periods of foreign exchange shortage, the

---

[8] The devaluation was at first small (10 percent) and temporary, but it was followed by the floating of the peso in 1933. In certain sub-periods it had multiple rate features as some foreign exchange transactions were taxed.

[9] In certain periods (in the initial transition and during the coffee boom of the 1970s), some multiple rate features have been temporarily maintained.

[10] A simple econometric exercise indicates that a time trend and the terms of trade explain half of the variance of the real import exchange rate during the period 1923-1987. See more complex exercises in Ocampo (1989c). In a comparative study of eight Latin American countries, using series for 1946-1985, Jorgensen and Paldam (1987) fail to get a significant trend. However, these authors obtain a significant upward shift of the real exchange rate in 1957, which may be interpreted as a step-wise upward shift.

Figure 9.3
The Exchange rate - Terms of trade link (Indices, 1980 = 100)

Sources: Terms of Trade - see Figure 9.1
Real Import Exchange Rate - 1923-40,.Ocampo and Montenegro (1984);
1940-86, Ocampo (1989c).

exchange rate has been used to generate incentives for "efficient" import substitution and export diversification and, in this way, to encourage the structural transformation of the economy.

In both cases, economic policy has followed signals in the foreign exchange market. It has also encouraged structural change by operating, however, on different aspects of the process in different phases of the coffee cycle—the supply side during booms and the demand side during crises. Such a role has been played with many inconsistencies and difficulties. In particular, the cyclical pattern of the real exchange rate may have had some adverse effect on sectors subject to dynamic economies of scale—manufacturing, in particular (see, for example, van Wijnberger 1984). On the other hand, it has encouraged the growth of coffee production during international coffee crises, despite the fact that the external demand for such a staple has not been infinitely elastic in the case of Colombia. This problem became quite important when the world coffee economy came to be regulated by successive international agreements in the late 1950s. The latter problem was basically "solved"—with strong resistance from the powerful coffee interests—by the taxation of coffee incomes, which have become relatively high since that time (see Table 9.6). It should be emphasized that such high taxation levels came after the slowdown of coffee production became clearly visible, and basically absorbed the long-run depreciation of the real exchange rate (Ocampo 1989c). The former problem was in a sense also "solved" by the use of complementary instruments of protection. However, such practice has generally reinforced

Table 9.6. Export and Import Policy Indicators

	Tax on coffee exports[1]	Subsidy for nontraditional exports	Average tariff rate	Proportion of imports under the prior licensing regime	Proportion of import licenses rejected	Prior import deposits as a % of imports
1910–14			47.4			
1915–19			30.3			
1920–24			24.5			
1925–29			30.6			
1930–34	2.6[2]		41.5			
1935–39	4.3		22.5			
1940–44	13.6		16.8			
1945–49	0.0	44.6[3]	11.1			
1950–54	7.1	32.5	18.3	21.0		4.8
1955–59	12.2	19.2	12.0	29.5		16.2
1960–64	24.7	29.3	14.2	50.4	15.5	21.2
1965–69	33.3	28.8	16.0	78.1	32.3	24.9
1970–74	32.2	28.9	14.3	70.0	8.8	13.7
1975–79	44.9	14.1	13.5	57.8	1.1[5]	5.7
1980–84	33.1	18.9	15.0	55.9	10.4	6.4
1985–87	41.2		16.7	65.4	25.7	10.2

[1] Ad-valorem tax, differential exchange rate and retention quota.
[2] 1932–34   [3] 1948–49   [4] 1959–63   [5] 1979
Source: Ocampo (1989c). Tariff rate in 1910–39 according to Ocampo and Montenegro (1984).

the effects of real exchange rate fluctuations induced by the coffee cycle.

In any case, as has been shown in this chapter, protectionism predated successful manufacturing development in Colombia. This is probably, as will be argued below, the most clear demonstration that industrial development had other roots. Moreover, rapid manufacturing growth also preceded the intensive use of both tariff and non-tariff protection. In fact, although a protectionist tariff reform was adopted in 1931—as the result of pressure by agricultural producers affected by the 1927 "emergency law" (see above)—it was rapidly eroded by inflation as it kept the traditional structure based on specific duties (Ocampo and Montenegro 1984, Chapter 5, and Table 9.6). Import rationing was used for the first time in 1937, but it was rather moderate up to the mid-1950s.

Thus, the most extreme forms of protectionism came rather late in the process as the result of the tariff reforms of 1950 and, particularly, 1959 and 1964 (Martínez 1986). The latter two were induced by the collapse of coffee prices in the mid-1950s and reinforced the effects of the real devaluation generated by the crisis. The foreign exchange shortage also encouraged the intensive use of non-tariff protection (see Table 9.6). Both forms of protectionism played an essential role in the third phase of industrialization outlined in the previous section. However, at the end of this period there was considerable "water" in the structure of protection for traditional consumer goods.[11] Among late manufacturing sectors, chemicals, basic metals, and metallic products received effective protection of 40-55 percent; it was only in electric machinery and transport equipment that effective protection rates were extremely high. Overall, effective protection used in Colombian manufacturing was, in fact, relatively low by Third World standards—25 percent (Hutchenson 1973). Moreover, despite the fact such a protective structure favored late industries, by the end of the 1960s, they were relatively under-expanded relative to the Kuznets-Chenery cross-country pattern (Syrquin 1987; Echavarría et al. 1983). In fact, comparative international surveys indicate that Colombia's structure was more akin to that of a small open economy than to a large import-substituting country during this period (Chenery et al. 1986).

The intensive use of protectionism induced by the collapse of coffee prices in the mid-1950s also led the government to adopt a complete set of policies to promote the diversification of exports. Preferential exchange rates for nontraditional exports were granted for the first time in 1948. After the mid-1950s, such preferential rates were complemented by a drawback system (1957), tax incentives (1960), and subsidized credit (1964). Up to 1967, these incentives were generally high (see Table 9.6) but unstable (Diaz-Alejandro 1976, Chapter 2). The famous Decree 444 of 1967 gave a stable shape to the system of incentives for nontraditional exports: it substituted the preferential exchange rate and existing tax incentives with a tax-free certificate, created the Fund for Export Promotion (PROEXPO), and improved the drawback system. Although average effective subsidies actually fell (see Table 9.6), the stability of the new incentives and additional real devaluation largely compensated for that fact.

Therefore, the policy package adopted in the late 1950s, and improved in 1967, combined protectionism with active exchange rate management and export promotion. A last component of such a package was economic integration, but its effects remained rather limited. The usual characterization of such a package as "inward-oriented" does not do justice to its global features. It was rather a mixed package aimed at a structural diversification of foreign trade. Although it relied more on import substitution in its early stages, this was largely a corollary of the highly concentrated initial export structure. After the process of export diversification took off, it started to play a more important role. However, up to 1974, it was never inconsistent with a parallel process of import substitution.

---

[11] This indicates that domestic prices for traditional consumer goods were not different from international prices—the traditional definition of "water" in the tariff structure. This does not mean, however, that protection had no significant effect on domestic production. In a context of imperfect competition, typical of manufacturing activities, it allowed local firms to exploit more fully the economies of scale which the domestic market permitted for those traditional goods. As the new literature on international trade suggests, its major welfare cost was the reduced variety of consumer goods available.

The implementation of this mixed package had remarkable effects. The rapid diversification of manufacturing, GDP, and exports has already been noticed. In terms of economic growth, after a very short recession in 1957-1958, the economy grew slightly above its long-run trend during 1959-1967 (4.9 percent), despite severe foreign exchange bottlenecks and unstable capital flows (Ocampo 1988). As a matter of fact, the latter were largely induced by the bilateral and multilateral aid agencies. This, finally, led to a confrontation with such agencies in 1966-1967 and the adoption of the autonomous foreign trade and exchange reform of that year—which included the crawling peg, the return to generalized exchange controls, and a stable export promotion system. It was soon followed by a very gradual liberalization of non-tariff protection (see Table 9.6). The success of the mixed policy package was made apparent between 1968 and 1974 when the economy grew at a healthy 6.3 percent. The steady flow of external lending helped the economy reach its highest recorded growth rate since the 1920s.

Non-Policy Dynamics of Structural Change

As the foregoing discussion suggests, economic policy played an important role in the rapid structural transformation of Colombia from the 1930s to the mid-1970s. However, it can hardly be given the determining role which some popular hypotheses claim. Rather, economic policy was ineffective when other preconditions for structural transformation were absent. Moreover, when it was effective, policy shifts and strategies came many times with a significant lag with respect to the processes they were supposed to affect. In fact, most policy shifts were forced by external events—particularly changes in conditions prevailing in the international coffee market—rather than a result of the implementation of a strategy of any sort. Actually, such "strategy" came rather late in the process as a rationalization of ongoing processes and policies.

This indicates that the structural transformation of the Colombian economy had a dynamics of its own. Such dynamics resulted from the interplay of two basic forces: (a) the external economies generated by the integration of the internal market and industrialization; and (b) the long-term cycle of coffee prices and the terms of trade. Given certain features of the country, this process followed an "unbalanced" Hirschman pattern—i.e., it was characterized by the build-up of structural imbalances, followed by phases of correction of existing disequilibria.

As mentioned earlier, geography largely determined the unbalanced features which the Colombian economy manifested in the 1920s. However, by the 1920s, geographically fragmented Colombia had for the first time the shape of a national economy. By itself, this fact would have had significant effects on manufacturing growth in the following decades as the external economies generated by the development of modern transportation made themselves felt. As we have seen, this process did in fact take place. However, it was significantly affected by the outbreak of the Great Depression. The relative price shifts generated by the collapse of international coffee prices, the maxi-devaluation of the peso and, to a lesser extent, the tariff reform of 1931, accelerated manufacturing development during the 1930s.

Once industrial development took off, its dynamics were determined by the external economies generated by the process itself. Two types of external economies played a crucial role in the process. On the one hand, industrial development and the integration of the domestic market reinforced each other. The former flourished in the integrated, national market, whereas the development (albeit slow) of an integrated modern transport infrastructure was largely possible thanks to the interregional trade generated by industrial development. The second type of externalities were the (mainly backward) linkages generated by industrialization itself. This process not only made possible the development of new manufacturing sectors, but also the modernization of non-coffee agriculture since the 1950s (Kalmanovitz 1978).

It is unclear whether this process and the economic policy which went along with it had by itself an intrinsic anti-export bias. Rather, it corrected for the pro-export bias generated by the absence of any type of national market up to the 1920s. In fact, it was only in the early 1960s that the structure of production finally assumed a normal shape according to the Kuznets-Chenery pattern (Londoño 1989a, 1989b). On the other hand, the slowdown of export growth in the 1940s was largely associated with events in coffee production and, thus, somewhat unrelated to industrial growth itself. Export diversification was slow, given the initial high comparative advantage in coffee and the lag of industrial and even non-coffee agricultural development, but it came as an additional by-product of the process after the late 1950s.

This transformation was by no means smooth. In fact, as in the rest of Latin America, industrialization eventually faced a foreign exchange bottleneck. Reduced import demands, generated by the domestic production of consumer and some intermediate goods, were overwhelmed by increasing demands generated by economic growth long before industrialization could contribute to the generation of new foreign exchange. The postwar coffee boom delayed the crisis by providing plentiful foreign exchange for a time. It also postponed, however, the process of export diversification. These disequilibria were only made explicit when the collapse of coffee prices in the mid-1950s was combined with the reduced dynamism of coffee production. However, this new disequilibria unleashed relative price shifts and a complex policy package which accelerated the transformation of the structure of production and trade. By the late 1960s, the economy finally reached a stage of structural transformation which seemed to make some sort of balanced growth possible. In a booming international economy, this was reflected in rapid economic expansion.

As Londoño (1989a) has shown, the sequence of disequilibria in the goods' markets had a parallel manifestation in the factors' markets, with important repercussions on income distribution. His results may be interpreted as a sign that rapid industrialization since the 1930s generated a faster response in the supply of physical rather than human capital, and in the supply of the former to manufacturing than to agriculture. The result was a significant income gap between skilled and unskilled labor and between urban and rural incomes which was reflected in the deterioration of income distribution. These gaps were largely (and fairly rapidly) corrected after the 1950s by rapid internal migration, the expansion of the school system, and the modernization of agriculture. The result was a reversion of trends in income distribution since the 1960s (somewhat later according to earlier studies—see Urrutia 1984; Misión de Empleo 1986; Reyes 1987).

A Structural Crisis (1975-1989)

The performance of the Colombian economy since the mid-1970s and, particularly, through the 1980s, has been praised in international financial circles. This reflects the fact that since 1975 the country has avoided the type of macroeconomic disequilibria that has plagued the region. As a consequence, it has also been able to avoid the costs of severe adjustment to the debt crisis.

This stereotyped image reflects the effects of conservative macroeconomic management in the face of favorable terms of trade shocks in the mid-1970s. The fairly rapid domestic supply response and the absence of quotas in the international market allowed coffee exports to increase until 1980. This fact, together with the boom of neighboring Venezuela and the drug trade, prolonged foreign exchange abundance for a few years when prices started to fall in the late 1970s. Controls on foreign indebtedness, combined with a significant accumulation of international reserves, were reflected in solid net external debt ratios in 1980.

Nonetheless, the performance of the Colombian economy since the mid-1970s has been far from satisfactory. Despite foreign exchange abundance, economic growth between 1976 and 1980 (5.4 percent) slowed down compared with the period 1968-1974 and was just above that of the period 1959-1967, when the economy faced severe exchange shortages. This process was related to the mild "Dutch-disease effects" of the coffee boom (Edwards 1984; Ocampo 1989c) that were reflected in the interruption of the structural transformation the economy had experienced in previous decades. Moreover, in the early 1980s, large macroeconomic disequilibria built up. Fiscal deficits reached postwar peaks and were partly monetized.

On the other hand, exchange rate appreciation and import liberalization, combined with adverse terms of trade, generated sizable current account disequilibria, also the largest in the postwar period. Thus, as external debt increased at rapid rates, eroding the strong net debt of the country, the economy entered the strongest and longest recession since the Second World War (Lora and Ocampo 1987, Figure 9.2).

Adjustment to existing disequilibria was adopted after 1983 and included a (temporarily variable) mix of contractionary fiscal policy, devaluation, and import and exchange controls (Junguito 1986; Garay and Carrasquilla 1987; Lora and Ocampo 1987). By late 1985, macroeconomic equilibrium had been restored. The country was, thus, able to use the temporary boost of coffee prices in 1986 to accelerate economic growth. Nonetheless, after a couple of years of fairly rapid expansion, the economy returned to moderate rates in 1988 and 1989.

Overall, economic growth during the period 1975-1989 (3.8 percent) has remained considerably below the trend rate for the 1925-1989 period (4.5 percent). Moreover, in open contrast to the development pattern typical in both the first decades of the century and the forty-five years of rapid industrialization that followed it, economic structure has experienced few changes. The modernization of the coffee industry and the growth of large-scale mining have been the most important of them. The former was the joint effect of technological innovation and the plantings induced by the coffee boom of the mid-1970s. The latter was the result of the change in oil exploration policy in the mid-1970s.[12]

The link between the slowdown of economic growth and the lack of significant structural transformation has become a subject of great concern in recent years. In a Schumpeterian or a Hirschmanite framework, the lack of a leading (or innovative) sector, with significant domestic links, should be a matter of concern. The two sectors that have experienced structural transformations in recent years can hardly play that role. Given the lack of dynamism of world demand and the fairly high share in the market, coffee could only temporarily play that part, as it did in the late 1970s. On the other hand, mining lacks the backward and forward linkages necessary to fulfill such a task.

A return to the mixed model implemented in the 1960s and the first half of the 1970s is, in this context, an open option. Policies implemented over the past seven years have resulted in a mix of import substitution and export promotion. However, some of the elements of such a model are absent. In

---

[12] The reform adopted in 1974 created a joint partnership contract between the government and foreign-owned multinationals, in which transactions are booked at international prices. A similar contract was adopted somewhat later for coal mining. Long-term investment induced by this new arrangement resulted in a mining boom in the second half of the 1980s.

particular, import substitution lacks the international and domestic support it had up to the early 1970s. Most importantly, however, after a prolonged crisis in the midst of rapid innovation at a world level, Colombian manufacturing has considerably lagged behind international standards.

The Colombian economy may, thus, be going through a "structural crisis." Although at a purely economic level it is certainly milder than that of its Latin American neighbors, its association with a deep social crisis is a matter of great concern. It is unlikely that such a crisis will be solved by a simple appeal to economic liberalization as predicted by the World Bank and many domestic economic and political observers. In fact, the appeal to liberalism may actually temporarily worsen the manufacturing crisis. Nonetheless, such a route may be followed in the near future for lack of coherent alternatives.

REFERENCES

Arango, M. 1982. *El café en Colombia, 1930-1958: producción, circulación y política*. Bogotá: Carlos Valencia Editores.

Archila, M. 1989. "La clase obrera colombiana (1860-1930)." *Nueva historia de Colombia*, vol. III, chapter 9. Bogotá: Planeta.

Bejarano, J. A. 1979. *El régimen agrario: de la economía exportadora a la economía industrial*. Bogotá: La Carreta.

Berry, A. 1983. "A Descriptive History of Colombian Industrial Development in the Twentieth Century." In *Essay on Industrialization in Colombia*, edited by A. Berry. Tempe: Arizona State University.

Brew, R. 1981. *El desarrollo económico de Antioquia desde la independencia hasta 1920*. Bogotá: Banco de la República.

CEPAL. 1957. *Análisis y proyecciones del desarrollo económico: el desarrollo económico de Colombia*. México: CEPAL.

_____ and FAO. 1958. *El café en América Latina: Problemas de la productividad y perspectivas*, vol. 1, Colombia y el Salvador. Mexico: CEPAL.

Chenery, H., S. Robinson and M. Syrquin. 1986. *Industrialization and Growth: A Comparative Study*. New York: Oxford University Press.

Deas, M. 1976. "Una hacienda cafetera de Cundinamarca: Santa Bárbara (1870-1912)." *Anuario Colombiano de historia social y de la cultura*.

Diaz-Alejandro, C. F. 1976. *Foreign Trade Regimes and Economic Development*. New York: National Bureau of Economic Research.

Edwards, S. 1984. "Coffee, Money and Inflation in Colombia." *World Development,* November-December 1984.

Echavarria, J. J. 1989. "External Shocks and Industrialization in Colombia," 1920-1950. Oxford University. Mimeo.

_____, C. Caballero and J. L. Londoño. 1983. "El proceso colombiano de industrialización: algunas ideas sobre un viejo debate." *Coyuntura Económica.*

Garay, L. J. and A. Carrasquilla. 1987. "Dinámica del desajuste y proceso de saneamiento económico en Colombia en la década de los ochenta." *Ensayos sobre política económica.*

Hirschman, A. O. 1958. *The Strategy of Economic Development.* New Haven: Yale University Press.

Hutchenson, T. L. 1973. "Incentives for Industrialization in Colombia." Ph.D.diss., Michigan University.

Jorgensen, S. L. and M. Paldam. 1987. "The Real Exchange Rates of Eight Latin American Countries, 1946-1985: An Interpretation." *Monetary Affairs,* December 1987.

Junguito, R. 1986. *Memoria del Ministro de Hacienda.* Bogotá: Banco de la República.

_____ 1989. "La deuda externa de Colombia en el siglo XIX: Implicaciones de la experiencia histórica." Bogotá. Mimeo.

_____ and D. Pizano. 1989. "Economía cafetera colombiana," 2d. ed., Bogotá: Federación de Cafeteros. Mimeo.

Kalmanovitz, S. 1978. *El desarrollo de la agricultura en Colombia.* Bogotá: La Carreta.

LeGrand, C. 1989. "El conflicto de las bananeras." *Nueva Historia de Colombia,* vol. III, chapter 8. Bogotá: Planeta.

Londoño, J. L. 1989a. "Income distribution in Colombia: Turning points, catching up and other Kuznetsian ideas." Cambridge: Harvard University. Mimeo.

_____ 1989b. "Agricultura y transformación estructural, Una comparación internacional." Bogotá: Fedesarrollo. Mimeo.

Lora, E. and J. A. Ocampo. 1987. "Colombia." In *Stabilization and Adjustment Policies and Programmes, Country Study no. 6.* Helsinki: WIDER.

Lucas, R. E. Jr. 1988. "On the Mechanics of Economic Development." *Journal of Monetary Economics,* July 1988.

Machado, A. 1977. *El café: de la aparcería al capitalismo.* Bogotá: Punta de Lanza.

Martínez, A. 1986. *La estructura arancelaria y las estrategias de Industrialización en Colombia,* 1950-1982. Bogotá: Universidad Nacional.

Mayor Mora, A. 1989. "Historia de la industria colombiana, 1886-1930." *Nueva historia de Colombia,* vol. V, chapter 12. Bogotá: Planeta.

McGreevey, W. P. 1971. *An Economic History of Colombia,* 1845-1930. Cambridge: Cambridge University Press.

Ocampo, J. A. 1984. *Colombia y la economía mundial, 1830-1910*. Bogotá: Siglo XXI.

_____. 1987. *Artesanos, comerciantes y política económica en Colombia, 1830-1880*. Bogotá: Academia de Ciencias Económicas.

_____. 1988. "Cuatro décadas de endeudamiento externo colombiano." In *Colombia y la Deuda Externa*, edited by José Antonio Ocampo and Eduardo Lora. Bogotá: Fedesarrollo-Tercer Mundo.

_____. 1989a. "Los orígenes de la industria cafetera, 1830-1929." *Nueva historia de Colombia*, vol. V, chapter 9. Bogotá: Planeta.

_____. 1989b. "La consolidación de la industria cafetera, 1830-1928." *nueva historia de Colombia*, vol. V, chapter 10. Bogotá: Planeta.

_____. 1989c. "Ciclo cafetero y comportamiento macroeconómico en Colombia, 1940-1987." *Coyuntura Económica*.

_____ and S. Montenegro. 1984. *Crisis mundial, protección e industrialización*. Bogotá: CEREC.

Ospina, L. 1955. *Industria y protección en Colombia, 1810-1930*. Medellín: Editorial Santa Fé.

Palacios, M. 1983. *El Café en Colombia, 1850-1970: una historia económica, social y política*, 2d. ed. Bogotá: El Ancora.

Reyes, A. 1987. "Tendencias del empleo y la distribución del ingreso." In *El problema laboral colombiano*, edited by José Antonio Ocampo and Manuel Ramírez. Bogotá: Contraloría General de la República-Departamento Nacional de Planeación-SENA.

Romer, P. 1986. "Increasing returns and long-run growth." *Journal of Political Economy*, October 1986.

Safford, F. 1965. "Commerce and Enterprise in Central Colombia," 1821-1870. Ph.D. diss., Columbia University.

Shleifer, A. 1989. "Externalities as an Engine Growth." Graduate School of Business, University of Chicago. Mimeo.

Syrquin, M. 1989. "Crecimiento económico y cambio estructural en Colombia: una comparación internacional." *Coyuntura Económica*, December 1987.

Urrutia, M. 1969. *Historia del sindicalismo en Colombia*. Bogotá: Universidad de los Andes.

_____ 1984. *Los de arriba y los de abajo*. Bogotá: Fedesarrollo-CEREC.

White, J. 1978. *Historia de una ignominia: la United Fruit Co. en Colombia*. Bogotá: Editorial Presencia.

CHAPTER TEN

THE SCANDINAVIAN MODEL
OF INDUSTRIAL POLICY

Lennart Hjalmarsson*

Introduction

The content and meaning of industrial policy has varied substantially between different countries and time periods. Using a broad definition, industrial policy may include the government's monetary and fiscal policy. More commonly, however, the concept is reserved for direct and detailed interventions by governments in industrial reorganizations, regional aid, employment, competition, trade, and research and development policies (R&D). Previously, industrial policy was closely connected with regulation and nationalization in some countries, but today more emphasis is placed on deregulation and privatization. Thus, industrial policy is the label used to describe a wide-ranging collection of micro-based supply side policies aimed at improving market performance and correcting market failures in a variety of ways.

The purpose of this chapter is to present the Scandinavian model of industrial policy in a theoretical as well as historical perspective. Scandinavian industrial policy differs from the more common, pro-competitive industrial policy in the sense that it emphasizes productive efficiency more than allocative efficiency. Productive efficiency refers to the efficient use of resources inside the firm, while allocative efficiency refers to the economic optimization of inputs and outputs. In other words, allocative efficiency deals with the questions of whether the input mix is cost minimizing, and whether different outputs are produced in the right proportions (so that prices are equal to marginal costs). The productive efficiency of an entire industry is characterized by its structural efficiency.

Historically, industrial policy in Scandinavia has concentrated on structural efficiency of various industries and on policy measures that should be taken to promote more rational industrial structures. Interest has focused on the modernity of capital equipment, the size of plants and firms, and the

* Comments on earlier drafts by Magnus Blomström, Ari Kokko, Patricio Meller, Martin Rama, Nils-Olof Stålhammar, Salvador Valdes and participants in the group are gratefully acknowledged.

extent of the division of labor and specialization. Government committees have been appointed to survey the structure of different industries and to recommend measures to accelerate the progress by so-called "structural rationalization," leading to more efficient industrial structures. Thus, structural rationalization policy has been directed towards a more efficient utilization of resources, especially labor and capital.

In the antitrust tradition, both productive and allocative efficiency is achieved by competition in the domestic product and factor markets. Productive efficiency is further enhanced by the pressure of an efficient capital market. This explains the emphasis on market structure. In the Scandinavian tradition, allocative efficiency is achieved by international competition which, historically, has been taken for granted there. Survival in international competition requires productive efficiency, which necessarily becomes the leading policy objective.

An important aspect of productive efficiency for small, open economies is scale efficiency. There is much evidence of considerable scale economies in many production sectors. Classical studies in this field are Haldi and Whitcomb (1967), Pratten (1971) and, for Sweden, Ribrandt (1970). More recent investigations have been undertaken in connection with the removal of trade barriers inside the European Common Market (EEC, 1988). The importance of scale efficiency seems to be less of a problem in the United States and in other large countries, but is an important issue for the small Scandinavian countries.

In industries characterized by putty-clay technology, the dynamic gains from economies of scale arise in the process of long-run capacity expansion, rather than in the more efficient utilization of existing capacity. The most relevant measures of scale economies are, therefore, engineering estimates of scale factors in the construction of new plants. Such engineering estimates usually indicate substantial scale economies in most manufacturing industries. Even in industries which are regarded as small-scale industries, e.g., metal manufacturing, economies of scale are important, but at a lower level. The number of products produced gives a false impression. At a reasonably detailed level of aggregation, economies of scale usually appear.

The chapter is organized as follows. The second section, which follows this introduction, presents the theoretical aspects of the Scandinavian model of industrial policy and contrasts it with traditional industrial policy, where the emphasis is on allocative efficiency. The case of Sweden, which is the clearest example of industrial policy with emphasis on productive efficiency, is reviewed in the third section. The Swedish labor market policy, which has been an important part of the industrial policy, is discussed in the fourth section, while the fifth section addresses other relevant aspects of Swedish industrial policy, particularly the role of the public sector. Finally, a summary of the issues discussed is found in the last section.

Theoretical Aspects of Scandinavian Industrial Policy

For many years, research in industrial economics focused primarily on different aspects of competitive failures in different markets on the basis of neoclassical micro-theory and what is normally referred to as the structure-conduct-performance (SCP) paradigm. In this tradition, industrial policy focuses on market failures of a particular kind, namely those connected with deviations of price from marginal cost, and the main objective of industrial policy is to reduce the social costs of monopoly power. From an efficiency point of view, the focus is on static allocative efficiency that is obtained by an efficient competition and antitrust policy (or direct price regulation) and that yields prices at marginal cost levels.

Within the SCP paradigm, productive efficiency is of less concern. Supposedly it is obtained by efficient monitoring inside firms and through capital market pressure, forcing the average firm to the efficient part of its production possibility set. Typical examples of this tradition are the antitrust policies of the United States and the United Kingdom and the regulation of utilities in the United States.

Industrial policy in Scandinavia has not been very much influenced by such ideas. Instead, a great emphasis has been placed on the productive efficiency of the manufacturing sector, and on the so-called structural rationalization policy of less efficient industry sectors. The focus on market structure in the antitrust tradition is replaced by the focus on productivity structure. Although the Scandinavian policy bears resemblance to some aspects of industrial policy in other countries, it seems to be more pronounced in Scandinavia. The theoretical underpinnings of this policy will now be addressed.

A Model of Structural Change

The early Scandinavian industrial policy was never based on an explicit theoretical model. However, the vintage, or putty-clay model is a good ex post rationalization of the main ideas and provides a convenient framework for a discussion of Scandinavian industrial policy in practice.

The crucial assumption in the vintage model is that of smooth substitution possibilities and free choice of capacity, ex ante, at the planning stage of an investment, but frozen capacity and technology ex post. When a new plant has been erected, capacity is fixed and substitution possibilities narrow. Technical progress is assumed to be capital embodied. Therefore, in the short run, an industry is characterized by a rigid capital structure. In the long run, this structure may be changed through a gradual process of investments in new technologies and scrapping of old capital.

Such a rigid industrial structure generally consists of a whole distribution of plant sizes and plant productivities, and there is a gap between best-

Figure 10.1

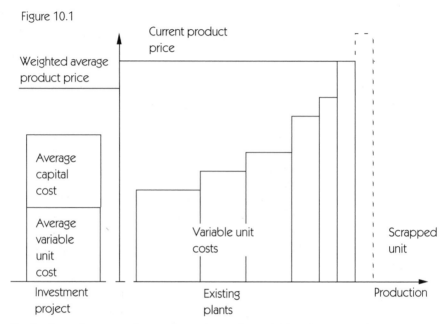

Production units arranged according to increasing variable unit costs on the
right-hand side, the investment project under consideration on the left-hand side.

practice and average productivity. Therefore, industrial policy focuses not
on the average firm, but on the development of the entire structure over time,
through its impact on the investment process and the closing down of old
plants and equipment.

The logic of the model is illustrated in Figure 10.1, which shows an
industry with a number of plants of different vintages and input coefficients
and, thus, different variable unit costs. Due to economies of scale at the
investment stage, modern plants are larger than older plants. The small, older
plants survive as long as they cover their operating costs. When operating
costs increase, or the product price level decreases, some plants are no longer
able to cover their operating costs and are closed down. New capacity enters
the industry gradually, and transforms its structure.

From an efficiency point of view, the focus is on productive and scale
efficiency of individual firms in general, and on the structural efficiency of
a whole industry in particular. Attention is especially directed towards the
efficiency of the dynamic process of structural change within industries, so-
called structural rationalization.

Economies of scale in combination with embodied technical progress are crucial for the size distribution of plants, or the distribution of input coefficients and technical progress at the best-practice frontier. The average productivity growth is determined both by the rate of structural change, i.e., the diffusion rate of best-practice technologies and the exploitation of scale economies, and by the rate of closing down old units.

In a dynamic model, exploitation of economies of scale depends on the size of the market and its growth rate, and a trade-off arises between the development of demand and scale economies. Therefore, there is a positive correlation between market growth and productivity growth.

This theoretical framework can be used as a basis for analyses of different aspects of dynamic efficiency, closely connected with Scandinavian industry policy, and especially for analyses of the importance of scale economies and scale efficiency as well as the determinants behind structural efficiency (Hjalmarsson 1973, Førsund and Hjalmarsson 1987). In fact, even the classical model of Swedish labor market policy, the Rehn-Meidner model, can be analyzed within this framework.

The intellectual history of the putty-clay approach is rather old. As a matter of fact, the Swedish economist Eli Heckscher introduced a diagram, similar to Figure 10.1, in which the firms' current average costs were sorted in increasing order as early as in 1918. On the basis of this diagram, Heckscher performed an analysis of the impact on industry structure of tariff changes (Heckscher 1918).

Another Swedish economist who made early contributions to the putty-clay approach was Åkerman. For instance, in a study from 1931, he analyzed the difference between the best-practice and average productivity of labor in Swedish saw mills. Among other things, he showed that between 1923 and 1926, the input coefficients of labor for the most modern plants were only 50 percent of that for the average of the industry.

The distance between best-practice and average practice is also discussed in an article by Svennilson (1944). It includes a thorough analysis of the determinants of the rate of growth of industry productivity and a simple model from which "ratios of inoptimality" are calculated. These ratios of inoptimality show the percentage ratio between the average and best-practice input coefficients for labor as a function of the rate of growth of production, the physical lifetime of equipment, and the input-coefficients of labor for each vintage of capital. A main point is the relationship between the rate of growth of production and the rate of productivity growth, which is also studied in an empirical analysis of Swedish industries.

For a long time, the vintage approach to analyses of industrial structure remained fairly descriptive. It was lacking rigor and did not receive much attention from the wider international audience of economists. The seminal work by Farrell (1957) on efficiency and Salter (1960) on productivity change, however, spurred the interest among economists for the vintage approach, but no formal theory was developed until Johansen (1972). He integrated different disparate theoretical elements into a formal production theory, which was further developed by Førsund and Hjalmarsson (1987). With this review of the vintage model in mind, there follows a discussion of Swedish industrial policy in practice.

A Brief History of Swedish Industrial Policy

The history of industrial policy in Sweden is one of controversies and battles between different opinions concerning:
- the use of selective measures versus general policy rules
- interventions in the production and investment processes of firms
- referring to Figure 10.1, "picking winners" in the left part of the capacity distribution through *ex ante* investment coordination and control, state-owned enterprises, and "bailing," as well as squeezing out losers in the right part of the capacity distribution through temporary subsidies, an active labor market policy, etc.

The history of actual policy can hardly be understood separately from the history of the industrial policy debate. Therefore, to enhance our understanding of the reasons for policy failures and successes, policy ideas will be contrasted with actual policies. The discussion will center on the period from the late 1800s to about 1970, concentrating on long-run ideas and policies.

Industrial Policy Before 1920

Until the mid-nineteenth century, the Swedish economy was rather regulated and protected by high tariffs. A successive deregulation and trade liberalization was initiated in the 1840s and 1850s, and a further step was taken in the 1860s, with free trade at its peak. This policy had a strong impact on the Swedish industry and provided strong incentives for the development of the forest-based industry, as well as the expansion of metal manufacturing (Heckscher 1941).

The import competition from the United States for grain led to a setback and a return to protectionism, not only for agriculture in the 1880s, but also for industrial goods in the 1890s. Trade agreements with Germany increased tariff protection further until the First World War.

The change in trade policy probably had a small impact on Sweden's economic development, but to some extent the protectionism may have contributed to a more diversified industrial structure, which became an advantage during the war. However, the protectionist trade policy also resulted in increasing concentration and market power in some industries, of which the sugar-trust, formed in 1907, is the most well-known (Heckscher 1941).

Although industrial policy issues were not ignored in Sweden during the first decades of the century, the economic policy debate at that time focused more on other issues. Inflation and unemployment, in addition to the problems created by the war, were discussed. To a large extent, industrial policy meant removal of regulations and taxes on industry.

Industrial Policy between the Wars

In the 1920s, Swedish industry experienced fierce competition both at home and in international markets. Most prices were falling during this period. The transition to an eight-hour work day for blue-collar workers, rising wages, and falling prices caused a severe profit squeeze. The reaction to this was an extensive industrial modernization, with exploitation of new innovations, rationalization, and many new firms entering the market. This fairly rapid structural change in the 1920s was followed by an extensive capacity expansion in new plants, equipment, and communications in the 1930s. In an international comparison, the economic growth in Sweden was exceptionally high during the 1920s and 1930s. Labor productivity increased by 4 percent per year during the 1920s and 3 percent per year during the 1930s (Dahmen 1950; Lundberg 1953).

In the 1920s, Swedish industry policy focused mainly on the impact of tariffs and exchange rates, but also on education and R&D, price regulation in agriculture, and general social policy issues. Due to rapid inflation during the First World War, the effective protection rates decreased substantially. As a result, Sweden appeared as a relatively free trade country in an international comparison when the war was over (Heckscher 1941). During the 1920s, there was also a lively discussion in Sweden about cartel and antitrust policy. However, this discussion did not focus on allocative efficiency, but rather on whether increased productive efficiency could be obtained by more competition in different markets (LO 1961, bil 1).

The political scene before 1920 was dominated by Liberal and Social Democratic governments and the ideological struggle between liberalism and socialism. The Marxist-oriented party program of the Social Democrats from 1920 proposed far-reaching nationalizations of the Swedish economy in order to strengthen productive forces and make standards of living more equal. However, the nationalization issue was gradually moderated and the emphasis was later placed on economic planning and efficient use of resources.

Between 1932 and 1976, Sweden was ruled by different Social Democratic governments. Among their activities was the establishment of a large number of committees to suggest measures of how to increase the efficiency of different sectors of the economy. One example of the outcome of such ad hoc committees was a report analyzing the economic situation and international competitiveness of the Swedish forest industries (SOU 1938:53). This study was based on a thorough analysis of input coefficients for labor and wood in different branches of the forest industry. Particularly, the impact of tariff protection in other industries on the profitability and competitiveness of the forest industry was discussed. One important conclusion of the study was that tariff protection of some industries created a burden for other export industries analogous to a tax.

One of the most controversial committees was the "Rationalization Committee" (SOU 1939:13). This committee proposed that the government stimulate the structural rationalization of industry and enhance the mobility of labor. However, in order to facilitate the process and decrease the social losses in the form of unemployment, the committee also recommended public control of rationalizations by a specific institute. This proposal caused strong opposition, both from employers and the political opposition. The government chose the cooperative road and did not follow up the proposal.

This was not the only case of cautiousness from the Social Democrats in real policy making. Though their ambitions were often far-reaching, actual industry policy measures were rather limited and confined to investment credits, export credits, subsidies, and tariff protection of some activities. In real policy, the Social Democrats chose the reformist and, to a large extent, cooperative road. The intense debate in Sweden about industrial policy issues from the 1920s to the 1950s is called "the economic planning resistance" (Lewin 1967).

Industrial Policy in the Postwar Period

For over forty years, from 1932 to 1976, the Social Democratic Party had a virtual monopoly on political power in Sweden. During most of this period, Sweden was ruled by purely Social Democratic governments, and the political scene was determined by the relationship between the Social Democrats and a fairly strong bourgeois political opposition. In spite of the generally cooperative atmosphere of Swedish society, there was a wide variety of political opinions. Particularly during the early postwar years, a relatively hostile political climate developed. This was primarily a reaction to the extensive planning ambitions of the governing Social Democratic Party (Lewin 1967).

A first important policy document from the Social Democrats from this period was the Postwar Economic Policy Program of the Labor Movement (1944). This was a radical program, demanding large-scale economic planning. Its point of departure was that the transformation of industry from war to peace could lead to a decrease in the growth rate of production and higher unemployment. In fact, within the Social Democratic Party, there were widespread expectations about a prolonged postwar recession. Therefore, Sweden's economic development could not be left to uncontrolled market forces.

The program of the Labor Movement proposed a thorough structural transformation of Swedish industry in order to increase its efficiency. To stimulate and control investment, a state-owned commercial bank was proposed, in addition to long-run investment planning in cooperation between industry, trade unions, and the government. Moreover, nationalization of the insurance companies was also proposed. State-owned enterprises (SOEs) were suggested in cases where strong monopolies could exploit their market power, decrease production, and cause low growth and high unemployment. In industries with a less efficient size distribution of plants, SOEs were also regarded as a tool to increase scale efficiency. Other proposed measures were low rate of interests, export credits, and an active labor market policy.

One consequence of this program was the initiation of a series of government committee investigations, so-called "structural studies," of different industries. Between 1946 and 1947, nine such studies were conducted. The main reason for these investigations was a perceived need to increase the economic efficiency of different industries. Interest focused on the modernity of capital equipment, the size distribution of plants, and the extent of the division of labor and specialization. It was found that important causes of inefficiency were the existence of too many small firms and unexploited potentials for specialization.

Compared with the 1930s, the proposed industrial policy in Sweden during the postwar period was more ambitious and theoretically much more founded. In terms of Figure 10.1, the industrial policy should promote rapid transformations of industrial structures, phasing out the right tail of the capacity distribution and switching resources to the left. The keywords were productivity, optimal structure, and structural rationalization. The attitude towards private ownership and nationalization was rather pragmatic. State-owned enterprises had a role to play only in the case of market or productive efficiency failures. An equitable income distribution should be achieved by public sector growth (LO 1961, bil 1; Hjalmarsson 1971 and 1973; Lewin 1967).

Most of these committee reports were published between 1947 and 1951, though a few committees interrupted their work before any report was published. The reports were fairly descriptive, and the policy conclusions and recommendations were often general and vague. There was never any analysis of the major issue, namely how to improve the efficiency of the dynamic process of structural change and how to do it better than the free market (SOU 1947, 14; 1947, 52; 1949, 44; 1950, 10; and 1951, 38).

Although many interventionist plans and ideas were discussed during this period, very little action was taken, mainly because it turned out to be much more difficult than expected to design an efficient structural policy. Therefore, industrial policy remained, to a large extent, indicative, and the proposed selective policy tools were substituted by more general policy rules (labor market policy was an exception).

Also, the political interest for more detailed regulation of industry decreased substantially over the years for several reasons. One was the hostile political atmosphere created by the Social Democratic proposals for more selective and detailed industry planning and regulation. The government had obviously underestimated the resistance for such changes from the political opposition and the industrial establishment. Another reason was that the expected recession did not materialize. On the contrary, the main economic policy problem was how to handle a strong boom with full employment. Rapid structural change occurred without government interventions (Lewin 1967).

At the end of the 1960s and the beginning of the 1970s, the planning ambitions rose again in Sweden. The main characteristic of this "new active industrial policy" was a shift from efficiency to distribution and equity, and a shift of power from industry to labor. The most concrete industrial policy measure was the creation of a state-owned investment bank. The equity objectives were supported by higher income taxes, more selective industrial or business subsidies to protect employment, and a more active regional policy. Security replaced mobility and efficiency as a key word. After a few years, however, this industrial policy also came to an end. The overall result of it was meager and by the late 1970s, opinion once again turned away from government interventions towards efficiency and market solutions.

The Role of Trade Unions in Swedish Industrial Policy

A typical feature of all Scandinavian countries are the strong and powerful organizations of the labor market. In Sweden, for instance, between 75 and 80 percent of all employees are members of a trade union, and the blue-collar trade union confederation (LO) has been particularly influential due to its high participation rate (about 95 percent). LO has also been influential in policy making, due to its close connections with the ruling Social Democratic Party. Traditionally, LO also has had its own economic expertise of well-educated, innovative, and independent economists. The importance of the white-collar trade unions is a more recent phenomenon. Therefore, this section will emphasize only the impact of LO on Swedish industrial policy making.

As early as in the 1920s, LO strongly promoted a productivity-enhancing industrial policy, emphasizing rationalization of firms. At the International Trade Union Congress in Stockholm in 1930, the International Trade Union Industry Policy Program was accepted. There one can read the following: "Trade unions should promote the planned development of industry, its structural rationalization into larger units, the financial reorganization, and the substitution of old machinery and methods by new plants and innovations." (Fackföreningsrörelsen, 1930:30, 100).

After the Second World War, the Postwar Economic Policy Program of the Labor Movement received strong support from the LO, as did all the proposals in the Parliament concerning industrial studies. LO was not, however, very satisfied with the activity level obtained, and in 1947 it proposed the following (LO 1961, 216-17):

1) Investigations of industrial efficiency should be performed on a larger scale.

2) After these investigations, more permanent industry councils, with representatives from society, firms, and trade unions, should be established.

3) A coordinating committee should be created to jointly organize and coordinate all investigations and planning work concerning the need for increased efficiency in industry and trade.

There were some efforts by the Swedish government to implement a coordinating committee, but because the Association of Swedish Industries refused to cooperate, no such committee was ever established.

Another important trade union policy document, "The Trade Union Movement and Full Employment," was published by LO in 1951. The call for further rationalization and closing down of less efficient firms in this document was motivated by the request for higher wages. LO, therefore, proposed an increase in efficiency-enhancing cooperation between the trade unions and the firms.

In the 1951 document, the view on industrial policy tools changed substantially from selective measures and detailed regulations to more general policy measures. In particular, competition was now recommended as a main policy instrument to increase productivity and force less efficient firms out of the market (LO 1961, 218-219). Structural change required movement of labor, and therefore, an active labor market policy was regarded as an important policy tool for increasing productivity growth. This issue will be further discussed later in the chapter.

It is interesting to note the anti-protectionist view of LO during this period. In the mid-1950s, LO strongly criticized two government committee reports, one on price regulation, and one on tariffs. In both cases, LO demanded a pro-competitive policy and it strongly criticized the latter committee for its protectionist view. LO argued that tariffs would decrease productivity growth, since it would protect stagnating and less competitive industries.

Another important trade union policy document, entitled "Coordinated Industry Policy," was published by LO in 1961. This study contained a thorough investigation of most of the determinants behind productivity growth. Several proposals on how to promote higher industrial efficiency were put forward. Among other things, an increased factor mobility was regarded as necessary. This would be achieved by:

- an active labor market and regional policy
- a free trade policy
- a growth inducing corporate tax policy

- a liberal credit policy
- a more positive attitude towards horizontal mergers and vertical integration

The attitude from Swedish industry towards all these industrial policy proposals from LO was generally negative, and during the early postwar period, directly hostile. The general political climate in Sweden during this period contributed strongly to this attitude. The negative and skeptical view towards industrial policy in general, and the pessimistic view concerning the practical problems encountered in pursuing an efficient structural rationalization policy in particular, were clearly expressed in SNS (1958).

In spite of all these conflicting views between industry, governments, and trade unions, a high degree of consensus has characterized the relationships. There has been a deep mutual understanding between the different groups, supported by friendly personal relationships across party and interest group lines. Although hard to identify, two important reasons for the cooperative climate in all the Scandinavian countries are probably the large income equality in a society with a homogeneous population and a fairly high and general education level.

Perhaps most surprising is the friendly and cooperative atmosphere that has prevailed between LO and the Swedish Employers Federation (SAF). During extensive periods, centralized wage negotiations were settled without conflicts, and the development of norms and rules in the labor market was done in a friendly atmosphere. A milestone was reached as early as 1938, when a cooperative agreement was made between LO and SAF determining the rules for labor market negotiations and the handling of conflicts without government intervention. Later in the 1950s, this agreement, which is still in effect, also served as a model for the relationship between the white-collar trade union (TCO) and SAF. Thus, the Swedish labor market from the 1930s to the end of the 1960s was characterized by strong labor market organizations that acted under great freedom and responsibility without government intervention and shared the same basic social values.

Another point that might particularly surprise a Latin American reader is that the Swedish trade unions have often supported efforts by firms to become multinational. Sweden has today a large number of multinational corporations, most of which employ more people abroad than at home. The prevailing view of the trade unions has been that foreign investment is necessary and positive for the overall competitiveness of the firms, and generates spillover gains to the domestic branches of the corporations.

It is not easy to assess the impact on actual economic development of the trade union industrial policy or to identify the trade union component in the rapid postwar economic growth in Sweden up to the 1970s. In any case, it is hard to imagine a more productivity-oriented atmosphere in any other country than that created by the Swedish blue-collar trade union. The LO was the driving force for increasing industrial efficiency. Coordination between labor market, regional, trade and other policies increased the mobility of resources, making it possible to shift resources from low to high productivity sectors. At the same time, LO accepted the consequences of closing down firms and temporary layoffs, which were regarded as the price for a rapid increase in real wages. There is no doubt in the documents from LO as to who would reap the gains from this policy. Real wages would increase at least at the same rate as productivity growth. Even if it is hard to measure, one would expect such a growth-oriented environment to have been of vital importance for the actual growth rates during this period.

The Swedish Labor Market Policy

One of the most important tools in Swedish industrial policy has been the labor market policy. The basic principles of this policy have been the work principle and the enhancement of mobility. The pressure put on the unemployed to accept jobs before they qualify for benefits has always been very strong. Unemployment should be alleviated by publicly organized or publicly supported activities—not by unemployment benefits without work. In addition, unemployment policy should also promote the mobility of labor. Since the 1920s these principles, particularly the former, have dominated the Swedish labor market policy (Axelsson et al. 1979).

Until the 1930s, labor market policy was in fact an unemployment policy, and usually regarded as part of the social security policy. Then the role of the labor market policy shifted and it came to be regarded as part of the general economic policy. An active labor market policy should, of course, primarily aim at full employment, but in addition to that, it should contribute to high economic growth and a low rate of inflation.

During the postwar period, the ambitions with this policy increased gradually. A first step was taken by the "Commission for Postwar Economic Planning," which especially stressed the need for mobility and adaptability obtained by public employment service, relocation benefits, education and occupational training (SOU 1945:36).

A few trade union (LO) economists, most notably Rehn and Meidner, played an important role in the postwar development of the Swedish labor market policy. They developed the famous Rehn-Meidner model which gradually grew out of several articles and was summarized in LO (1951). The main objective of the Rehn-Meidner model was to move the Phillips curve closer to the origin so that full employment could be obtained with low inflation. At the same time, it would permit high wage increases and rapid economic growth. Labor market policy thereby became closely connected with industrial policy.

The main components of the Rehn-Meidner model were:
- contractionary aggregated fiscal policy

- firm wage policy
- active labor market policy
- investment stimulating policy

The purpose of this model was to decrease, through a firm policy, the total amount of current economic surplus, represented in Figure 10.1 by the area between the rectangles in the histogram and the price level. High and uniform wage increases, achieved by nationwide centralized wage negotiations, should cause the less efficient firms to the right in the histogram to close down. Capacity expansion, in the left part of the diagram, should restore full employment. To obtain this, the profit squeeze should be countered by selective, publicly controlled, investment incentives, and the required movements of labor should be stimulated by an active labor market policy—not by an aggregate expansionary fiscal policy. Thus, a rapid structural change of Swedish industry, which would lead to a high growth rate and scope for rapid increases in real wages, was inherent in the Rehn-Meidner model. The increase in real wages should at least amount to the productivity growth.

This model, which obviously was very closely related to the general industrial policy model discussed above, became rather influential in Swedish development during the 1950s, 1960s, and the first half of the 1970s (Axelsson et al. 1979). This is particularly true for the firm wage policy and the active labor market policy, but less so for the contractionary fiscal policy and, in the 1970s, the investment policy. In Figure 10.2 the development of the wage spread for blue-collar workers is depicted.

The upper level in Figure 10.2 shows the percentage distance from the industrial average to the average for those sectors that are above this average, and the lower level shows the percentage distance for those sectors which are below the industrial average. The figure reveals a remarkable compression of the wage structure during a twenty year period (SOU 1981: 44, 133).

This period also saw a rapid increase in labor market policy activities, with a strong emphasis on public employment service and job matching through "job centers," occupational education, and strong relocation incentives to increase regional mobility. The Swedish system puts workers seeking jobs and firms seeking workers in touch with one another through centrally collected information available on computer terminals in local employment centers. These centers handle a flow of about 500,000 to 700,000 vacancies a year, representing up to 60 percent of all job openings (compared with 10-20 percent in most other countries), and about 12 to 18 percent of the total labor force. Those who decline a "reasonable" job offer do not receive unemployment pay.

The number of workers in labor market education and training increased rapidly from about 1,000 in the late 1950s to more than 40,000 in the early 1970s, with a high priority of "bottleneck training" where there was a shortage of skilled staff. When training is considered inappropriate or when

Figure 10.2
Wage Dispersion in Sweden, 1959 - 1979

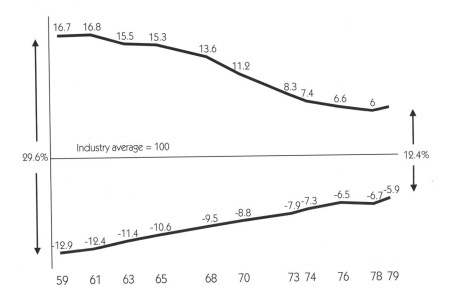

Source : SOU 1981:44, p.133.

Table 10.1. Expenditure Distribution of Swedish Labor Market Policy, 1950–1970
(Percent of Total Budgetary Expenditures)

Year	Employment creation	Protected works	Employment service	Labor market	Mobility enhancing education support
1950	19.1	38.4	35.9	0.2	1.1
1955	30.1	43.0	23.9	0.1	0.1
1960	70.6	16.2	6.8	3.9	1.1
1965	52.7	24.7	8.6	9.1	2.9
1970	32.8	39.3	7.8	15.6	2.5

Source: Axelsson and Löfgren (1979).

jobs cannot be found, people are offered "relief jobs" or "protective employment" organized by a state-owned enterprise.

The employment service is still a public monopoly, mainly because of the opinion that labor markets work best when all information is centralized and made easily available to all parties through local employment centers. All these activities are not without costs. The labor market policy budget increased its share of the total government budget from 4 percent in 1960 (0.8 percent of GNP) to about 8 percent in 1970 (2.2 percent of GNP). The allocation of public resources under different types of labor market policies between 1950 and 1970 is presented in Table 10.1.

A general characterization of the Swedish labor market policy up to the 1970s is its strong supply side, market perfecting feature, particularly through its vast labor market retraining and education activities, and its strong growth orientation aimed at a rapid mobilization of resources from low productivity to high productivity areas. The professional composition of labor supply should be made consistent with the composition of demand through education and retraining, and the regional demand for labor should be satisfied by a high labor mobility. From a productivity point of view, the result was successful. During the 1950s and 1960s Sweden experienced steady economic growth and a very low unemployment rate, around 2 percent.

The Role of the Public Sector in Swedish Industrial Policy

State-Owned Enterprises

Excluding natural or technical monopolies (railways, postal service, telecommunications, electricity, etc.), the publicly-owned share of Swedish industry has always been very small, between 2 and 6 percent of total industry employment. Part of this share includes corporations that are subsidiaries of the technical monopolies. One reason for public ownership has been the control of fiscal monopolies (tobacco, wine and liquor, and lotteries). Another reason, important during the Second World War, was defense-oriented motives (weapons, steel, and domestic energy production) (SOU 1978: 85).

In the 1950s and 1960s, and more so in the 1970s, public ownership was usually motivated by employment protection. The number of SOEs increased substantially in industries that were in a crisis (shipyards, textile, steel, and pulp production). This trend continued until 1979, when it was reversed. Except for this period, nationalization of industry has had a very low priority in Swedish industrial policy. SOEs outside the technical monopolies have not been very popular among the trade unions. The trade unions, in general, have regarded the state as an ineffective employer and a competitor with the private sector. The basic attitude from both the government and the trade unions has been not to nationalize the economic activity, but to nationalize the income generated from this activity. What has mattered is not the formal ownership, but the efficiency. Therefore, Sweden has one of the smallest SOE sectors among the industrialized countries.

Publicly-Owned Monopolies and Public Procurement

Communications and electricity have traditionally been high priority sectors in the Swedish economy. Bottlenecks in these sectors have been removed swiftly and the price levels have been favorable. In an international comparison, Sweden ranks among the very high per capita consumers of telecommunications services as well as electricity. The former sector has been developed by a public monopoly, while in electricity production, the public share amounts to about 50 percent. The latter may exemplify the working of an efficient market, which in most countries is characterized by serious distortions.

The electricity market is characterized by a mix of short-run competition between about ten large producers and long-run coordination of capacity expansion. The market is implicitly regulated by the rate of return requirement on the SOE and its price leadership, and there is no price regulation. This model has been very favorable both for long-run dynamic efficiency, with full exploitation of scale economies in electricity production, and for short-run efficiency in the utilization of the existing system (Hjalmarsson and Veiderpass 1987).

One of the most productivity-enhancing rules in the Swedish public sector is the Public Procurement Act, which determines the conditions and rules for procurement to the public sector, including publicly-owned monopolies in electricity, telecommunications, etc. According to this act, public procurement rests on competition between different suppliers and is not permitted to favor domestic suppliers. Swedish firms must compete, on equal terms, with international firms. The Public Procurement Act is another example of the reliance on international competition to achieve allocative efficiency. It is based on the fact that the welfare of a small country is due to its efficient use of comparative advantages and specialization in a few products in international markets.

The importance of this act for public sector efficiency and, thus, for Swedish welfare, can hardly be exaggerated. It accounts for the very low price levels in telecommunications and electricity markets. This opinion is also supported by recent calculations of welfare gains from further European integration and reduced protection in the public sector (EEC 1988; Geroski and Jacquemin 1985; Geroski 1989).

Concluding Remarks

This chapter has presented the theory behind the Scandinavian model of industrial policy and has shown, in a historical perspective, how this model has been applied in Sweden. The main characteristic of the Swedish industrial policy up to the late 1960s was its heavy emphasis on productive efficiency. This was obtained by rapid diffusion of new technologies, extensive exploitation of scale economies, full exposure to international competition, and a fast, continuous adjustment of industrial structure to changing comparative advantages in international markets. The objective was to maximize the growth of total output and to use a large share of national income for redistribution purposes.

From an international perspective—and particularly from a Latin American perspective — the following aspects of Swedish industrial policy seem to be most striking:

- the very active labor market policy
- the blue-collar trade unions acting as the driving force
- the trade unions proposing a free trade policy
- the trade unions' positive attitude toward investments abroad by Swedish firms
- the insignificant role of public enterprises
- the Public Procurement Act.

An important part of this industrial policy has been aimed at creating a structure of highly productive, large-scale plants, and large, internationally competitive firms. Scale efficiency has been promoted both by a corporate tax policy, which has stimulated horizontal mergers and vertical integration, and a liberal trade policy, which has extended the size of markets. The attitude towards monopolies and "big business" has also been quite different in Sweden compared to, for example, that in the United States. The Swedish industrial policy has been pro-trust, with fiscal incentives (tax exemptions) for merging firms, rather than anti-trust. This has given Sweden a disproportionate number of successful multinationals (Bourdet 1989). Because of their small domestic markets, the Swedish multinationals are dependent on overseas production for their prosperity, and the trade unions have accepted that these companies make acquisitions and green-field site investment abroad to defend and expand their market shares. Generous tax deductions have also stimulated R&D and capacity expansion. Retained profits in the large companies have served as a basis for internal credit markets, an important complement to the less developed financial markets in Sweden.

In summary, Swedish industrial policy has mainly been indicative. It has been based on general policy measures, such as trade, credit and tax policy, but it also has been supported by a strong and selective labor market policy, with high ambitions to adapt the structure of labor supply to the occupational and regional structure of labor demand. Main features of this policy have been to encourage industrial restructuring and train redundant workers for new jobs rather than try to prevent them from being fired. During some periods, the interventionist ambitions rose, but deceptive and unfulfilled expectations forced the policy back to the mainstream road of more general policy measures. Most attempts to beat the market have failed, as have attempts to increase its dynamic efficiency, and activate a "picking the winner policy" by government coordination and control of investments by activating SOEs. Therefore, industrial policy has never been permitted, nor gained enough confidence to replace the free market. A prospering, privately-owned industry merged with the welfare state has remained the hallmark of Sweden.

REFERENCES

Åkerman, G. 1931. *Den industriella rationaliseringen och dess verkningar*, SOU 1931:42. Stockholm.

Axelsson R., K-G. Löfgren and L-G. Nilsson, 1979. *Den svenska arbetsmarknadspolitiken under 1900-talet*. Stockholm: Prisma.

Bourdet, Y. 1989. "Policy Toward Market Power and Restrictive Practices in Sweden." Department of Economics, University of Lund. Mimeo.

Dahmén E. 1950. Svensk industriell företagarverksamhet. Stockholm: IUI

EEC. 1988. *The Economics of 1992*. Brussels: EEC Commission.

Farrell, M.J. 1957. "The Measurement of Productive Efficiency." *Journal of the Royal Statistical Society*, Series A, 120.

Fredriksson, B. and G. Gunnmo. 1985. *Våra fackliga organisationer*. Stockholm: Raben & Sjögren.

Førsund, F. R. and L. Hjalmarsson. 1987. *Analyses of Industrial Structure: A Putty-Clay Approach*. Stockholm: IUI.

Geroski, P. A. 1989. "European Industry Policy and Industry Policy in Europe." *Oxford Review of Economic Policy*, vol. no. 2.

_____, and A. Jacquemin. 1985. "Industry Change, Barriers to Mobility, and European Industry Policy." *Economic Policy*, no 1.

Haldi, J. and D. Whitcomb. 1967. "Economies of Scale in Industry Plants." *Journal of Political Economy* 75(4).

Heckscher, E.F. 1918. *Svenska produktionsproblem*. Stockholm: Bonniers.

_____ Svenskt arbete och liv. 1941. Stockholm: Bonniers.

Hjalmarsson, L. 1971. "En precisering av begreppet strukturrationalisering." University of Oslo. Memorandum.

_____ 1973. "Optimal Structural Change and Related Concepts." *Swedish Journal of Economics* 75 (2).

_____ and A. Veiderpass. 1988. *The Market for Electricity in Sweden*, Gothenburg: University of Gothenburg Press.

Johansen, L. 1972. *Production Functions*. Amsterdam: North Holland Publishing Company.

Lewin L. 1967. *Planhushållningsdebatten*. Uppsala: Almqvist & Wicksell.

LO. 1951. *Fackföreningsrörelsen och den fulla sysselsättningen*. Stockholm.

_____. 1961. Samordnad näringspolitik. Stockholm.

Lundberg E. 1953. *Konjunkturer och ekonomisk politik*. SNS.

Pratten, C.F. 1979. "Economies of Scale in Manufacturing Industries." Department of Applied Economics, Occasional Papers, no 28. Cambridge: Cambridge University Press.

Ribrant, G. 1970. *Stordriftsfördelar inom industriproduktionen*. SOU 1970: 30: Stockholm.

Salter, W.E.G. 1960. *Productivity and Technical Change*. Cambridge: Cambridge University Press.

Scherer, F.M., A. Beckenstein, E. Kaufer, and R.D. Murphy. 1975. *The Economics of Multi Plant Cooperation. An International Comparisons Study.* Cambridge: Harvard University Press.

SNS 1958. *Branschrationalisering.* Stockholm.

SOU *Statens Offentliga Utredningar.* Stockholm.

Svennilson, I. 1944. "Industriarbetets växande avkastning i belysning av svenska erfarenheter." *Studier i ekonomi och historia tillägnade.* Eli F. Heckscher 24-11-1944. Stockholm.

Author Index

Subject Index

A

Advantages of backwardness thesis. *See* Convergence hypothesis
Agrarian reform
  Denmark, 6
  Scandinavia, 6
  See also Land reform
Agrarian Union, Finland, 192
Agricultural processing industry, Denmark, 8-9, 11
Agricultural sector
  Chile, 53
  Colombia, 213-15, 219-23
    performance of, 226, 228
    See also Banana industry; Coffee industry
  Denmark, 11
    exports (1870-1900) of, 69, 70
    farmer self-support system in, 70-71, 74-77
    performance and size of, 68, 75-77
    political circumstances affecting, 71-73
  Ecuador
    exports from, 160, 172
    foreign firm participation in, 174
    performance of, 163-66
    See also Banana industry
  Finland
    effect of protection and support for, 190-94
    historically, 182, 184-86
    shift in emphasis: post World War II, 198-200
    See also Resettlement policy, Finland
  Norway, 130
  Scandinavia, 1, 6
  Sweden
    change in nature of, 19
    historical incentives of, 15-17
  Uruguay, 106
    See also Cattle-raising industry, Uruguay
Allocative efficiency, 245-46
Aluminum industry, Norway, 134, 144
Andean Pact, 170, 174
Antitrust policy, 10
Artisan production, Colombia, 215, 217, 228, 231

B

Balance of payments
  Chile, 47, 52
  Denmark, 81-83, 91
  Finland, 204-5
  Sweden, 26, 28, 32, 35
  Uruguay, 103-5
Banana industry
  Colombia, 219
  Ecuador, 163-66, 175
Banking system
  Denmark, 77
  Ecuador, 161
  Norway, 137, 145
  Sweden, 22
Bargaining economy, Norway, 149-53
Birkeland-Eyde process, 137-38
Budget deficit
  Colombia, 239
  Denmark, 92-93
  Ecuador, 167

C

Cacao industry, Ecuador, 160-63
Capital goods, Ecuador, 172
Capital markets
  Colombia, 225, 236
  Ecuador, 161
  Norway, 137
  Sweden, 19, 23, 27, 28
Cartegena Agreement, 174
Cattle-raising industry, Uruguay, 102-3, 106-9
Central Trade Unions (CTU), Denmark, 86-90
Central Union of Manufacturers (CUM), Denmark, 86-88
Civil War, Finland (1918), 184, 187, 188-89, 195
Coalition formation, Scandinavia, 149
Coffee industry, Colombia, 213-14, 215, 219-23, 239-40
Collective bargaining
  Norway, 142
  Sweden, 31, 35
COMECON. *See* Council for Mutual Economic Cooperation (COMECON)
Convergence hypothesis
  conditions to realize, 12, 183